I, Lobster

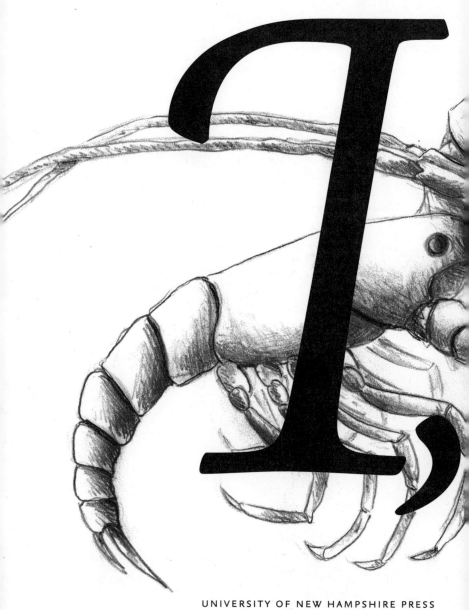

I,

UNIVERSITY OF NEW HAMPSHIRE PRESS

DURHAM, NEW HAMPSHIRE

Lobster

NANCY FRAZIER

A Crustacean Odyssey

University of New Hampshire Press
An imprint of University Press of New England
www.upne.com
© 2012 Nancy Frazier
Manufactured in the United States of America
Designed by Eric M. Brooks
Typeset in Adobe Jenson and Seria Sans
by Passumpsic Publishing
Lobster drawing © Makarova Olga | Dreamstime.com

University Press of New England is a member of the
Green Press Initiative. The paper used in this book meets
their minimum requirement for recycled paper.

Selection from "New Religion," by Bill Holm, from
The Chain Letter of the Soul: New and Selected Poems
(Minneapolis: Milkweed Editions, 2009). Copyright
© 2009 Bill Holm. Reprinted with permission from
Milkweed Editions (www.milkweed.org).

Library of Congress Cataloging-in-Publication Data
Frazier, Nancy.
I, Lobster: a crustacean odyssey / Nancy Frazier. — 1st ed.
    p. cm.
Includes bibliographical references and index.
ISBN 978-1-58465-962-4 (cloth: alk. paper) —
ISBN 978-1-61168-323-3 (ebook)
1. Lobsters. I. Title.
QL444.M33F72   2012
595.3'84—dc23   2012012527

5 4 3 2 1

To

ED KNAPPMAN,

a dear man and wonderful

literary agent

CONTENTS

I, Lobster

Introduction

I am sitting at a window in Waldoboro, Maine, looking out at the Medomak River. The powdery blue sky is banked with low-lying clouds edged in gray and pink. It's four o'clock on January 25, 2008. The temperature is zero and falling. About an hour ago a bald eagle flew toward the opposite shore, skimming down to the water's surface before vanishing on the far side of a small island.

It's high tide. The river is empty. No birds or seals or boats are visible now, but mainly it is forlorn because the lobster buoys have been taken away. I'm so used to seeing them bob, decorating the river like lollipops. But the lobsters started heading out to deeper ocean hideouts in the fall, and by early November the Medomak lobstermen and women were pulling their traps out of the water. It will be early May before our river starts coming back to life.

The lobsters are gone, true, but they still have my undivided attention. A few years ago I started thinking about occurrences of lobsters in art, literature, and history. I already had several notions about them in my mind, as most art historians would. Lobsters are almost a cliché when you start looking at seventeenth-century still-life paintings from Europe because lobsters epitomized luxury in the Low Countries where those paintings flourished. One purpose of the still life was to simultaneously celebrate the widespread taste for opulence and materialism among members of the new merchant class and scold them for it.

When I am not in Waldoboro, I live near Amherst, Massachusetts, where I pay regular visits to one of the most stunning of such paintings: Frans Snyders's epic *Still Life*, which belongs to Amherst College's Mead Art Museum. In the painting's cast of characters are heroic animals, most dead—including a doe, a swan, and a peacock—and two live hunting dogs still nervous from the intensity of the chase. In the background an apprehensive servant carries a large charger with a huge boar's head. But mainly it is the lobster—brilliant red, its beady eye nearly burning a hole in the canvas—that makes the scene roar with sensual excess.[1]

I loved those still lifes with lobsters when I was a graduate student at the University of Massachusetts Amherst more than a decade ago (after a career in journalism), but even then I think they set off a silent alarm in my mind. Whether surrounded by silver or gold pitchers and platters, bright oranges and gleaming grapes, silks and velvets, or hunters' dead game, the lobster stands out as an anomaly—often the only sea animal, and cooked at that. Still, my attention wandered elsewhere, and the concept of self-portraiture was the subject of my dissertation.

In 2001 my husband and I bought our house on the Medomak River, a rich lobster fishing ground. The full lobster alert didn't actually sound for me until the fall of 2006. It was tripped during discussions of Trevor Corson's fascinating *The Secret Life of Lobsters: How Fishermen and Scientists Are Unraveling the Mysteries of Our Favorite Crustacean.*[2] My thoughts lurched back to those show-stopping lobsters, and I knew there was *much* more to them than meets the eye.

So began my research project. First, I looked for images of lobsters, and before long I had over two hundred on my computer—starting with an ancient Roman wall mosaic of fishermen standing in their boats on a sea teeming with life. A lobster has pride of place in the center of the composition; it is the same size as the boats that surround it. Later, I found several paintings of imagined Roman feasts painted from the Renaissance on, in which the lobster platter was the magnet, the *pièce de résistance.*

Whole red lobsters are the aesthetic rule, even though, as almost everyone knows, red lobsters are usually dead lobsters. There are the standout works by famous Renaissance, baroque, and modern artists (including Picasso, Willem de Kooning, and Salvador Dalí). In addition, some oddities—even favorites—in my collection include a beautiful, moody, and very strange early-nineteenth-century watercolor by Charles-Frédéric Soehnée of a man riding a lobster, slouched like a weary cowboy, though his eccentric, burnoose-style outfit makes him look as if he should be riding a camel. In stark contrast is a drawing from the early Nazi era lampooning Adolf Hitler, titled "Hitler Advances." In it, the *Führer*, astride a lobster, waves his riding crop like a flag and appears to be proceeding toward a blistering sunset, or sunrise, emblazoned with the word "DIKTATOR." But the point of the caricature is that he is instead going "backwards like a lobster, and would never reach a dictatorship in such a manner," writes Randall Bytwerk. Bytwerk continues: "Events turned out entirely differently. Hitler and his Nationalist lobster moved forward so quickly that the opponents not only had to retreat, but committed suicide."[3]

Then there is the picture that hung above my head at the Rockland Cafe in Rockland, Maine, one day at lunch. In it, a lobsterman is pulling up a trap in the back of his boat, blissfully unaware that the King Kong of lobsters, having advanced from stem to stern, is poised above his head, prepared to take revenge on behalf of its species. The picture was a faded copy of a copy of a painting, all the more ominous for its ghostly, yellow-brown hue. And there is a 2002 poster for a harvest festival in Westport, Massachusetts, with a lobster milking a cow. A lobster milking a cow!

The exponential growth of my lobster collection is not really surprising since I was constantly on the alert. New pictures showed up even when I wasn't looking for them. For instance, it was after we discussed my project during a Labor Day cookout that a neighbor e-mailed me a copy of the poster with the hilarious lobster milkmaid, which he had photographed at the Westport festival. On another occasion, having learned that I would be giving a talk on lobsters in art at a local club, a member showed me what looked like an original drawing by Dalí that she'd bought for her husband thirty years earlier. If the lobster milking a cow was outlandish, at least it had an underlying rationale: the town of Westport's pride in both its dairy and seafood commerce. But Dalí's image seemed inexplicable. In the background, a horse with blinders carries skulls on its back; in the foreground is a sewing machine; and in the middle ground is the head of a man with a handlebar moustache and a lobster holding fast to his bald pate.

My cache of lobster images was a virtual cabinet of curiosities, a visual museum filled with treasures like those that explorers brought home during the Age of Discovery. But the larger my inventory grew, the more I wanted. Not just fine and graphic arts — what about other arts? Were lobsters interesting in literature? Poetry? How about the movies? Photography? The decorative arts? Yes. Yes. Yes. Yes. And yes. Even high fashion. Not to mention haute cuisine.

Each of the arts makes its own claims on and has its own use for one of the strangest creatures to parade across the face of the earth — or, more accurately, beneath the surface of the sea. It scurries both backward and forward on its five pairs of walking legs, the first two of which, on the lobsters we know best, are awesome claws that it raises in defense and challenge. It hides in dark places, protecting its territory, threatening everything from a passing lobster to a submarine.

Backward and forward also describes the way that people characterize and feel about this creature, a relationship that surely parallels the human presence on earth since lobsters preceded us here, and we had to try to figure them out. We still do.

Lobsters are arthropods. Their ancestry dates back nearly four hundred million years to the Jurassic period, when they kept company with dinosaurs. Though the lobster, along with giant spider crabs, is today the largest of arthropods, it would have been just a crunchy snack, a potato chip, to its prehistoric predator, the giant sea scorpion. In 2007 an international team of scientists discovered the fossil claw of a sea scorpion they estimated to have been over eight feet long.[4]

In order to survive, Jurassic scorpions had to severely downsize. For their part, lobsters diversified and evolved. Most familiar on our shores is *Homarus americanus* — also known, according to the US Fish and Wildlife Service, as the American lobster, Maine lobster, northern lobster, blueshell, old shell lobster, blackshell, crack backer (when it's ready to molt), shedder, soft shell, new shell, shadow rubber shell, paper shell, and (recently molted) buckle shell.[5] This creature roams the coastal and oceanic waters of the Atlantic Ocean from Labrador to North Carolina and, I'm proud to say, may be nowhere denser than in my stomping grounds, the Gulf of Maine.

The ferocious distinction of the American lobster is its killer claws. One is popularly known as the slicer, and the other is the crusher — and when you look closely, you recognize that not only the names but also the shapes illustrate the rule that form follows function. The slicer is smaller, and its serrated edges are sharper than those of the hefty crusher.

The slightly smaller European version of *Homarus americanus* is *Homarus gammarus* or *vulgaris*. While most American and large European lobsters are a dark brownish-black- or blue-green, there are variations on the theme, including red, white, black, and calico (marbled black and orange/yellow), as the US Fish and Wildlife Services describes them.[6]

Adult lobsters are inclined to migrate seasonally, moving to deeper bottom terrain as winter approaches. There the temperature is relatively constant and milder, and the water is calmer than it is inshore, where freezing surface temperatures and icy winds strongly affect the shallower bottom water's temperature and turbulence. I don't wonder at their departure. The Medomak River is too cold for a dip almost all summer long, and although it infrequently freezes over, it must be unimaginably cold during the winter.

But, of course, winter is relative: consider the Caribbean (sometimes called Florida) spiny lobster, *Panulirus argus*, which enjoys the tropical and subtropical waters around south Florida, the Bahamas, and down into the Gulf of Mexico. Tropical or not, during the autumn thousands—I repeat *thousands*—of these lobsters line up in single file, antenna to tail, and march along the shallow ocean floors to deeper water. What a parade! It's a behavior familiar in ants and some bird flocks, but *Panulirus argus* seems to be unique among crustaceans in this eccentricity.[7]

Homarus americanus migrates without the military rigor and melodrama of its southern relative. Populations of lobsters from the northern East Coast have been tagged and tracked from location to location. Most, apparently, don't stray very far from where they are released. However, some do. Among them are relentless hikers who choose to traverse the coast rather than move to and from the shoreline. Among those long-distance trekkers, the award for the most tenacious traveler goes to an American lobster that logged 496 miles between the Gulf of Maine and the Bay of Fundy during a journey that lasted three and a half years.[8] Who knows how much farther it might have gone had it not been captured in a lobster trap?

One name the US Fish and Wildlife Service does not use for lobsters is "bug." But Linda Greenlaw does in *The Lobster Chronicles*, an absorbing story of her early years of fishing for lobster around Isle au Haut, Maine.[9] "Bug" and "spider" are among the fond — and not so fond, depending on the situation — names that lobstermen and women attach to their quarry.

Neither they nor US Fish and Wildlife Service use the nickname "locust," but as it happens the locust is the lobster's namesake. For that we may thank the Roman chronicler Pliny the Elder, who lived from about 23 to 79 CE. His exact birth date is not known, but the day he died is burned into history: it was during the eruption of Mount Vesuvius, and Pliny's intention to record that event ended in his early death. His heroic thirty-seven-volume work *Natural History* was published two years prior to the eruption. In the preface he noted that, during his research, he had read two thousand volumes by Greek and Roman authors.

Chapter 30 of the ninth volume of Pliny's magnum opus is titled "Of the Many Foot Fish Called Ozaena, of the Nauplius, and Locusts of the Sea, or Lobster."[10] So, one way or the other, the etymology of "lobster" is traced back to Pliny's *locusta* through the Old English *loppestre*.

Whatever their name, lobsters are definitely not kosher:

> You shall not eat anything abhorrent . . . These you may eat of all that live in the water: you may eat anything that has fins and scales. But you may not eat anything that has no fins and scales: it is unclean for you."[11]

Insects were prohibited, too. Perhaps it's partly because lobsters and insects look alike that both are proscribed, but more likely it is because, like birds of prey — which are also abhorrent — lobsters will eat dead meat. They are bottom feeders, and not as discriminating as one might wish.

That didn't trouble the empire-building ancient Romans. In fact, very little interfered with their boundless, hedonistic appetites for vast conquests, including the lands of Judea, colossal entertainments, and almost unimaginable feasts, as we will see in the next chapter.

Nor did it bother Zanino di Pietro in 1466 when he painted a

Zanino di Pietro, detail from Last Supper fresco, 1466. Chiesa di S. Giorgio, San Polo di Piave. Photo: Cameraphoto Arte, Venice / Art Resource, NY.

fresco titled *Last Supper* for the church of San Giorgio in San Polo di Piave, a region north of Venice known for its wine production and bountiful crayfish. Both fresh and saltwater crayfish (sometimes called spiny lobsters) are in the lobster family and are also forbidden to Jews. Yet they are plentiful in Zanino's rendering of what was supposed to be the Passover table of Jesus and his twelve apostles. John Varriano points out that usually little attention was paid by artists to particular dishes: "In most depictions of the Last Supper, bread is on hand, as are wine and perhaps a prepared dish or two, but the meal is usually a spare one."[12] However, in addition to several carafes of wine and loaves of bread, there are platters of fish and bright red crayfish boldly set out on Zanino's long white tablecloth. Though two of the apostles hold glasses of wine, no one is drinking or eating. Rather, almost everyone is seated at the far side of the table (facing us), gesturing and pointing meaningfully.

But Judas sits alone on a low stool on the near side of the table, his gaze fixed on Jesus—who is bent over with his eyes closed, as if in mournful anticipation of the inevitable betrayal.

The appearance of crustaceans in a portrayal of the Last Supper seems exceptional, but nonkosher offerings appear in other Last Supper compositions, including a suckling pig and clams. Even in the most renowned of all renditions, that of Leonardo da Vinci, what formerly looked like bread came under scientific scrutiny in 1997. Varriano reports that experts decided the "bread" was more likely grilled eel with decorative oranges.[13]

Jewish proscriptions from "graven images" to eating seafood without fins or scales lost their meaning in the Christian world and so rendered historical authenticity irrelevant. But why choose eel or crayfish for Christ's Last Supper? Whether Leonardo ate it or not—there is some evidence that he was a vegetarian—Varriano points out that eel was popular in Renaissance Italy and that Leonardo was quite familiar with contemporary taste. And Zanino's crayfish, Varriano suggests, must be a reference the regional bounty.[14]

Beyond that rationale for the scarlet minilobsters scattered artfully on Zanino's table, the fact that they are made present and witness to the most famous supper in the history of the Western world is what counts.

What began as my reflections on the representations of lobsters in art has evolved into an absorption with the world of lobsters. That is perforce our world, for it is we who have created lobsters as monsters the size of elephants, the centerpiece of gluttonous feasts, emblems, and metaphors of the world's uncertainties. We used "lobster" as a contemptuous name for a British Redcoat, or (uncooked) for the blue-uniformed English policeman. The French poet Gérard de Nerval was famously and widely reported to have walked his pet lobster at the end of a blue ribbon in the gardens of Paris's Palais-Royale. Doris Day chased her pet lobster around the house in the movie *It Happened to Jane*. And years later, in one of the funniest movie scenes ever, Woody Allen at his manic best chased several lobsters around the kitchen in *Annie Hall*.

Consider the words of Heinrich Wölfflin: "It is true, we only see what we look for, but we only look for what we can see."[15] Wölfflin lived from 1864 to 1945 and revolutionized the study of art. That's a provocative phrase, a prompt to look deeper rather than for more. But deeper where? And how? What will make sense of this overwhelming, interdisciplinary and international cabinet of curiosities?

Wölfflin again: "Not everything is possible in every period."[16] That is, the things that we can see, that can be seen, change according to the characteristic spirit, mood, ideas, and beliefs of a specific time and place. We must deeply breathe an era in, absorbing its sensibilities and emotional, philosophical, and political currents, if we are to hear the lobster speak.

As we listen to what it says, we must remember that the lobster's voice is really our own. It expresses our fears, our struggles with good and evil, and our madness, and it gives us clues to how we inhabit our worlds. That is why the lobster is so interesting. I know the theme: it is self-portraits.

We do not just see ourselves in mirrors, we see ourselves everywhere. Most dramatically, I believe, we see ourselves in lobsters. Although or *because* we don't "see" the lobsters in their world, we conjure them up in ours. We portray them in all kinds of human situations and adventures. Our imagination is the beginning and usually the end of our understanding of lobsters, as it is of ourselves.

In this book I intend to demonstrate what fascinating lobsters we can be. I hope that you will be as interested, pleased, astonished, amused, and even horrified as I am by the lobster personas awaiting discovery — from medicine to poetry, raw sex to cooked food, and fact to fancy; from Zanino's *Last Supper* to *Alice's Adventures in Wonderland*.

Now is the time to put ourselves in Alice's shoes and pay attention to the Mock Turtle as he speaks to her — to us — through his tears. He begins:

"You may not have lived much under the sea—" ("I haven't," said Alice) "— and perhaps you were never even introduced to a lobster — " (Alice began to say "I once tasted" but checked herself hastily, and said "No, never") " — so you can have no idea what a delightful thing a Lobster-Quadrille is!"[17]

Shall we dance?

I Consider the Cult of the Lobster

In the second century Pausanias — the ancient Greek geographer, traveler, and author — wrote: "The lobster was generally esteemed sacred by the Greeks and was not eaten by them; if the people of Seriphos caught a lobster in their nets they put it back into the sea; if they found a dead one they buried it and mourned over it as over one of themselves."[1] These words took me by surprise. What could he possibly mean? Why was the lobster sacred? There is no clue in Pausanias or in other ancient writers, including Aelian, who earlier commented on this contention of the lobster's deification. It appears to be unchallenged. Surely an explanation should be available.

Seriphos is one of the Cyclades, a rough circle of some 220 islands in the Aegean Sea. Seriphos was visited by J. Theodore Bent, an English traveler who was born in 1852 and died from malarial fever just forty-five years later. Bent chronicled his explorations in archeological articles and in books that ranged from the *Life of Giuseppe Garibaldi* to travel guides with social commentary. In 1885 he published *The Cyclades, or Life among the Insular Greeks*. It sounded promising to me.

However, Bent's book said nothing at all about the sacred lobster. Even worse, he wrote that of all the towns in the Greek islands he visited, Seriphos was the filthiest. The main street he described as a sewer, literally, and said it was occupied by pigs.[2] He was unfavorably inclined toward Seriphos partly because he visited during the winter season, when the vineyards — for which the island is renowned — were barren. "The long straggling vines which in the islands are trained along the ground to get what protection they can from the summer winds, do not in winter present a very lovely appearance," he wrote.[3] He described the traditions, practices, and specifics of winemaking on Seriphos, but if he had the pleasure of tasting any wine there, he doesn't mention it. He recounts several Nereid myths that the islanders told him with conviction, but nothing — nothing at all — about lobsters.

One legend that Bent did mention is that Seriphos is where Danaë and Perseus washed up after being thrown into the waves. This story eventually led me to the only possible explanation I have found for the deification of the lobster on Seriphos.

A prophecy that the son of his then-childless daughter Danaë would kill him led the king of Argos to imprison Danaë in a bronze tower as a preventive measure. Foolish man — nothing could deter the lustful Zeus when he set his mind on what he wanted. Transforming himself into a shower of gold, Zeus ravished Danaë in her prison and impregnated her. She gave birth to a son she named Perseus. When the king learned he had a grandson, he ordered that mother and child be locked in a wooden trunk and cast out to sea.

A fisherman on Seriphos rescued the castaways, and Perseus grew up on that island. But then Danaë's beauty attracted the attention of the king of Seriphos, Polydectes, who determined to get rid of young Perseus in order to seduce his mother. Polydectes dispatched Perseus on a mission to kill Medusa, a gorgon (from the Greek word for "dreadful") whose glance could turn anyone who looked at her to stone.

Perseus used a highly polished shield borrowed from Athena as a mirror so that he did not have to look directly at Medusa, and with her reflection to guide his aim, he succeeded in cutting off her head. Proudly he returned to Seriphos with his trophy, only to find his mother in the arms of Polydectes. In revenge Perseus held up Medusa's head, directing its gaze at Polydectes and then at the entire island. So it was that Polydectes and his kingdom of Seriphos were transformed into the rocky, barren landscape Bent so disparaged (Perseus eventually, though unintentionally, killed his maternal grandfather in accordance with the prophecy). Even today Seriphos is one of the more desolate and least visited and appreciated of all the Greek islands.

The Evil Eye

Because I had nothing else to go on, I looked for clues about the lobster that Medusa might hide. Before becoming a gorgon, Medusa was a beautiful young woman whose gorgeous hair was especially admired. Poseidon, god of the sea, raped her in the temple of the virgin goddess Athena, where Medusa was a priestess. Enraged, Athena (who later loaned Perseus her shield) turned Medusa and her two sisters, also priestesses, into gorgons. Pictures of gorgons show them as monsters with huge eyes; a gaping mouth, often with the tongue sticking out; and, most grotesque of all, live snakes emerging from their heads.

In some of the older images the "snakes" look more like arms, and suggest an alternative. They are "not snakes, but the writhing tentacles of the horrible Octopus," announced the folklorist F. T. Elworthy when he brought his idea to light in 1902.[4] "Those who have studied that monster, the Octopus, at close quarters, as I have," Elworthy went on, "will find no difficulty in appreciating the awfully fascinating glance, in the baleful eye of that odious creature, an eye in itself conveying the most frightfully malignant expression of any living thing upon which I have ever looked."[5] An expression that could turn anyone stone cold with fear. Elworthy convincingly argued that Medusa evolved from the horrible octopus.

And the horrible octopus is the mortal enemy of the lobster.

The violent clashes of lobster and octopus were well known in ancient times. Pliny the Elder, invaluable chronicler of everything from insects to art, wrote that if a lobster just *sees* an octopus, "he evermore dieth for very woe."[6]

The fishermen of Seriphos would have been familiar with both the octopus and the lobster and could have witnessed deadly combat between the two. The story of that battle would have been told and retold. In any case, it was a favorite theme in ancient art. Two similar and wonderful examples are mosaic compositions excavated at Roman villas in Pompeii. The fight, in which the glaring octopus grips the lobster with its tentacles, is surrounded by a variety of other Mediterranean sea creatures; their coloring and movement, the pattern and silvery sheen of their scales, the shapes of fins and other physical characteristics were all carefully observed and recreated with tesserae, tiny pieces of colored stone. Even the depth of the underwater scene is suggested by the use of lighter blue tesserae toward the water's surface. Not only is the mosaic drama powerful and dreadful, but there is also a clever suggestion of another violent chapter in store. This is the depiction of a large and ferocious eel speeding into the fray.[7] The lobster may or may not live to see another day, but now it is the octopus that is in mortal danger.

The mosaics of Pompeii predate an astonishing literary interpretation of the same three-way engagement between lobster, eel, and octopus written by the poet Oppian toward the end of the second century. Oppian's blow-by-blow account of the prolonged battle is as excited and detailed as the rant of a ringside announcer, and far gorier. Oppian begins when an eel attacks an octopus, sinking her deadly teeth into him. The octopus hasn't got a chance but fights back nevertheless, wrapping his tentacles around the eel—who easily slips through his embrace. It is, Oppian writes, like two wrestlers exerting all their force against each other, but the eel consumes the octopus even as he fights against her. The octopus grabs onto a rock for purchase and changes color as if to camouflage himself. The eel seems to mock him, as if to say, Who do you think you are fooling? Oppian now turns maudlin:

> She fixes him in the curved hedge of her teeth and devours him, pulling him all trembling from the rock. But he, even while he is rent, does not leave the rock nor let go. Coiling he clings to it till only his suckers remain fast. As when a city is sacked by the hands of the foemen, and children and women are haled away as the prize of the spear, a man drags away a boy who clings to the neck and arms of his mother; the boy relaxes not his arms that are twined about her neck, nor does the wailing mother let him go, but is dragged with him herself; even so the poor body of the Poulpe [octopus], as he is dragged away, clings to the wet rock and lets not go.[8]

Soon after our compassion for the octopus reaches a peak, Oppian introduces a lobster "breathing hostile breath" and issuing a challenge that the eel, "quivering with wrath," accepts. And now it is the eel's turn to be humiliated, for her teeth merely bounce off the lobster's shell, while the lobster grabs and slices away at her flesh and grasps her by the throat. Sometimes, if the eel's teeth are able to find a grip and hold tight, the pair seem locked together in deadly combat, as if they would finally perish together. But for the most part the lobster is the eel's nemesis.

In the last act, the lobster succumbs to the octopus, which leaps onto his back and winds his eight tentacles around the lobster's body. Though the lobster swims and stops and struggles, swims, stops, fights again, and beats against sharp rocks in an effort to dislodge his foe — the octopus holds on until the victim collapses. Then the octopus sits beside the dead lobster and, in Oppian's words, "feasts, even as a child draws with his lips the sweet milk from the breast of his nurse; even so the [octopus] laps the flesh of the [lobster], sucking and drawing it forth from its prickly vessel and fills his belly with sweet food."[9]

As unpleasant as this stilted humanizing may seem, it follows a tradition reaching back to Hesiod in the eighth to seventh century BCE: "obey the voice of justice and always refrain from violence. / This is the law Zeus laid down for men, / but fish and wild beasts and winged birds / know not of justice and eat one another."[10] One of the oldest proverbs in history, this is a succinct international lesson, a maxim found in art, literature, popular culture, and business: *big fish eat little fish*. Sometimes it crops up in strange places.

Henry Lee, a nineteenth-century naturalist, reported that the first octopus received at the Brighton Aquarium was caught in a lobster pot at Eastbourne in October 1872.[11] Although the true octopus, *Octopus vulgaris*, is not a common visitor to England, in 1899 and 1900 octopuses were so plentiful along the country's southern coast as to be a veritable plague. They were also all too present along France's western coast, up into the English Channel. One hypothesis was that unusually warm springs and hot summers had encouraged this invasion. Whatever the cause, the result was that lobster pots hauled up during those years were often bereft of lobsters but inhabited by their predator, the octopus, and the remains of its victims: "One fisherman took in a single week 64 specimens of octopus and only 15 living uninjured lobsters."[12]

It's true that the bite of an octopus can poison a person, but unless the animal has been frightened it is unlikely to attack. Yet the cover of Lee's book shows an octopus as big as the three-masted schooner it is about to bring down. As far as a confrontation between lobster and octopus goes, the odds generally favor the octopus. But if Medusa might have represented the octopus, and she was slain by Perseus — her mortal enemy, who might have represented the lobster — doesn't it make sense that the battle between octopus and lobster was localized by storytellers on Seriphos and led to the victorious lobster's becoming sacred to the island? Supporting this conjecture is the notation by Pausanias (citing Aelian) that the people of Seriphos called the lobster a "plaything of Perseus."[13] It is tempting to take a further step: the story of Perseus killing Medusa is not only a metaphor for the triumph of lobster over octopus but also, by extension, of good over evil. The caveat is that the pagan gods were never simple enough to be labeled either good or evil.

Lobsterworld

In book 7 of Milton's *Paradise Lost*, after the archangel Raphael warns Adam against Satan's temptations, he tells Adam about the creation of the world. Milton's account is largely based on the biblical Genesis as he describes the beginnings of the undersea world:

> Forthwith the sounds and seas, each creek and bay
> With fry innumerable swarm, and shoals
> Of fish that with their fins and shining scales
> Glide under the green wave, in schools that oft
> Bank the mild sea; part single or with mate
> Graze the sea weed their pasture, and through groves
> Of coral stray, or sporting with quick glance
> Show to the sun their waved coats dropped with gold,
> Or in their pearly shells at ease attend
> Moist nutriment, or under rocks their food
> In jointed armour watch.[14]

Milton hears a new world teeming with life, sees it in motion and in colors, lights, and textures, though by the time he wrote this he was blind. He describes the animals but identifies very few — perhaps because Adam had not yet named them — but he knows and envisions them in his mind's eye. We can picture them, too, and recognize as lobsters those covered in "jointed armour" and hiding under rocks.

This is the fifth day of creation, when all the creatures that fly through the air and live under water came to be, a wonderful and dramatic day. The drama especially moved Gustave Doré during the nineteenth century. In all Doré made fifty woodcuts to illustrate *Paradise Lost*. They were transferred onto metal by engravers, and these form a prodigious and brilliant accompaniment to Milton's work. Doré did not illustrate the lines quoted but an earlier passage:

> And God said: Let the waters generate
> Reptile with spawn abundant, living soul
> And let fowl fly above the earth.[15]

For this Doré drew the sun as if shooting its rays through the clouds and a thick flock of birds, before dropping a floodlight onto the turbulent water and its reptilian, monster fish. He also illustrated a later passage:

> There leviathan,
> Hugest of living creatures, on the deep
> Stretched like a promontory, sleeps or swims,
> And seems a moving land; and at his gills
> Draws in, and at his trunk spouts out, a sea.[16]

The leviathan of this woodcut, unimaginably large, follows the curves of a long hilly divide, beyond which is the bold ocean, and in front of which is a rocky cove. In this cove, deep down, is where the armor-plated lobsters hide.

Milton first published *Paradise Lost* in 1667, describing God's creation. In 1866 Doré interpreted Milton's creation. In 1986 Franco Ferrucci published *Il mondo creato*. It was translated and published in English in 1996 as *The Life of God (as Told by Himself)*. The book begins: "For long stretches at a time I forget that I am God. But then, memory isn't my strong suit. It comes and goes with a will of its own."[17]

Ferrucci's God veers from humor to anger, from exasperation to bliss. As narrator of his life, God lets us know that he was just an infant, not an old man with a white beard, when he became aware that he was alone—and lonely. The creation of the world to end his solitude did not at happen at once; he wandered through darkness for "light years" before letting out a cry that rose "like an arrow, reaching the center of the heavens and exploding into fragments that became stars."[18]

With the creation of light, God understood that what is done cannot be undone: he may be God, but he cannot destroy what he has made. Once the sun exists, it will remain, a curious reflection of the "light years" between his own infancy and the realization that what he brings about is self-reproducing "like a host of mirrors reflecting whatever I do."[19] It was at one of his lowest moments that God climbed a cliff until he was high above the sea and let himself fall over the edge: "I had wanted to die, and this was itself an act of creation: I was creating my own end."[20] He swam among schools of fish and wandered through "labyrinths of the ocean": "The flash of the lamprey and of the bass fleeing the shark's pursuit; the cod disappearing into the maw of the hammerhead, and the sudden shadow above me, like the heavy sky, during the regal passage of a blue or sperm whale . . . and the incredible lobster that couldn't laugh at itself lest it choke, like a boy hiding inside a suit of armor in some museum."[21]

And at this moment, God judges the underwater drama for what it suddenly seems to be: all these creatures "driven by the urge to eat another and by the fear of being eaten." He determines to escape, which is not easy since he is a fish. But he is encouraged, attended to, and befriended by a jellyfish. Finally, with reliable lungs, his "watery purgatory" is over.[22]

It was often said that Bill Holm was "larger than life," maybe because at six feet eight he was certainly bigger than most people, but also because he grew up on the Minnesota prairie and had views, passions, beliefs, and sentiments that were as vast as it was. His compatriot Garrison Keillor called him the "sage of Minnesota." Holm taught there and wrote poetry. And he loved his ancestral home, Iceland, where he spent summers and surely where he came to know the sea intimately. Holm died of pneumonia at sixty-five in 2009, the same year this poem was published:

This morning no sound but the loud
breathing of the sea. Suppose that under
all that salt water lived the god

that humans have spent ten thousand years
trawling the heavens for.
We caught the wrong metaphor.
Real space is wet and underneath,
the church of shark and whale and cod.
The noise of those vast lungs
exhaling: the plain chanting of monkfish choirs.
Heaven's not up but down, and hell
is to evaporate in air. Salvation,
to drown and breathe
forever with the sea.[23]

The idea in this poem is so unexpected — to look down to the
ocean bottom for god, or God, rather than up to the heavens —
that it is revolutionary. Holm has thrown thousands of years'
worth of history into a state of tumult. Look down to what you
cannot see at all, he says, rather than up at the sky that you can see,
or think you can see. Both go deeper and farther that our instruments or imagination can penetrate.

Ise Ebi

From 1603 to 1868, the Tokugawa shogunate ruled Japan with a
tight grip on the social, class, and legal system. The seat of government was Edo, which later became Tokyo. Besides closely regulat-
ing its subjects, the shogunate banned virtually all foreign trade
and influence, not to mention visitors (the Japanese were allowed
to do some trading with the Dutch, but all foreigners' freedom of
movement was severely limited).

Nevertheless the arts blossomed in the Edo period, especially
the kabuki theater and the pictorial arts known as *ukiyo-e*, most
renowned of which was a form of woodblock printing. The Japanese characters that signify kabuki refer to song, dance, and skill,
but it is also thought that they derive from the verb "to lean," as in
deviating from the norm or the ordinary. *Ukiyo-e* means pictures
from the floating world, an allusion to evanescent pleasures. Besides representing courtesans, tea houses, other entertainments,
and landscapes, *ukiyo-e* prints illustrated kabuki dramas and their
starring actors.

It was a woman, Izumo Okuni, who developed the sensual and suggestive style of dance, song, and drama that was named kabuki — in fact it was first named Okuni Kabuki. She and her troupe of women became extremely popular but were ultimately considered a threat to public morality by the shogunate, which in 1629 banned women from performing in public.[24] Previously men and women had acted in the few licensed theaters, but thereafter only men were permitted to perform, and they played both male and female roles. Youthful males were usually cast as attractive females. Theaters were closely monitored by the shogunate, which also instituted sumptuary laws. Kabuki directors set and followed their own conventions of color, pattern, movement, timbre, and meaning, as well as embracing specific symbolic imagery and tradition. Kabuki was visually striking and stylized, often to a point of great exaggeration.

Ichikawa Danjūrō I (1660–1704) was the founding ancestor of a line of kabuki actors that continues to this day with Danjūrō XII. Most Danjūrō actors were blood relatives though some were adopted. Danjūrō I was a playwright as well as the mastermind behind *aragoto* (wild style) acting, and he was the most influential of all kabuki actors. Asked to explain *aragoto*, according to legend, Danjūrō I smashed a shoji. Whether that's true or not, the expressions of ferocity in *aragato* are manifest in story, action, sound, costume, and makeup. Danjūrō I's face was colored red, and his eyes appeared to bulge with intense fury. An innovation of his son Danjūrō II was to cover his face with white foundation, on which thick, shaded stripes of paint followed and intensified natural lines of expression, emphasizing feelings such as anger, fear, and tension.

And the lobster.

"'Shrimp' is ebi and 'lobster' is ise ebi in Japanese. The leading or second leading Ichikawa actor [that is, the next in line of succession] has been called Ebizō from the time of the second Danjūrō. The stripes on a shrimp or lobster are compared to aragato makeup. Aragato acting and makeup were passed down to Danjūrō II from his father," writes Laurence Kominz, a leading scholar of kabuki.[25]

Actors of the Danjūrō lineage were worshiped as gods and shamans, and people thought that hanging pictures of them might cure illness, while being touched by them was a blessing. Even they were not immune to persecution by the shogunate, however. Ebizō Danjūrō VII was banished from the stage for breaking the sumptuary laws with his luxurious lifestyle.[26] After seven years his son, Danjūrō VIII, went to see him in exile. He carried a banner with the face of Shoki (the ancient Chinese foe of demons adopted in Japan), replaced by the bright red face of Ebizō Danjūrō VII, whose emblem was a curled red lobster.

In the play "Ya No Ne" (the arrow sharpener), the hero Goro says of his adversary, "Even if [he] is as powerful as the whale in my New Year's soup, I'll be a killer whale disguised as the decorative lobster, for my lobster-red face was handed down to me by my father."[27]

In both Japan and China, lobsters — with their backs bent over as if by the weight of years — have been emblematic of old age and were accordingly revered. "May you live until your head is bent forward with age as a lobster's" is a time-honored well-wisher's greeting. At the new year in Japan, a model of a lobster is among the most conspicuous of the many symbolic decorations. Oranges that represent past and future generations often accompany it. During the nineteenth century, Georg Heinrich von Langsdorff described the traditional decorations:

> As the next day was the beginning of the Japanese new year, on this day . . . two fir trees were planted before the door of every house . . . Over the entrance of the doors was placed a trophy of platted straw-work, representing a lobster, an orange, or a cabbage. The lobster, on account of its powers of re-production, since a whole claw, if torn off, will grow again, and of its fine red colour, is considered by the Japanese as the emblem of health. The orange is called in their language *dai-dai*, the same word which signifies posterity, the increase of which is to be looked forward to in the new year.[28]

Japan was still officially closed to outsiders in 1805 when Langsdorff traveled there in the role of ship's physician on the first Russian circumnavigation of the world. The mission included an effort to open an embassy and trade with Japan. Although after much negotiation a few men were briefly allowed ashore, their efforts toward diplomacy and commerce were unsuccessful. No doubt Langsdorff did see the New Year's decorations he describes, but his interpretation is questionable. It is true that lobsters are able to regenerate lost claws, but neither that nor their "healthy" red color (which generally means they're dead) are typically cited as the reason the lobster was iconic in Japan. Could the mistake have been a purposeful ruse on the part of an interpreter with instructions from the Tokugawa shogunate to misinform foreigners? Or just a problem of translation?

Besides their symbolic role, lobsters — often accompanied by shrimp — not only appear on banners and the boldly colored robes of kabuki actors, but also on delicate Japanese tea bowls of breathtaking beauty and in *ukiyo-e* color prints. Among the latter is *Lobster and Shrimp* (circa 1833) by Ando Hiroshige in which everything, even the columns of calligraphy, seem to be gracefully drifting in a balletic underwater world.[29]

Rockland, Maine

The very idea of Maine is inseparable from that of the lobster, even though that idea shines the spotlight only on the coastal region. Since we bought our house along the coast in 2001, I've come to recognize a contemporary version of historic cults. For dancing around the golden calf, substitute carousing at a lobster festival. Then think of Rockland.

Rockland, Maine, a city with a population of nearly 8,000, is the commercial center of what's called the midcoast region — which includes our relatively modest town of Waldoboro. Rockland is sandwiched between upscale Camden to the north and Thomaston to the south, with its wide main street and an enormous green field where the old state prison stood until recently. Rockland has a busy working harbor with a ferry terminal, a Coast Guard station, and a boatyard. The harbor is also the home of the largest passenger-carrying windjammer fleet in the United States.

In 2001 the credit card company MBNA opened a Rockland branch office in a splendid harborside building. As a grace note, they added a public pier and boardwalk. Then, in 2005, they closed shop. That hurt, MBNA having been the city's biggest taxpayer, but Rockland is still a great town with good downtown restaurants, antique shops, clothing stores, galleries, and a first-class museum of American art, the Farnsworth Art Museum.

There is lobster kitsch of some kind in just about every Rockland establishment: shiny black galoshes with small red lobsters crawling all over them; key chains with dangling lobsters; stuffed plush lobsters; lobster books for children and adults; place mats with instructions on "how to eat a lobster" and bibs to use while doing so; and lobster designs painted, printed, woven, embroidered, silk-screened, etched, or carved on every kind of material, for any kind of purpose one can imagine. As Seriphos once did, this town worships the lobster. Rockland (along with the Canadian town of Shediac, in New Brunswick) has named itself "The Lobster Capital of the World." In contrast to the idolatry of ancient times, however, neither its citizens nor its flocks of visitors feel the prohibitive force of any lobster taboos. On the contrary, all are invited—in fact, encouraged—to eat as much lobster as possible, as often as they possibly can. That is especially obvious during the carnivalesque Maine Lobster Festival, an annual celebration that has taken place for the past sixty-four-plus years. Here's the pitch: "What do you get when you mix nine tents, the world's greatest lobster cooker, a sea goddess, a big parade, top notch entertainment, an international crate race, fine art, talented crafts people and vendors, US Navy ship tours, all you can eat pancakes, free shuttle service, US Coast Guard Station tours, professional and amateur cooking contests, marine heritage, road races, kids events, over 20,000 pounds of lobster, *plus* over 1,000 volunteers and a group of dedicated directors?"[30]

What you also get is as many as 100,000 visitors during four or five days of carousing. In 2004, 69,600 people bought admission tickets costing $7 to $10. During that year's four-day festival, twelve tons—24,000 pounds—of lobster were sold.[31] At roughly $6 per pound, that would bring in about $144,000. (Several tons of other shellfish and finfish were also eaten, and it's a good bet that a lot of children and some adults in the crowd did not buy lobster, so it is difficult to calculate how the twelve tons were distributed.) Add to the income from lobsters more than $487,000 from ticket sales plus sales of miscellaneous items, and the 2004 festival had gross receipts of roughly $1 million.[32] That parses out to an expenditure of a little more than $14 per person. All to celebrate lobster!

What must it be like to be there? In 2003 David Foster Wallace covered the Maine Lobster Festival for *Gourmet* magazine. The article he wrote, "Consider the Lobster," was published the following year in time for the next festival. It caused a clamor not only among the festival's promoters, sponsors, and happy customers but also among a cross-section of others whom Wallace rubbed the wrong way.

Wallace described the festival's "constant Disneyland-grade queues" and the scene under the main eating tent, where "friend and stranger sit cheek to jowl, cracking and chewing and dribbling." It is hot and steamy, and the smells "are strong and only partly food-related," he writes, leaving the other malodorous sources to his reader's imagination. A substantial part of the high noise level is "masticatory," and there are not enough napkins, "considering how messy lobster is to eat, especially when you're squeezed onto benches."[33]

The carnival atmosphere Wallace describes evokes the same severe discomfort I feel while looking at James Ensor's enormous painting (8¼ by 14 feet) called *Christ's Entry into Brussels in 1889*, in which a tightly packed throng of people with grinning, masklike faces pushes through the city ostensibly to see the Second Coming—but they are oblivious to the small figure of Christ who is already among them, having ridden in on his donkey unnoticed.[34] *Christ's Entry* is loud and lurid, a *danse macabre*—and, like Wallace's lobster festival, a celebration gone bad.

Both Ensor and Wallace lodge their complaint against human nature in scathing pictures of crowd behavior. And each man identifies himself with the victim of the crowd's ignorance: Christ's face, behind which the sun forms a halo, is Ensor's self-portrait. Wallace speaks in proxy for the lobster: "After several days in the midst of a great mass of Americans all eating lobster and thus to be more or less impelled to think hard about lobster and the experience of buying and eating lobster, it turns out there is no honest way to avoid certain moral questions."[35] One such question becomes the fulcrum of his essay: "Is it all right to boil a sentient creature alive just for our gustatory pleasure?"[36]

In depth, with details, and at length, Wallace investigates whether and how lobsters may suffer pain and the various ways of killing them that may cause more or less pain. He discusses their nervous system, veering from objectivity to subjectivity. Assuming the point of view of a cook who, having just plunged some live lobsters into a pot of boiling water, watches them try to get out, he imagines how he might feel and act under those circumstances: "The lobster, in other words, behaves very much as you or I would behave if we were plunged into boiling water."[37] He finds it "hard to deny in any meaningful way that this is a living creature experiencing pain and wishing to avoid/escape the painful experience."[38]

Wallace isn't strident or dogmatic. The path that the Maine Lobster Festival took him down troubles him. He would like to find a way to eat lobster without being so distressed. So he concludes his essay by peppering his readers with a barrage of difficult questions, beginning with: "For those *Gourmet* readers who enjoy well-prepared and presented meals involving beef, veal, lamb, pork, chicken, lobster, etc.: How much do you think about the (possible) moral status and (probable) physical suffering of the animals involved?"[39]

Here is my answer. About twenty years ago, I came upon an announcement that paired a full-color photograph of a juicy hamburger and another of a winsome calf. As I remember, the text said something like: "This hamburger once had big brown eyes." That was when I stopped eating beef. Soon after I also renounced veal, lamb, and pork.[40]

Already in the back of my mind was a prompt that, I now think, must have contributed to my decision: a short story by James Agee called "A Mother's Tale," published in *Harper's Bazaar* in 1952. The story is told by a cow to her son and a group of other calves, who are all excitedly watching a cattle drive they see in the distance. Reluctantly at first, the mother recounts an ancestral legend about the roundup — the long, terrible train ride without food, then the fattening, and the ever narrowing path that takes the cattle into the slaughterhouse where a man with a hammer, standing on a bridge beneath which the cattle must pass, smashes their skulls in, one by one. But a single victim, rendered senseless, hung upside down on a meat hook and stripped of his hide like all the others, somehow regains consciousness. Driven by supernatural commitment, he escapes and miraculously returns to warn the herd of their fate and exhort them to save themselves.

Common to the three vividly graphic depictions of Ensor, Agee, and Wallace is the struggle of a would-be savior/reformer against the ignorance of the masses . . . to no avail.

"Be apprised, though, that the Maine Lobster Festival's democratization of lobster comes with all the massed inconvenience and aesthetic compromise of true democracy," Wallace wrote just before launching his complaint about the disgustingness of the Rockland scene.[41] If the revelers at the Rockland festival had been thoughtful, well mannered, and restrained instead of so odious to him, would Wallace have been less sensitive to the lobsters' fate?

Another problem is that although he proclaims he finds it difficult to deny that lobsters experience pain when thrust alive into boiling water, Wallace also writes: "Since pain is a totally subjective mental experience, we do not have access to anyone or anything's pain but our own."[42] Yet it is human nature to project what we do know as sentient beings onto beings whose levels of sentience may not, and often do not, resemble our own.

My decision to stop eating beef was emotional, not rational. I think Wallace's emotional state during his prolonged exposure, cheek by jowl, to people he found offensive is what drove him to consider the lobster compassionately, although his sympathy was expressed in the objective terms of neuroscience as well as with the subjectivity of an eyewitness chef.

The misbehaving masses sabotaged Wallace's outing and he, in turn, sabotaged the festival. His unflinching editor at *Gourmet*, Ruth Reichl, stood by Wallace and his article, though she had not expected it to be a disquisition on bioethics. She even left intact a footnote in which Wallace predicted that the footnote itself would "not survive magazine editing."[43] It did survive. Footnote digressions are characteristic of his style, and this one raises another challenging idea: it discusses how being a tourist destroys the very unspoiled thing you have ventured forth to see. Whether Wallace meant it to or not, that parallels the situation in which going to a giant lobster cookout can wring every bit of pleasure out of one's enjoyment of eating lobsters, at least temporarily.[44]

*O*n the island of Seriphos the lobster was a totem, worshiped and not eaten. In Japan (where it is not only eaten but sometimes eaten alive) it became the emblem of many generations of a kabuki family who were honored and revered for their cultural importance, a status that the lobster enjoyed by association. In Milton's poem the lobster is one of God's sea creatures, and as such it invisibly haunts the deep pools in Doré's illustrations of *Paradise Lost*. Playing God, Ferrucci also creates the lobster. And most uniquely, Holm turns God's firmament upside down when he plants the notion of heaven and salvation not in the sky above, but in the lobster's domain, the deep-breathing ocean below.

As for the lobster festival in Rockland, Maine, there the totemic power of the lobsters of Seriphos is another inversion: the more lobster that is eaten, the happier it makes the believers, and the unhappier it makes unbelievers.

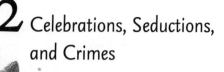

2 Celebrations, Seductions, and Crimes

Lobster is more than food: it is an idea, an event, a challenge, a happening, a celebration, an indulgence. And, more often than imagined, it is an opportunity to misbehave.

The movie *Tom Jones*, starring Albert Finney when he was devilishly young and irresistibly handsome, was a clue that eating lobster could be X-rated. Though based on Henry Fielding's novel *The History of Tom Jones, a Foundling* and set in the eighteenth century, from its irreverence and promiscuity to Finney's tousled hair, leather vest, and rakish headband (really a bandage), the movie has the feel of the 1960s when it was made.

The famous scene, still a brilliant chapter in cinematic history, takes place in a bawdy tavern where Finney, playing Tom, sips spoonfuls of soup from a pewter bowl and dunks bread in it, pausing in between to grin at his companion, the seductive Mrs. Waters. Then he picks up a lobster, turns it belly up, chops off a claw and hammers it with the blunt end of his knife. With flirtatious looks and sensual bravado, he snaps the shells open between his fingers and plays with the lobster meat as he eats it. Mrs. Waters reciprocates, giggling and upping the ante with each sly glance and insinuating taste of her food.

The erotic pantomime gets lustier with succeeding courses — chicken and oysters, fruit and wine — but the die was cast when the lobster took the situation out of bounds, *way* out of bounds.

Why lobster?

The taste of lobster is the taste of ocean depths, but there is a mysterious sweetness added to the salty broth. Along with more familiar love potions like caviar and oysters, lobster has a reputation as an aphrodisiac. That's understandable since it comes from the sea, like Aphrodite, the Greek goddess of love. Unlike Aphrodite, a lobster is not at all beautiful when it emerges from the ocean bottom in its dark mottled shell, brandishing its ungainly claws and flailing its spidery legs. Only when it is cooked and turns brilliant red does it become desirable. Then it has a taste that is incomparable. Irresistible. Expensive.

One of the world's first books devoted to food, written in the fourth century BCE by the Greek poet Archestratus, was called *The Life of Luxury*. Among the fragments of this text to survive is this blunt epicurean advice: forget the other trifles — buy lobster. It's significant that lobster has been pricey and coveted for most of human history. The Roman satirist Juvenal scorned a wealthy host who ordered that he be served a huge lobster garnished with asparagus, while his lowly guest was given a small crab and half an egg.

Tom and Mrs. Waters ate their lobster straight from the shell. We usually dip ours in butter because . . . well, because that seems enough. But I'm reminded that members of the upper class in both Greece and Rome reclined on couches, supporting themselves with one arm while using the other to eat one-handed with their fingers. That made lobster served in the shell, with nutcracker and bib, somewhere between unlikely and impossible. Of course, it *is* possible that ancient banqueters were hand-fed shelled lobster meat by their servants. What is certain is that Roman feasts were opulent and extravagant, and Roman appetites so excessive as to be considered gluttonous.

With a touch of humor, evidence of Roman gluttony was incorporated into the very floors of Roman villas: *trompe l'oeil* mosaic floors in the rooms where meals were served were sometimes made to look as though the their surfaces were littered with garbage: the skeleton of a fish, scraggly foot of a chicken, snail's shell, and bits and pieces of other shells, including a lobster's claw. In one case, there is even the detail of little opportunistic mouse investigating some of the debris.[1] While mosaic artisans may have viewed the mess with a sense of humor, the floors do contribute to the Roman reputation for stepping beyond the pale.

The Romans' uncontrolled hedonism is parodied by Petronius, an arbiter of taste during the rule of Nero in the first century CE. The purported host was Nero's friend Trimalchio, a freed slave whose liberation brought him great wealth and led him into enormous ostentation. On the menu were dormice flavored with honey and poppy seeds, a garden warbler inside an egg made from pastry, which was inside a duck carved out of wood. More than sixty-two separate kinds of food have been counted in the parody, among them the contents of a tray decorated with the twelve signs of the zodiac. Above each sign the chef placed theoretically related dishes: Over Gemini were kidneys and testicles — explicable if, upon reflection, aesthetically and otherwise unsavory. Over Virgo was the uterus of a sow — appalling. And over Capricorn was a lobster. Why?

Whoever answers that question will be celebrated, if not with a Nobel or Pulitzer Prize, at least with the gratitude (or envy) of classical scholars. Could Petronius's astrology be faulty? Was he trying to show the ignorance of his cast of characters? Or was he devising a rebus, or perhaps it was some kind of play on the word "lobster"? One scholar has written: "Petronius was never an ordinary classic. The sexual license of his characters, the difficulty of his vocabulary, and the many out-of-the-way objects and customs he described all called for commentary."[2] This call was heard before the seventeenth century and echoes still.

Croquettes

The largest trove of ancient recipes for lobster was assembled under the name of Apicius, an author whose actual identity is unknown. Speculation is that the recipes were collected in Roman times, building on both Greek and Roman cooking practices. In an English translation by the scholar and chef Joseph Dommers Vehling, the lobster section comes after "Stuffed Dormouse" and is followed by instructions for preparing ray (or skate). There are six lobster entries, including croquettes, the perfect finger food for a reclining sybarite.

The Apicius recipes do not resemble those in contemporary cookbooks — there are no measurements or timing cues, let alone instructions on how to proceed — but they do excite the senses. For the croquettes, for example, the instructions are to have leaves ready so that, after mincing the tail meat and combining it with broth, pepper, and eggs, it can be wrapped in the leaves and fried.[3] Other examples include "A sauce for shellfish — chopped scallions fried lightly, crush pepper, lovage, caraway, cumin, figdates, honey, vinegar, wine, broth, oil, reduced must [new wine that has been boiled down]; while boiling add mustard"[4] and "Boiled lobster — cooked with cumin sauce and, by right, throw in some pepper, lovage, parsley, dry mint, a little more cumin, honey, vinegar, broth and, if you like, add some [bay] leaves and malabathron [a cinnamonlike aromatic used in cosmetics as well as food].[5]

The Apicius collection of recipes from imperial Rome was assembled during the late fourth or early fifth century CE. Roughly a thousand years later, in 1570, Bartolomeo Scappi, personal chef to Pope Pius V, published a monumental work with about a thousand recipes — *Opera [Works] di M. Bartolomeo Scappi*. Scappi introduces different ways to cook lobsters that include unusual ideas such as plugging up the holes in the lobster's tail with cotton before cooking, so that the water won't get in. He also offers a variation on croquettes in the form of *tomacelle* (small sausages) or fishballs and "pears," which are croquettes shaped into pears. It seems an odd recipe: "Get the flesh from the tail and claws of the lobsters and, raw, beat it small. For every pound of it, put in three ounces of boneless, salted eel flesh, along with common spices, raisins, a little sugar, oil or butter, beaten mint, sweet marjoram and wild thyme. With this mixture make up the shapes of *tomacelle*, pears and fishballs."[6] For cooking, Scappi refers us to an earlier recipe for *tomacelle* of sturgeon flesh, where he suggests flouring them and frying them in butter or oil, turning them so they cook "above and below." He instructs us that when done, they should be served hot with orange juice and sugar poured over them.[7]

The sweetened savories of imperial Rome have flavors in common with the papal Rome of the Renaissance. Regardless of their scolding satirists, and periodically discouraging sumptuary laws, the ancient Romans didn't suffer much guilt or remorse for their sins of gluttony, and during the Renaissance, when curiosity about ancient Greek and Roman culture absorbed intellectuals in Italy and Northern Europe, those appetites were actually celebrated. Artists were inspired and commissioned to represent ancient myths. Lobsters played their part in this flourishing, often hedonistic culture, particularly when imagining the feasts of Neptune and the river gods.

Peter Paul Rubens in collaboration with Jan Brueghel the Elder,
The Feast of Acheloüs, 1615. Image © The Metropolitan Museum of Art /
Art Resource, NY.

Painting the exploits of pagan gods was an opportunity to take
liberties — especially in portraying nudity — that were not con-
doned for images based on the Bible. An outstanding case in point is
a painting by Peter Paul Rubens in collaboration with Jan Brueghel
the Elder. *The Feast of Acheloüs* of 1615 illustrates a tale from book 8
of Ovid's *Metamorphoses*. The hero Theseus (naked except for a red
cape) was sailing home to Athens after slaying the Minotaur when
his voyage was interrupted by a storm. This detour was staged by
the river god Acheloüs, as an excuse to offer Theseus shelter and
a five-star seafood spread. Rubens painted his characteristic ener-
getic, robust figures while Brueghel encrusted Acheloüs's grotto
with every kind of shell and set food on the table — notably those
sexual stimulants, cooked lobster and raw oysters.

One particular lobster, if it catches your attention, takes the
scene into the danger zone. It is on the lower left-hand corner of
the canvas, where a pretty, buxom nymph is emerging from the sea

with a platter full of shellfish for the table. She is closely followed by a bedraggled fellow who is holding a large, live lobster with an open claw alarmingly close to her bare behind. The detail could be missed, but when discovered it's as shocking as it is unexpected and inexplicable.

Rubens's reconstruction of Acheloüs has something besides lobsters in common with the movie version of Tom Jones: with a wink and a nudge (in a Monty Python mode), each makes the audience complicit in the scene's sexual insinuation.

Still Life with Lobster

The seventeenth century in the Netherlands was known as the Golden Age: the Dutch were exploring, colonizing, and importing everything from spices and silks to pineapples and lobsters. (Their own sandy shores were not good lobster grounds, so most lobster was brought in from Norway.) This is when still-life painting came into its own: "No other period or country produced still lifes in such quantity or quality, and no other branch of painting reveals more clearly the Dutch devotion to the visible."[8] These gorgeous compositions, piled high with expensive fruits and vegetables, also showed off the finest silver platters, pitchers, porcelain, and beautiful fabrics. A brilliant red lobster, incongruous or not, was often the star of the show.

Still Life with Fruit and Lobster, painted around 1648 by Jan Davidsz. de Heem, is the epitome of this type of work.[9] The objects on the tabletop gleam against a dark background, as if they were painted with some radioactive substance. It is a landscape of fruit, although the scene is indoors and everything is meticulously arranged. Most of the fruit is on a large platter that is barely visible. Dramatically lighted from the lower left, the still life shows green grapes, black grapes, red grapes, pears, nectarines, and peaches; an orange cut in half trails a ribbon of its peel along the edge of the table. This abundance from nature is mounded with a just-off-center balance, a faultless display of baroque technique. A grape vine skims the top of the mound almost like a chorus line of dancing figures. Shimmering glasses of different shapes hold white wine or maybe champagne; on top of a sizable blue box, delicately detailed with white trim, sits a large, pearly pink nautilus.

The silky black fabric draped in the upper right corner suggests a stage set and emphasizes the theatricality of the composition.

Slightly isolated on the right is a tall, slender, elegant golden pitcher. And in front of it is the grand diva, a large red lobster. Its claws hang over the edge of the table as if to grab you if you get too close.

I always think of de Heem's *Still Life with Fruit and Lobster* as a large painting, perhaps because it contains so much and I always think I've missed something in it, like the little bell that hangs above the nautilus, the crayfish just behind the lobster, and what I think is a shrimp near the crayfish, seeming about to fall off the edge. Is de Heem making a joke in this corner of the table? The painting is only about three feet high by four feet wide, but it has a sense of monumentality. Looking at a reproduction of it, we expect it to be at least twice as big as it really is.

The message of such still lifes was *memento mori*, Latin for "remember you must die." In other words, worldly goods and pleasures are passing fancies, and you can't take them with you. The still lifes are also called *vanitas* paintings as in Ecclesiastes: "Vanity of vanities; all is vanity." It is to the point that the glistening grapes and velvety peaches and the brilliant cooked lobsters are at the peak of ripeness and edibility, but on the verge of turning rotten. In French the term for "still life" is *nature morte* — dead nature.

Besides the vanity of materialism and the immorality of overindulgence, there is another cautionary footnote: because their legs carry them now forward and now backward, lobsters were symbolic of indecision and the uncertainty of life, as well as sin and the devil, who also walked backward.[10]

But don't despair. There is always the other side of the coin. If heads is *memento mori*, tails is *carpe diem* (seize the day). Live for the moment! Or, as the bold lettering on T-shirts worn at a gathering of bikers along Route 1 in Maine last year shouted out, "EAT LOBSTER."

And the Dutch of the Golden Age did. There was lobster enough to satisfy the appetites of those who could afford it. The author of the definitive seventeenth-century Dutch cookbook, *De Verstandige Kock* (the sensible cook), is anonymous, but Peter G. Rose has translated its text into English. Included are instructions for cooking lobster: "Take water, vinegar, salt, and pepper-powder, let it cook well together [let it come to a rolling boil], add the lobster. . . . It will have beautiful color."[11] Interesting, but it pales next to Apicius.

Lobster Palaces

When English, Dutch, and French explorers made their way to the New World during that same period, they found so many lobsters along America's rocky Northeast coast that in some places they could just reach down into the tidal pools and pick up enough for a banquet. And the size! Some weighed twenty pounds.

Sadly, that didn't last. By the end of the nineteenth century, American lobster was a luxury, and that's when lobster palaces made their debut. It was called the Gilded Age, maybe as a parody of the Dutch Golden Age. Parody or not, American excess and ostentation matched that of both ancient Rome and Renaissance Holland.

Lobster palaces were restaurants patronized by newly and fabulously wealthy American tycoons and their trophy showgirls. Earliest in the genre was Delmonico's, in New York City. It started in 1825 at 23 William Street, first as a wine shop, then a cafe serving pastries, coffee, teas, and liqueurs. In 1831 the Delmonico brothers expanded again, hired a French chef, and introduced French cuisine and wines to America in an elegant, sophisticated restaurant with a menu in both French and English that ranged from seven to eleven pages. The first restaurant burned down in the great fire of 1835, but the brothers reopened two years later at Beaver and South William Streets.[12] Delmonico's started a trend and was at the hub of it for almost a century. It was here that a favorite specialty was named Lobster à la Wenberg, in honor of the patron who introduced it to the Delmonicos. But a damning incident (maybe too much alcohol, a political argument, or raucous behavior) led to Ben Wenberg's disgrace and banishment from Delmonico's. What to do about the lobster dish on the menu that was such a big hit? By sleight of anagram, it became Lobster à la Newberg.[13]

Still popular today, Lobster Newberg's ingredients vary from chef to chef, but its rich flavor depends on butter, heavy cream, egg yolks, nutmeg, and alcohol—usually rum, sherry, or brandy alone or in combination. Imagine flaming it in a chafing dish as a finishing touch.

The theater district became the location of choice for lobster palaces, so that the Broadway area also became known as Lobster Alley. A popular vaudeville duo named Weber and Fields toured successfully and became wealthy enough to open their own music hall in 1896. One of their well-known routines was about the chorus girl who was asked if she ever found a pearl in an oyster. She replied, "No, but I got a diamond from a lobster over in Rector's last night."

Lillian Russell, who was one of the most famous actresses and singers in America, joined the Weber and Fields Music Hall in 1899. Russell was born in Iowa under the name Helen Louise Leonard; Russell was her stage name. Her parents separated and her mother—Cynthia Leonard, a feminist—became the first woman to run for mayor of New York City. Russell was the toast of the town, as beautiful as she was talented; in fact, she was known as "the American Beauty." For forty years she was the companion of Diamond Jim Brady, who made a great fortune selling equipment to the railroad companies. Russell and Brady were in the highest tier of lobster palace society, and especially devoted to dining at Rector's.

Rector's was opened by Charles Rector on September 23, 1899, on Broadway between 43rd and 44th Streets. It's been written that the restaurant was the star of Times Square and that "it was to other lobster palaces what Lillian Russell was to the Floradora Sextet—a shade more lush, more vibrant, more exciting."[14] A giant illuminated griffon, the Rector's logo, hung outside the building. Inside, the restaurant was decorated with green and gold and mirrors—which allowed those already seated to watch everyone else, especially newcomers emerging from the first-ever revolving doors. The Irish table linens were hand woven and stenciled in silver especially for Rector's. "I found Broadway a quiet little lane of ham and eggs, and left it a full-blown avenue of lobsters and champagne," Rector once bragged.[15]

It was with the encouragement of Diamond Jim that Rector moved from Chicago to New York, and Brady's patronage was a significant bonus. Brady's nickname came from his jewelry. Rector's son George commented that when fully outfitted, Brady "looked like an excursion steamer at twilight."[16] That might have referred to his avoirdupois as well as his sparkling gems, for his appetite and size were both historic. At lunch he'd put away two lobsters, deviled crabs, clams, oysters, and beef and finish with several pies. The menu was expanded and numbers were multiplied to astonishing integers at dinner, including six or seven lobsters. Rector described Brady as his best twenty-five customers.[17]

And Lobster Tricks

The New York press covered the rich and famous of the lobster palaces and coined a related phrase of its own, "lobster trick." In the 1940s, the newspaperman H. L. Mencken was asked for help in drawing up a definition of the term, which by then was outdated. He described it as a work shift that started after midnight: "In those days anyone who was astir at 2 a.m. was regarded as a gay dog, and gay dogs were currently supposed to spend all their time after midnight eating lobster and drinking champagne with chorus girls. It is thus quite possible ... that the lobster trick at the start meant a tour of duty during the lobster hours."[18]

As the lobster slips into the later morning and midday hours, it loses some of its edge as an aphrodisiac and takes on a more restrained demeanor — more affectionate, perhaps, than exciting. It seems, for example, that a dish called Eggs Drumkilbo has been a favorite on the menu of the British royal family. The recipe combines cooked and cooled lobster meat with hard-boiled eggs, tomatoes, mayonnaise, ketchup, Worcestershire sauce, gelatin, sherry, shrimp, and parsley.[19]

This was a favorite of the Queen Mother and of Queen Elizabeth, who served it to former Presidents Ronald Reagan and Gerald Ford and other American politicians on the royal yacht *Britannia* in 1991. It was also served at the wedding breakfasts of Princess Anne and Captain Mark Phillips on November 14, 1973, and Prince Andrew and Sarah Ferguson at Buckingham Palace on July 23, 1986. The wedding breakfast following the marriage of Prince Charles and Lady Diana on July 29, 1981, changed the menu but did not neglect the lobster tradition: the first course was brill (a flatfish, like turbot or sole) in lobster sauce. But in the erratic, erotic, and *vanitas* tradition of lobster, those royal marriages did not last.

No lobster is listed on the lunch menu for the 650 guests invited to celebrate at Buckingham Palace after the April 30, 2011, wedding of Prince William and Kate Middleton — probably a wise decision.

That's how it is with lobsters. They make a big impression. They attend and ramp up extravagant behavior in human affairs. I can't say they bring out the best of human nature, but I believe they do contribute to its extremes, such as breaking the Ten Commandments and committing a few of the Seven Deadly Sins. To more vividly illustrate this point, I return to the Gilded Age when lobster was so often synonymous with the fast life and bad behavior.

Stanford White, one of America's premier architects and a celebrity in high society, was often seen dining on lobster and drinking champagne at various lobster palaces. He was a voluptuary, aesthete, and art collector. He also collected girls. He kept an apartment in New York City for his conquests. Its decor was darkly luxurious and sensually extravagant; its most famous furnishing was a red velvet swing on which he launched his young paramours to the ceiling.

Evelyn Nesbit was sixteen, an exceptionally beautiful and unsophisticated artists' model and novice showgirl when White first arranged to have her brought to his apartment for lunch in 1901. To impress her, he ordered Lobster Newberg sent in from Delmonico's. One might almost say "of course." He took his time in courting Evelyn and her widowed mother with extravagant gifts, and they considered him a generous benefactor, a kind of father figure. But one night when Mrs. Nesbit was out of town, White poured Evelyn glass after glass of champagne, perhaps laced with something else. She passed out and awoke no longer a virgin.

In 1905 Evelyn was married to the millionaire Harry Thaw, another familiar face at lobster palaces. Thaw hated White and was madly jealous of his affair with Evelyn and maniacally vengeful. In 1906 he shot White three times in the head, point-blank. The crime was known as the murder of the century, a scandal that absorbed the nation.

It was then the twilight of the Gilded Age, of lobster palaces and lobster tricks. And it's possible that the company it had kept tarnished the lobster's mystique for a time. But didn't almost everything lose its glitter with the First World War and the Spanish flu pandemic of 1918? Then, beginning in 1919, Prohibition finalized the demise of the lobster palace era.

Red Lobster

While lobsters were adding glitz to the later nineteenth century in New York City, in Italy Carlo Collodi (the pen name for Carlo Lorenzini) was writing *The Adventures of Pinocchio*. During the course of his frightening, near-catastrophic adventures, the wooden puppet Pinocchio was tricked by the wicked Fox and Cat. They persuaded Pinocchio that if he buried his five gold pieces in the Field of Wonders, the coins would multiply overnight to thousands. But first they took him on a long hike to the Inn of the Red Lobster, where the two animals ate copiously. With the complicity of the innkeeper, Fox and Cat stole off while Pinocchio slept, leaving the bill for him to pay. But that was the least of their evil schemes, for they hid in the woods, intending to murder Pinocchio and steal his remaining gold pieces. Even in Italy a place named for lobster had some unsavory associations.

It is likely that Collodi had a real Inn of the Red Lobster in mind in 1880 when he wrote the story of Pinocchio's exploits, first published as a series in an Italian weekly newspaper for children. It is not likely that William (Bill) Darden had *Pinocchio* consciously in mind in 1968 when he founded The Red Lobster Inns of America and Red Lobster restaurants in Lakeland, Florida. Darden was from Georgia, where his first venture, a lunch counter twenty-five by thirty feet called The Green Frog, opened in 1938 when he was nineteen years old. It promised "service with a hop."[20] Thirty years later, things kept hopping and happening with his successful Red Lobster ventures. Providing the capital Darden needed, General Mills bought the Red Lobsters in 1970, opened a company headquarters in Orlando, and named Darden its president. Then the Red Lobster boom really started.

Bill Darden died in 1994. In 1995, while holding on to Cheerios, Wheaties, Betty Crocker mixes, and other food products, General

Mills spun off its restaurant business to a separate entity called Darden Restaurants, which celebrated its first official day of trading on the New York Stock Exchange on May 30 of that year.

Darden operates more restaurants — including six separate chains — than any other company in the world. On November 28, 2011, according to a quarterly filing with the Securities and Exchange Commission, the leading holdings were 693 Red Lobsters and 735 Olive Gardens in the United States and Canada. That equals 1,428 of the 1,852 total restaurants.[21]

Rich merchants, industrialists, and chorus girls, all dressed to the nines, patronized the lobster palaces, but Darden's Red Lobsters were traditionally family-oriented and middle market. I checked the menus at two Connecticut restaurants and noted that both offered a dinner selection called the Ultimate Feast, which includes split Maine lobster tail, steamed snow crab legs, garlic shrimp scampi, and something called Walt's Favorite Shrimp.

Who is Walt?

"Walt was a customer who ate at the first Red Lobster in Lakeland, Florida. He loved the breading on the shrimp and went there to eat it every day, so it was named after him," the friendly manager at the Wethersfield, Connecticut, restaurant told me.

Where Rector's chef used a chafing dish to finish its Lobster Newberg, Red Lobster has a "grill master" who works over an open flame — what Red Lobster calls its "signature wood fire grills." And, as for decor, forget Irish linen and mirrors:

> In 2008, Red Lobster unveiled a new look, inspired by Bar Harbor, Maine. Within the restaurants, guests will find cozy, dark-wood paneling; warm-toned fabrics; attractive, soft lighting; and nautical décor such as signal flags and seaside-inspired artwork. New exterior features include shingle and stone towers, ship lanterns, flags snapping in the breeze, and Adirondack-style benches, all intended to transport guests' minds to the coast. Going forward, all of the nearly 700 Red Lobsters in the United States and Canada will share this redesigned atmosphere.[22]

To tell the truth, there is not a single Red Lobster restaurant in Bar Harbor or anywhere else in Maine. The only Red Lobsters in New England are in Connecticut.

One of journalism's most scathing critics of everything—whose tirades are balanced only by his self-mockery—is Joe Queenan. In 1996, at the age of forty-five, he came to the conclusion that he was "growing weary of the elite, effete subculture that I had for so long occupied."[23] He decided to put aside the *New Republic*, ignore performances by Placido Domingo at the Metropolitan Opera, and avoid the long-winded, high-toned dinner conversations with friends that he was accustomed to enjoying. He resolved to "throw off the mask of the urbane sophisticate and plunge headfirst into the culture of the masses."[24]

One place where he fetched up on this dive into the mainstream was the local Red Lobster, somewhere in Westchester County, New York. A disaster. "Red Lobster, I quickly learned, was a chain geared toward people who think of themselves as a little bit too upscale for Roy Rogers," he wrote. But it wasn't just the decor or ambience that bothered him. He complained about everything. Especially the food: "The Red Lobster menu consisted almost entirely of batter cunningly fused with marginally aquatic foodstuffs and configured into clever geometric structures . . . Technically, my dinner—The Admiral's Feast—was a dazzling assortment of butterfly shrimp, fish filet, scallops, and some mysterious crablike entity. But in reality, everything tasted exactly like Kentucky Fried Chicken. Even the French fries."[25]

Plunging into the culture of the masses can be a terrible disappointment, as Queenan learned and David Foster Wallace would discover seven years later. "Democratization of lobster comes with all the massed inconvenience and aesthetic compromise of true democracy," is how Wallace put it.[26] Moreover, their experiences were entirely without the erotic pleasures of eating lobster in the bawdy tavern shown in *Tom Jones*, or of feasts such as the one Rubens designed for the gods, and it goes without saying that they enjoyed none of the social cachet of a lobster palace or a British royal spread.

But guess what, Joe? Things are changing at Red Lobster since you were there! Not only has the interior you thought garish and phony been remodeled, but so has the food. It isn't just because of the "signature wood fire grills" that, Darden executives hope, will draw a younger crowd, but also because they're trying to get away from their old fried food image. They are aiming "to create a fresh brand that will deliver sustainable growth for many, many years to come," as Red Lobster President Kim Lopdrup told a reporter for the *Orlando Sentinel* in February 2009. The headline for the *Sentinel* article is "Red Lobster Fishes for Upscale Diners."[27] That Ultimate Feast now costs $25. And to improve chances of reaching their goal, upgrades include improving maintenance and improving the quality of live lobsters.

You should give it a second chance, Joe. Or maybe you already know all this. Maybe you were responsible for the change.

Let us not be fooled, however. Regardless of how it changes from one century to the next and one eating establishment to another; whether the lobster we order represents human sexuality, excess, exclusivity, good or bad taste (in terms of either flavor or deportment, or both), it does so not as a metaphor but as the embodiment of those things. Yes, our lobster is a crustacean chameleon reflecting our perceptions, thoughts, and behavior. Perhaps only when it is visited in its natural habitat can a lobster be just a lobster.

3 "Natural" History

In book 9 of Pliny the Elder's *Natural History* is a brief statement of inquiry as conceptually sweeping as his encyclopedic masterpiece as a whole: "Why the Sea should breed the greatest living Creatures."[1] This statement compels us to consider an idea that we might not ordinarily think about, let alone question.

Yet before we have time to do either, Pliny follows his statement with explanations: "The Waters bring forth greater Abundance of living Creatures, and these also of a larger size, than the Land. The Cause is evident, in the excessive Abundance of Moisture . . . [I]n the Sea, which is so widely spread abroad, so soft and proper to yield Nourishment and increase, and receiveth the Causes of Propagation from on high, Nature is always framing some new Creatures."[2] Pliny elaborates. Not only is there more water than dry land on the surface of the earth, but life that might barely survive on solid ground flourishes and multiplies in number, size, and kind in the embrace of the sea because that is where "Seeds and universal Elements" are propelled by wind and the tumble of waves. In retrospect, his imagery suggests natural selection theory — evolutionary Darwinism almost two thousand years before the fact.

"It may truly be said," Pliny adds, "that whatever is bred in any Part of Nature is to be found also in the Sea." Examples are things that resemble bunches of grapes, or that look, smell, and even taste like cucumbers, and some things standing out like "horse-heads."[3] As the sea cucumber is named after the vegetable it reminds us of, and the sea horse miniaturizes one of our most familiar domesticated animals so, in the first century CE, the lobster reminded Pliny of a locust. Thus he named lobsters *locusta*, locusts of the sea, and his naming influenced what we call them today: lobster is from the Old English for locust, which was spelled *lopustre*, or *lopystre*, or *loppestre*.

Part of Pliny's legacy is the intensely satisfying hypothesis that things that *look* alike *are* alike. Appealing as it is, this premise doesn't work. In the universe of understanding initiated by Carolus Linnaeus with the publication of *Systema Naturae* in 1758, the land cucumber is in the plant kingdom and the sea cucumber is in the animal kingdom, so they are not even distantly related. Early classification of the horse's genus was *Equus*, and its species *caballus*. When sea horses were assigned a genus later, in 1816, it was *Hippocampus*, and there are more than thirty species of this fish whose only relationship to Black Beauty or Mr. Ed, apart from the vague though enticing similarity in the shape of their heads, is that they are all in the animal kingdom. The connection between locusts and lobsters is only a rank closer — both are animals, and both are arthropods — but, Pliny and popular names aside, that is the extent of their relationship.

Linnaeus devised a hierarchical system of five orders for naming, ranking, and classifying groups of organisms that takes into account how they look in very specific ways. Lobsters in general fall in the phylum Arthropoda, which consists of invertebrates with jointed appendages and an external skeleton that the creature must molt in order to grow. The lobster's class, Malacostraca, refers to the form of a animal's shell, which is soft and flexible (compared, say, to that of an oyster or a scallop). The order, Decapoda, counts the lobster's ten legs; and the family name, Nephropidae, refers to the lobster's possession of claws.

Thus, the Linnaean classification of the American lobster, in the kingdom Animalia, looks like this:

Phylum	Arthropoda
Class	Malacostraca
Order	Decapoda
Family	Nephropidae
Genus	*Homarus*
Species	*americanus*

The two last classifications finalize the distinctions with the most significant contribution of the Linnaean system: binominal nomenclature. The combination of generic name with species name effectively consummates what is unique about particular kinds of animals. There are both American and European lobsters in the genus *Homarus*, but they are distinguished by their species names: European lobsters are *Homarus gammarus* (sometimes called *vulgaris*). The species' geographical range (the western versus the eastern Atlantic) and size (*americanus* runs slightly larger) are the main differentials.

As neatly arranged as the Linnaean system might seem to be, there are continuing challenges, discussions, controversies, and changes within the ranks. Still it persists, satisfying a human compulsion to forever categorize and recategorize, organize and reorganize, define and describe and then redefine and redescribe the world we live in. For instance, for some two hundred years there was a third species of lobster in the *Homarus* genus.

Homarus capensis was found in shallow coastal waters around the Cape of Good Hope, South Africa, and was scientifically described in 1793, but it was very rare — no more than fourteen dead specimens were available for research until the 1990s, when new, living specimens were discovered. After careful comparative studies with its presumptive close relatives, significant differences emerged, both genetic and structural, such as *capensis*'s extremely small size (about 47 millimeters compared to *americanus*'s average 229) and divergences in details such as the tail fan, eyes, and teeth. One of the most persuasive pieces of evidence for the reconsideration of *capensis*'s classification were the hairy bristles on the surface of *capensis*'s shell, where *americanus* and *gammarus* are smooth. "Results of our studies indicate that this species should be removed from *Homarus* and placed in a genus of its own," researchers concluded.[4] Happily, the pangs of separation are softened: the outcast's new binominal nomenclature, *Homarinus capensi*, seems a comforting suggestion that the apple hasn't fallen that far from the tree after all.

Homarus sounds like an original Latin term, but is not. *Homarus* is from the French word for lobster, *homard*, which was "borrowed" not from Latin but from the Old Norse word for lobster, *humarr*, or the Danish *humme*, probably during the ninth or tenth century CE, when the Viking fleets invaded Frankish territory and settled in what is now Normandy. According to Ferdinand de Saussure, the adopted word "acquired a final -*d* by analog with

French words ending in -*ard*." This was an application of what the author calls "popular etymology," which takes place when a foreign word is given a familiar gloss to usher it into popular speech. That, he says, is to "make some kind of sense of an embarrassing word by connecting it with something known."[5]

Buffon's Challenge

Governed by rules that work their way down from the most to the least inclusive, the classification system of Linnaeus prevailed because "his nested and hierarchical scheme . . . could be slotted into the genealogical interpretation — the arborescent tree of life, with twigs on branches, on boughs, on trunks — that the discovery of evolution would soon impose upon any formal system," as Stephen Jay Gould puts it.[6] Though born some forty years after Linnaeus died, Darwin did read Linnaeus's writings while working on his theory of evolution. But Linnaeus was famous long before Darwin studied him and celebrated during his lifetime, with admirers in his native Sweden and in other European countries, including France.

France, however, was also home to Linnaeus's most formidable rival, a naturalist who, though arguably as great as Linnaeus, was far less famous in his day or later: Georges-Louis Leclerc, comte de Buffon. Both men were born in 1707, but they died a decade apart, Linnaeus in 1778 and Buffon in 1788. Buffon is the genius behind a forty-four-volume work titled *Natural History*, the last nine volumes of which were published after his death. Rather than a symptom of his insignificance, Buffon's relative obscurity is a sign of how well integrated into our culture his ideas have become: as Gould writes, we now take his innovations for granted and forget their source. "We must not equate the fading of a name with the extinction of a person's influence," Gould insists. "In so doing, we propagate one of the many errors inspired by our generation's fundamental confusion of celebrity with stature."[7]

Though Buffon's name isn't attached to a particular theory, discovery, or movement, his vital influence lives on in his masterpiece, *Natural History*, which was used to teach "students throughout the world as a primary text for more than a century — often in pirated editions that didn't acknowledge [Buffon]."[8]

Buffon was not against classifications, but he believed that Linnaeus's hierarchical streamlining and simplifying of categories was wrongheaded, and that instead of focusing on the independence of the taxonomical orders, natural historians should recognize and attend to their interdependence. Labels setting the boundaries of organisms are not intrinsic to the organisms themselves; they are arbitrary abstractions created by the human mind. Buffon wrote: "The more one increases the number of divisions in natural things, the closer one will approach the truth, since there actually exist in nature only individuals and the Genera, Orders and Classes exist only in our imagination."[9] "Individuals" and "our imagination": these words are key. They may even mean more to us than they did to Buffon's circle.

In nature, in the world, there are only individuals. Every rock, every plant, every person, every lobster is an individual. No matter how similar they may seem, each individual is distinct in genetics, size, shape, color, patterning, behavior — in one way or another — from every other individual. In what is essentially a philosophical argument between Buffon and Linnaeus, Buffon sees individuals as part of a continuum, a chain of relationships in the natural world. To Buffon, that makes it impossible to construct "a perfect systematic arrangement, not only for Natural History as a whole, but even for a single one of its branches."[10]

What is preeminent in Buffon's approach to natural history? That priority be assigned and described according to each organism's importance to humanity. Since it is human invention and imagination that designs and names the system, any system should reflect what humans value, and how: "[The] most natural order of all, is the one we have decided should be followed . . . and we believe that this simple and natural means . . . is preferable to the most highly refined and elaborate taxonomic methods, because none of these is not more arbitrary than our own."[11] The central thesis of this book — that the lobster as we know it is a reflection of ourselves — is in harmony with this quotation from Buffon.

So, according to Buffon, the Linnaean methodology is more arbitrary and less "natural" than his own. Instead of defining distinctions, Buffon wanted to concentrate on and know everything about the history and behavior of living animals.

The entry for "The Lobster" in *Natural History*, though written after Buffon's death by one of his collaborators, is nevertheless a splendid example of the Buffonian spirit and style — if Buffon is well known for anything, it is for his aphorism *le style c'est l'homme même* (style is the man himself) — descriptive and appreciative at the same time, resembling an ode to the lobster more than a scientific text. Simple, natural, yet in every way celebrating complexity, surprises, interactions, and comparisons, it marvels at the lobster's voracious appetite and commiserates with the animal's suffering during the painful process of molting:

> Just before casting its shell, it throws itself upon its back, strikes its claws upon each other, and every limb seems to tremble; its feelers are agitated, and the whole body is in violent motion: it then swells itself in an unusual manner and at the last the shell is seen beginning to divide at its junctures. It also seems turned inside out; and its stomach comes away with its shell. After this, by the same operation, it disengages itself of the claws, which burst at the joints; the animal, with a tremulous motion, casting them off as a man would kick off a boot that was too big for him.
>
> Thus, in a short time this wonderful creature finds itself at liberty; but in such a weak and enfeebled state, that it continues for several hours motionless . . . Every animal of the deep is then a powerful enemy, which they [lobsters] can neither escape nor oppose.[12]

On the scale of its significance in the lives of people, the lobster — or any other crustaceous invertebrate — might not have seemed as important to Buffon as, say, a domesticated animal. Nonetheless, but he honors the lobster with the same attention, compassion, and respect as he grants other individuals.

Darwin's Bulldog

After Darwin published *On the Origin of Species* in 1859, his ideas preoccupied almost everyone within and many outside of the natural sciences. After reading it and anticipating the controversy that would follow, Thomas Henry Huxley wrote Darwin a letter of praise and thanks for his new ideas and vowed to defend Darwin against the opposition that Huxley knew would be forthcoming. That he did so with passion gave him the nickname of "Darwin's Bulldog."

Huxley had virtually no formal education, but the fierce devotion he promised Darwin was evident in his determination to educate himself. He learned languages and studied philosophy, history, and science. At the age of fifteen, he became a medical apprentice in a London hospital; at twenty-one, as assistant surgeon, he joined the crew of a ship that embarked to chart the oceans around Australia and New Guinea. During the voyage, Huxley began collecting information on marine invertebrates, mailing his findings back to England. This work brought him recognition by the English scientific establishment, which he joined when he returned home in 1850.

Huxley argued relentlessly on behalf of evolution, education, and the natural sciences that were just progressing from the status of rich man's hobby to that of a profession. In 1861, when he was thirty-six, Huxley delivered one of his most important lectures at the South Kensington Museum, urging his audience: "Let us turn away . . . from abstract definitions. Let us take some concrete living thing, some animal, the commoner the better, and let us see how the application of common sense and common logic to the obvious facts it presents, inevitably leads us into all branches of zoological science."[13]

Which common animal did he choose? The family dog? A pesky raccoon? Or garden snake?

No.

A lobster.

"I have here before me a lobster," Huxley remarks,[14] as if to say, "What could be commoner?" But there can be little doubt that the attendees were taken aback.

It was surely not a live one, but still, how common could any lobster be to the audience of teachers whom Huxley hoped to recruit? Even people familiar with lobsters are likely to be surprised at seeing one unexpectedly and out of context.

"When I examine it, what appears to be the most striking character it presents?" Huxley immediately asks.[15]

Claws! Its claws are by far the lobster's most striking feature! Literally. Even when pegged they're daunting.

No.

Huxley's answer: "Why, I observe that this part which we call the tail of the lobster is made up of six distinct hard rings, and the seventh terminal piece."[16]

With brilliant rhetorical strategies, talking about the extraordinary as though it were everyday, confounding expectations, Huxley moves segment by segment along the lobster's tail, both top and underside, and then over the rest of its body, looking carefully at each part and its appendages and reaching the "very remarkable conclusion that a unity of plan . . . pervades the whole organization of its skeleton."[17] He also traces this plan through the development of a lobster's egg. The lobster is considered in comparison with other similar and dissimilar animals; it is traced archaeologically; and it is considered as a living, moving organism. Using the lobster as his model, Huxley acquaints us with the field of zoology and with his philosophy of education.

In the end, the lobster is a signifier of scientific discovery, and its claws are now a perfectly coherent part of a wonderfully developed, unified system of perfect symmetry and beautiful design.

Hands, Fingers, Knees, and Toes

The design is perfect, but here is a puzzle. Everyone talks about lobsters as decapods — that is, as having ten feet. But are they feet? Or are they hands? Or mouths? True, the five pairs of jointed appendages on the lobster's carapace support its ramblings on the ocean bottom, but all ten of the "feet" at the end of those so-called "legs" are actually multitask attachments. They rummage around in sediment looking for food, and incidentally the lobster's unsavory reputation as a scavenger for dead meat is not entirely deserved. Lobsters eat live, fresh food such as the flesh of shellfish, which they crush in order to draw out the meat; sea urchins now and then; worms — a lobster in an aquarium was even found munching on the tail of a passing skate, as it struggled to get away. Adult lobsters can't swim in pursuit of food, so they grab what they can. If they're hunting for food and they happen upon a lobster trap baited with smelly dead herring, they don't walk away.

On January 13, 2006, the National Public Radio program *Pulse of the Planet* broadcast a mini-lesson on lobsters' eating habits by the marine biologist Jelle Atema:

> So, all their little feet have hairs on them, at the tips. And each one of those hairs is both a tactile and a taste receptor. And they can make very nice taste discriminations between all sorts of different mixtures of food. They crack a shell and use their little feet to pluck the meat out of the bivalve. And then you have two mandibles that can be used to cut the meat up in smaller pieces. Mandibles would be literally like our teeth.
>
> And then it goes inside the mouth, and believe it or not they can again taste what's in the mouth before it goes all the way down to the stomach.
>
> And you can get these really conflicted lobsters. A lobster that has just fed and you give him a piece of this really strong smelling, old, quite rotten fish, they will go for it and their little feet with all the taste sensors, will pick it up and hand it over to the mouth.
>
> Then they have other taste sensors in their mouth, and those are saying "oh no! This is awful!" And they throw it away. But then the little feet pick it up again and they say, "no, no, no! It's good, I told you! Here!" And they give it back to the mouth. The mouth then manipulates it again and says, "ew! Awful!" And they throw it away.
>
> And this can go on several times back and forth and [the lobster] usually ends up not eating it.[18]

Atema teaches at Boston University, where he and his students investigate how lobsters use their senses to explore the world, mate, gather food, and avoid danger. One thing they learned is that individual lobsters recognize one another through their sense of smell, specifically by detecting pheromones in urine. This is extremely helpful information because, as has long been known, lobsters continually fight for dominance. And the question was, after half an hour of winning or losing numerous fights, how do they figure out or remember with whom they have fought, and who won?

Even though their eyes are on movable stalks that expand their range of vision, lobsters don't see very well in the low light of their habitual environment. Their sense of smell, however, is just fine. On either side of the front of a lobster's head is an antennule, split into two slender threads, or flagella. These contain the lobster's chemosensory organs, or "nose." With a whiff of another male's urine, a lobster can remember where he stands in chain of command. At least until a new, unknown contender shows up.

All for One—One for All

The winner of the battle for lobster-in-chief can choose the best real estate in the neighborhood, and once he does, he begins a landscaping and reconstruction project to make it fit his desires. Usually that means making it secure and private, and to keep it that way he pugnaciously guards the entrance against visitors, male and female alike. In choosing a mate, however, the female is the decider. Whether he likes it or not, the male's dominance and homestead attract a number of females who take turns paying him visits. They come to the entrance and send him seductive wafts of pheromones. Once he admits a female, an odd event occurs. She approaches him, "puts her claws on his shoulders and for a few seconds stands there and then walks away again," Atema says. "What we think is happening is that, at that moment, the female is blasting the male with chemical information. Because where the chemical information is produced is right under her head, so by putting her claws on his shoulders, she is literally blowing this odor straight into his nose."[19]

A female lobster cannot mate until she molts, which she will do anywhere from a few hours to a few days after moving in with her chosen partner. Molting is not only the painful, exhausting process that Buffon described, but it leaves her soft body unprotected and vulnerable. Considering the male's aggressive nature and the fact that he is still fully armored, the mating process could be very dangerous for her, but it proceeds carefully and without injury—to the best of our knowledge. Monitoring lobster copulation has not so far been possible in the animals' natural environment. What is known about it derives from research conducted in aquariums. There, observers report, once the female's shell has hardened enough for her to stand, perhaps half an hour after molting, the male helps her to turn over, gently cradles her, and injects his sperm via a forked pleopod, or swimmeret, into her seminal receptacle, which is located between the third and fourth pairs of walking legs (and in proximity to the opening of her oviducts). Copulation lasts only a few seconds, and then the female moves away.

Having mated, the female stays in the male's shelter for a day or so. Then she leaves to find a safe place of her own, where she waits until the new shell is strong enough to protect her. The sperm is stored in the seminal receptacle until she produces eggs, perhaps fifteen months after mating, and then the eggs are fertilized as they flow past the sperm. The tiny fertile eggs, pine green in color, adhere to the swimmerets along the underside of the female's abdomen (mistakenly called the lobster tail) until they are ready to hatch.

Meanwhile, a succession of females has followed her into the dominant male's shelter as each one was ready to molt and mate, a routine known as sequential monogamy — or, depending on your point of view, sequential polygamy.

The "berried" lobster, as the female bearing fertilized eggs is called, carries the eggs for some nine to thirteen months, and then she rhythmically fans her swimmerets to release them. As the eggs rise toward surface waters, moved about by currents and waves, they molt into the first of their larval stages. By their fourth molt, they are no longer larvae and are strong swimmers. Thereafter they begin to make their way to the ocean bottom, finding or devising hideaways in dark places from which they venture out for food. At somewhere between seven and eleven years of age, they reach adulthood and begin their own forays into the mating game.

Individual Individuals

Though every lobster, like every person, is an individual, as Buffon intuited, some are more individual than others. Such is the case with members of the exotic lobster collection that the Lobster Conservancy of Maine inadvertently began when local lobstermen presented the organization with yellow, blue, and even polka-dotted lobsters.

Collecting oddities is interesting (and some of them end up in museum aquariums), but it is not the primary goal of the conservancy, which was founded in 1996 by Diane Cowan, a marine biologist and educator. It is a nonprofit organization devoted to maintaining a successful lobster fishery that involves the community as well as scientific research.[20]

The conservancy, also known as TLC, began a Juvenile Lobster Monitoring Program along the Maine coast in 1993. Three years later volunteers began expanding the monitoring sites, and by early 2010 there were 120 well-trained volunteers on the rolls who were monitoring twenty-two sites.

During low tides in the spring, in designated areas running parallel to the water's edge, the volunteers find their subjects about 1.18 inches below the average low water depth. They record each lobster's size, sex, molt stage, handedness, and missing appendages or shell damage, if any. They also measure and record water and air temperature, salinity, and weather conditions. (Hourly temperatures are also recorded remotely.)[21]

The 2010 report of the previous year's findings confirmed that the numbers of juveniles were still increasing and still generally highest in summer, but that "abundance in recent winters rivals what it was in the first several summers of the census." And "highest densities are found along the mid-coast of Maine."[22] Cowan's analysis of the statistics is encouraging:

Census data gathered by volunteers and scientists at The Lobster Conservancy are valuable as indicators of changes in settlement success and early survival of juvenile lobsters along the Gulf of Maine Coast. Time-series data like these can help us understand the ups and downs in the availability of lobsters by contributing baseline records. In the early years, I was impressed with average numbers of one or two lobsters per square meter. Not anymore. With peak densities hitting an order of magnitude higher in recent years, I begin to wonder where the ceiling might be. This puts qualifiers like a high year and a low year in perspective. Ten years ago I had no concept of what "high" could be. It makes me realize that it may be critically important to have many decades of data before we can begin to truly understand what is driving the trends in lobster abundance.[23]

This report is accompanied by a photograph of the palm of someone's hand on which six very small lobsters, most less than an inch long, are crawling around. One of the lobsters, somewhat larger than the others, is spread over the first three fingers, while its front legs, already tipped with tiny claws, are dangling over the side of the index finger — much as someone sitting on the end of a dock might dangle her feet over the edge to splash lightly in the water.

4 Life, Death, and
Medical Conditions

April 10, 1982. *Saturday Night Live*, season 7, episode 16. A historic, inspirational, and notorious skit written and performed by Eddie Murphy. Murphy holds up, live and kicking, Larry the Lobster for judgment in the court of public opinion. Viewers are given two telephone numbers, both beginning with a 900 exchange, and told to vote by calling one number to spare, and the other number to cook, the lobster. Almost 500,000 calls come in, and AT&T is nearly overwhelmed by the spike in traffic.

It's a pretty close call, but Larry is saved by some 12,000 votes.

The *Saturday Night Live* episode was historic because polling an audience like that was unprecedented. It marked the beginning of interactive television.

It was inspirational because five years later, after the televangelist Oral Roberts warned that if his loyal followers didn't contribute to his medical missionary work, God would call him home. He raised $5 million.

It was notorious because the outcome was a disaster for both Murphy and Larry. During the following episode, Murphy talked about the mail he'd received protesting Larry's treatment, especially a nasty racist letter that read, "I didn't even know you people liked lobster." That letter prompted Murphy to rescind Larry's stay of execution. Murphy showed everyone a boiled red lobster on a plate. And then he ate it.

*A*mong the many fables attributed to Aesop, there is one about a mother and daughter who are at the seashore, where the daughter sees the red shell of a lobster. She tells her mother she will never be happy until she is thus beautifully clothed, instead of being dressed like the rest of her kind, dull and undistinguished. The mother scolds her severely for being so vain and covetous and points out that such finery was won only by the poor victim's death.[1] Be careful what you wish for is the lesson of this fable.

Red, for lobsters, is a question of life and death. They go into a pot of boiling water with dark, morosely colored shells and come out with a sassy red hue. The mysterious process is analogous to a renowned New England autumn event, the turning of leaves from green to a variety of stunning reds, yellows, and golds. Those colors are present in the leaves all summer, but the green of their chlorophyll is more dominant until the season changes. Similarly, a live lobster's dark greenish shell, mottled brown or black, contains the pigment astaxanthin bound in protein chains. Cooking the lobster causes the protein chain to unwind the astaxanthin; thus liberated, it is able to reflect the wavelength we see as lobster red.

The main source of astaxanthin is a form of microscopic algae found in the sea that is eaten by the seafood that the lobster feeds on. The US Food and Drug Administration has approved astaxanthin as a food supplement for humans. It begins to sound like a magic wand, an antioxidant with a multitude of effects that range from benefiting the cardiovascular system to fighting cancer. It may be useful in counteracting neurodegenerative diseases such as glaucoma and Alzheimer's.

Color is the most attention-getting feature of the cooked lobster, but the shell material of a lobster is remarkable in its own right — marvelous, really, from a structural perspective. Like other arthropod exoskeletons, its chief ingredient is chitin, along with various proteins. Chitin "is one of the, if not the most abundant structural biomolecule [an organic molecule produced by a living organism] found in nature."[2] Due to its dimensions — remember that lobster is the largest extant arthropod — *Homarus americanus* provides the best shell to study, according to researchers at the Max Planck Institut. One goal of their research is to understand how nature arrives at so light, protective, and at the same time multifunctional a material as a lobster's shell, so that scientists can design new structural materials inspired by biology.

Max Planck scientists have looked at different parts of lobster shells with various tools, including electron microscopes. Among their discoveries is that the pattern and design of chitin in the lobster's shell contains anisotropic components. The opposite of something that is isotropic — in which elements such as fibers all go in the same direction — an anisotropic object is one in which such elements are laid out in different, nonparallel directions. The best example of the latter is wood, in which the direction of the grain determines the strength of the sample — the wood is stronger along the grain than it is across the grain. The scientists also discovered honeycomb configurations and what they call "twisted wood" arrangements. They conclude that the "interaction of different construction principles can be used as a template for the design of novel high performance materials."[3]

The composition of chitin in different parts of the lobster shell varies according to specific need. The functions of the main body segments are to provide support for the animal and to serve as a protective shield against predators. These segments are microscopically distinct from the parts of the animal that move, slice, dice, and chomp. Looking at the micrographs of various chitin cells brings Thomas Henry Huxley and his description of a lobster's structural symmetry to mind. These pictures of the microstructure of chitin reveal the opposite, something more like abstract chaos rather than balanced orderly organization.

Besides clothing lobsters and potentially leading to new, high-performance structural materials, chitin has been investigated for other uses. As summarized by an article in *Science* in 1981, "research on chitin as a marine resource is pointing to novel applications for this cellulose-like biopolymer."[4] Spinning filaments of chitin to make surgical sutures was one of the suggestions. Though I am unable to find evidence of the manufacture of suture thread derived from chitin, the clinical usefulness of chitin-based products in both human and animal medicine is otherwise impressive, especially since it is enhanced by chitin's biodegradability and biocompatibility. Biomedical applications include the regeneration of various kinds of tissue, including skin, bone and cartilage, liver, cardiac, vascular, corneal, and nerve.[5] Other applications under discussion include chitin's use as a food additive and in agriculture as a protection for seeds and plants and as well a fertilizer. Even paper may be made with chitin: US patent number 4392916 proposes a unique paper-making process that uses regenerated chitin fibers.[6]

The benefits of a lobster's exoskeleton begin to seem limitless until its very real constraint is remembered: the shell limits the lobster's growth. That is why it has to be shed periodically. Monster lobsters are the creation of myths, but how big can lobsters really get?

Truth or Consequences

In February 2005, a twenty-two pound lobster was caught off the coast of Nantucket, Massachusetts. It was delivered to Robert Wholey's seafood market in Pittsburgh, Pennsylvania, where it was named Bubba.

If Eddie Murphy's Larry, a regular one-and-a-half pounder, were to shake claws with Bubba, Larry would be about the size of one of Bubba's big claws. Here are Bubba's vital statistics: weight, twenty-two pounds; length, twenty-one inches from the tip of his nose to the end of his tail; age, estimated to be between fifty and a hundred years.

Wholey might have sold him for a dinner party of about fourteen lobster lovers, or to the woman who offered $500 to buy Bubba and return him to the sea. Wholey was under pressure to do neither from many people, some sympathetic to Bubba because of his age, and others members of People for the Ethical Treatment of Animals. Finally, Wholey decided Bubba should be allowed to retire to Ripley's Believe It or Not! Museum in Myrtle Beach, South Carolina. Bubba's way station was the PPG Aquarium, at the Pittsburgh Zoo, which agreed to take care of him. Bubba died after spending about a month in human custody, which included a week at Wholey's market and less than twenty-four hours at the aquarium.

Linda Wilson Fuoco covered Bubba's story for the Pittsburgh *Post-Gazette*. On April 6, 2005, she reported that the zoo had commissioned an independent laboratory to do a necropsy, or animal autopsy, to determine the cause of death. It was discovered that Bubba had died from a severe bacterial infection. The necropsy also confirmed that Bubba was male lobster and, in fact, an "active male"—he was still producing sperm at the time of his death.[7]

On April 16, 2010, I spoke with Bob Wholey and asked how Bubba happened to come his way. "I challenged one of my fresh fish buyers with a $5 bet that he couldn't find me a lobster over fifteen pounds," Wholey said. "A month later, the buyer showed up with Bubba." Wholey called CBS News when Bubba reached his market in 2005, and when a news crew came to check the lobster out on March 2, he not only showed them Bubba, but with perfect aplomb he set an ordinary lobster next to him. The contrast, as mentioned above, was impressive.

Bubba was big, but not the biggest lobster in documented history. The record is still held by an individual caught off the coast of Nova Scotia, Canada, in 1977. It weighed over forty-three pounds and was about forty-one inches long. It might have been well over a hundred years old. I thought I had tracked that honorable specimen down when I found a news story about a big lobster called Sammy that was the star attraction at Marine City in Tanabe City, Japan.

On December 5, 1989, the headline of a newspaper story on page 21, illustrated with a gargantuan lobster, screamed "Seafood Lover Jailed for Eating 41-Pound Lobster" (Sammy had apparently lost weight). It was a disturbing account: "A hungry seafood lover got into hot water when he fished a 41-pound lobster out of a Sea World–style aquarium and ate it for dinner! Toshiro Sato was jailed on charges of theft and cruelty to animals in the death of the monstrous, three-foot crustacean."[8] Sato, who worked as a night watchman at the aquarium, netted Sammy and clubbed him to death after the other employees had gone home. Then he chopped the lobster up and broiled him in the aquarium's kitchen.

The newspaper also considered Sammy's past: "'Sammy was no ordinary lobster — he was almost human,' Yasuro Nagat, director of the aquarium, told newsmen in Tanabe City. 'We flew him in from the United States in 1973. Over the years he grew and gained weight and became king of the aquarium.'"[9]

Just a minute! These statistics don't compute. Our record lobster wasn't caught until 1977, and if it had gained weight it would have been more than 43 pounds. I was both disappointed and relieved when I finished reading the article and realized that Sammy couldn't have been the record-breaking lobster from Canada. I believe the whole story was a hoax. The article appeared in the *Weekly World News*, a sister paper of the *National Enquirer*—

both are located in Lantana, Florida—that was published from 1979 to 2007. The *Weekly World News* was devoted to weird and fantastic stories.

Forty-three pounds is still the largest lobster on record, but nobody knows just how large a lobster can get, or how long it can live. It is known that molting slows as lobsters grow older, so size does not necessarily correlate to age. In addition, lobsters don't show evidence of aging: their metabolism doesn't change; and they don't lose their energy, appetite, or sex drive as they grow old. No wrinkles either, perhaps thanks to astaxanthin and/or chitin. Though juvenile lobsters are vulnerable to almost everything in the sea with an open mouth, adults don't have many serious predators besides people and codfish, and since people are decimating the codfish population, cod is becoming less of a threat to lobsters. Other potential ocean-dwelling enemies of the lobster include seals, octopuses, haddock, and sometimes other lobsters. But if they don't get sick from diseases caused by parasites, bacteria, or chemical pollution—from sources such as plastics, detergents, and cosmetics[10]—lobsters could just live on and on, theoretically.

Medical Guidance

+ Galen (129–99 CE) was a prolific writer, researcher, scholar, and the most influential of ancient physicians (his patients included Marcus Aurelius). Galen remarked about lobsters that "their flesh is hard throughout and because of this they are both difficult to digest and nutritious, provided of course that they be boiled beforehand in fresh water."[11] He believed that the salty juice from all shellfish acted as a laxative.
+ According to information on The Lobster Conservancy website, during the Middle Ages and Renaissance, the lobster's rostrum—the flattened section that ends in a beaklike projection between the eyes—when roasted, pulverized, and dissolved in wine was prescribed for treating urinary diseases, purging kidney stones, and other human problems. And the gastrolith, "a calcerous 'rock' found in the stomachs of lobsters preparing to shed their shell, was used for eye inflammations and as a remedy for stomach aches and epilepsy."[12]
+ Although Robert Burton does not comment on lobster

specifically in his monumental survey, *The Anatomy of Melancholy*, he reports that many people believe all shellfish contribute to the malaise. However, the sixteenth-century physician Timothy Bright, in his *Tract on Melancholy*, excepts lobster.[13] Michel Foucault takes a further step, noting that "the principal task is to dissolve the fermentations which, having formed in the body, give rise to madness," and he reports that in 1758 the French physician Joseph Raulin recommended powdered lobster claw as a "dissolvent" as well honey, chimney soot, Oriental saffron, wood lice, and bezoar.[14]

+ In 1813 the Scottish physician William Charles Wells was visited by a "female of the white race of mankind, parts of whose skin resembles the skin of a negro." The cause, according to her family and neighbors, was that her mother had "received a fright while pregnant with her, by accidently treading on a live lobster."[15]

+ Substitute turbot for lobster, recommended Horace Benge Dobell, another nineteenth-century physician, since turbot is "much more easily digested than lobster, and when eaten cold with pepper and vinegar, the flavour is remarkably like that of lobster." Dobell suggested cutting the turbot into strips and tinting the outside with beet juice: "In this way invalids, fond of lobster but unable to digest it, may have their taste pleased and appetite thus promoted."[16]

+ You may have noted that a lobster's claws are now banded when it is caught, rather than wedged shut with a wooden peg. Here is an explanation for the change: the practice of pegging became necessary for shipping lobsters alive, to prevent them from mauling and killing one another during their travels. It was discovered that the pegs broke into the lobster's flesh and introduced bacteria or infection. In the 1980s pegs were abandoned, and fishermen began to routinely use rubber bands to clamp the lobster claws shut.

+ "Sarah Mitchell, a servant, . . . 25, of the sanguineous temperament, was seized at two o'clock in the afternoon on Monday, May 21, with severe pain in the region of the stomach, and sickness, almost immediately after eating a small portion of lobster . . . Her friends gave her some gin and warm water two or three times without any relief; the pain became intolerable; a friend then administered forty drops of laudanum, but without any relief," before the physician, Samuel H. Bibley, was called in, as he reported in the *London Medical Gazette* in 1838. Despite his ministrations, the patient died less than twenty-four hours later. An autopsy disclosed stomach ulcers, one of which was "big enough to admit one's thumb." The doctor concluded: "The principal features of this unfortunate case were that the whole system was collapsed from the very commencement." However, the lobster may have been the coup de grâce.[17]

+ Four days before visiting Dr. Charles Schram of New York, a twenty-nine-year-old married woman of Russian birth and good health, the mother of two, ate boiled lobster, as did other members of her family. Three days after eating the lobster, the woman had begun to vomit uncontrollably. Other symptoms were constipation, headache, dizziness, excessive thirst, ringing in the ears, and pain—both gastric and abdominal pain and pain in her limbs. When he examined her, the doctor noted her pallor and thickly coated tongue. He prescribed calomel, a compound of mercury and chloride that can be toxic because of the mercury but was much used for its purgative and antibacterial properties, and beta naphthol-bismuth, a powerful intestinal antiseptic. The crisis of the illness came three days after she visited the doctor: a salt-water enema had produced a piece of lobster; the patient developed a severe chill, collapsed, and seemed to have no pulse. When the doctor arrived at her home, she was in a cold sweat, had a feeble but regular pulse, and was on her way toward recovery. According to the title of the paper that Schram read in October 1897, at a meeting of the Harvard Medical Society of New York, it was "A Case of Poisoning from Eating Lobster."[18]

+ Roy Atwell (1878–1962) was an American actor and comedian. His distinctive voice was heard as Doc, the head dwarf, in Disney's *Snow White and the Seven Dwarfs*. In 1915 he wrote and recorded a gem of a poem called "Some Little Bug Is Going to Find You." It begins: "In these days of indigestion / It is oftentimes a question / As to what to eat and what to leave alone; / For each microbe and bacillus / Has a different way to kill us, / And in time they always claim us for their own." The poem lists water, air, cucumber, radishes, not to mention "huckleberry pie . . . a pleasant way to die." And wouldn't you know it: "Eating lobster cooked or plain / is only flirting with ptomaine."[19]

+ At least the lobster is exonerated in this connection. The Gulf of Maine Research Institute answers the question about whether lobster is safe to eat during a shellfish ban: "Yes. Lobsters, unlike mussels, oysters, and clams, are not 'filter feeders.' Filter feeders pump seawater, and any plankton or pollution it carries, through their bodies. Any toxins in the water will be concentrated in their flesh. Meat eaters like lobsters, crabs, and fish do not filter plankton from seawater, so they are safe to eat during an outbreak of red tide."[20]

+ Tomalley, the soft green substance in the lobster's body cavity that acts as the liver and pancreas — often enjoyed and included in recipes — should be avoided. In July 2008 the US Food and Drug Administration advised that dangerous levels of toxins responsible for paralytic shellfish poisoning had been found in tomalley. The poison does not affect the lobster's white meat.[21]

+ If a lobster's claw is lost or compromised in some mishap — an attack by another lobster, for example — it will shed the claw, and another will grow in its place. This very beneficial process is called epimorphic regeneration. It has been studied for centuries in the hope of applying it to humans. In the early twentieth century, scientists discovered that a group of cells forms at the location of the crustacean's missing part; these cells multiply and differentiate into components for replication of the lost limb. A human equivalent hasn't yet been developed, but stem cell research may solve the problem some day.

Claws

Ectrodactyly, known as lobster claw syndrome or clefting syndrome, is a genetic abnormality of the human hands and feet. The usual configuration involves the absence of one or more of the central digits, though there are variations of the condition. Its name comes from the Greek words for "damage" and "finger."

Bree Walker was born in 1953 with ectrodactyly. She has had a successful career in radio and television as a news anchor and talk show host. She is a social activist and defender of the rights of people with disabilities.

Grady Stiles, who was born in 1937, had clefting syndrome too, but his life was very different from Walker's. True, he was also on television — but as an oddity, not an employee, and after his death. The Arts and Entertainment network featured him in an episode of its series called *City Confidential*. The promotional description reads as follows: "A city. A mystery. A story. Every seemingly normal city hides a mystery — an event that has changed it forever. City Confidential scours the country to find these intriguing places and unearth their mysteries."

Stiles's story was set in Gibsonton, Florida. If you look up Gibsonton, you'll probably see it referred to as the Circus Freak Wintering Town. Its post office has a counter designed to accommodate dwarfs.

The *Sarasota Herald-Tribune* published an article titled "Everybody Fits In In 'Gib-town,'" on February 23, 2008. According to the article, it was in the 1930s that this town became known as "Freak Town." The newspaper quoted a resident who remembered that time nostalgically: "Everybody fit in. People came here because they weren't looked at or talked about or asked questions." Gibsonton's permissive zoning "allowed people to keep trailers on the street and elephants in their yards."[22] That's where Grady Stiles, also known as the Lobster Boy, lived a terrible life — a violent alcoholic, he abused his wife, Teresa, his children, and his stepson (who was conceived during a period when Teresa and he were separated and then divorced; they subsequently remarried and lived together again). And Gibsonton is where on November 29, 1992, Stiles was murdered in the living room of his trailer. Teresa had given her eighteen-year-old son, Harry Glenn Newman (Grady's stepson) $1,500 to hire someone to kill Stiles. Teresa, her son, and Chris Wyant, the hit man, were found guilty of the murder and sentenced to prison — Teresa for twelve years, her son for eighteen, and Wyant for twenty-seven.[23]

A lobster needs its claws for everything from collecting and eating food to fighting for dominance or self-protection. Maybe it's because they are so basic and important that the claws can be reproduced by each lobster for itself. There is no real equivalent to claws on humans, so when a genetic irregularity causes a malformation of hands or feet and they cleft rather than developing fingers or toes, those malformations — and the people who have them — become anomalies. The result could be called crab or scorpion claws, or likened to any other object resembling scissors or a clamp. But an ever-present analogy for human catastrophe seems to be the lobster.

Is it a catastrophe or a conquest? Stiles capitalized on what could have been disadvantageous and used it to identify and promote himself. In his Lobster Boy performance Stiles turned his disability into a career, and he piqued the audience's morbid curiosity by telling them that his clawlike hands and feet were caused by parental incest.[24] He was evil and violent, but also very clever. In medicine, teratology is the study of abnormalities; in popular culture, it is the study of monsters. When the two fields collide, as in freak shows, the result is dark and sinister — what Douglas Biklen, dean of Syracuse University's School of Education, calls the "pornography of disability."[25]

5 Man-Eating Monsters

Semiconscious, Roland Deschain doesn't know if he is dreaming or drowning. Suddenly he is shocked by icy cold water washing all the way up his legs to his gun belt. Thus alerted, his first clear thought is to save his guns and shells, though he's peripherally aware of a dangerous monstrosity off to his right.

Roland lies on the shore of the Western Sea, at the western edge of the world. The Cyclopean Mountains run parallel to the beach. Roland, the last gunslinger, is on a quest to reach the Dark Tower — a quest that matters more to him than people, love, pain, or life. Roland is a cross between Jesus Christ, Captain Ahab, and Harrison Ford. The situation in which he finds himself that I have just described is from the opening scene of *The Drawing of the Three*, published in 1987 as the second volume of Stephen King's Dark Tower series; Roland is King's antihero. The approaching danger, at first glance some eight yards away, is four feet long and one foot high and weighs about seventy pounds. It fixes him with stalked eyes and begins to make noises that sound human; sounds like "plaintive even desperate questions." It asks: "*Did-a-chick? Dum-a-chum? Dad-a-cham? Ded-a-check?*"[1]

It is and it isn't a lobster, though it is more like a lobster than anything else. King calls it a "lobstrosity." But before Roland can attend to it, he has to get beyond the tide to protect his gun shells. He hears the roar as a huge wave approaches, and he sees the monstrous creature raise its claws against the breaker in the defiant, belligerent way that lobsters have. Roland is reminded of the so-called honor stance with which boxers open a match. Too weak and numb to stand, propelling himself in much the way the lobstrosity moves, by clawing into the sand, Roland creeps away from the crashing wave.

Moving faster than expected, the creature suddenly attacks him, clamping down on and tearing away the first and second fingers of Roland's right hand. When the gunslinger manages to stand, the creature tears into his calf. He kicks it, and the animal takes off his boot and most of his big toe. Left-handed, Roland painfully removes his gun, aims, and pulls the trigger — but the damp shells don't fire. At last, as the lobstrosity fulfills its compulsion to rise in honor of or in protest against another roaring wave, Roland wrenches a large rock from its sandy bed, raises it, and crashes it down on the creature. The first blow crushes the animal's back. Its subsequent death throes, plus the gunslinger's grinding the creature beneath his remaining boot heel and his methodical stomping on the shattered, scattered remains are horrific. So is Roland's raging pain, later compounded by poison from the lobstrosity's bites, which bring on long fevers and "shuffles" in and out of consciousness.[2]

That was just the first of the battalions of lobstrosities that lurk in this monster-horror fantasy: lobster things that resemble scorpions and are poisonous, though instead of stingers they have jagged, edged beaks. Unafraid of humans, they confront and challenge them with plaintive, inquiring voices. The oddity of their speech seems a rhythmic, musical refrain, and paradoxically it is so unlobsterlike as to be funny. The creatures do not emerge with the tides but come out of the waves as the sun sets and darkness approaches.

Each time a wave breaks, they all raise their claws. And is that not as peculiar and pathetic as their imploring "Did-a-chicks"?

Even without literary modification, lobsters are exceedingly strange. When do they become monsters? When they are supersized. When they talk. When they cross borders between species. When they are deformed or in some other way step beyond the characteristics that we recognize and expect them to have.

As noted in the previous chapter, teratology — the Greek word for the study of monsters or marvels — is the study of abnormalities in medicine and biology. In mythology, literature, and history, teratology refers to the study of marvels, prodigies, monsters, and other wondrous plants and animals. Nathan Bailey's 1731 edition of *The Universal Etymological English Dictionary* defines teratology as "when bold writers, fond of the sublime, intermix something great and prodigious in everything they write whether there is a foundation for it in reason, or not, and this is what is called bombast."[3] Categories meet, as Buffon would say, in our imagination.

Welcome, Stephen King.

A brief article called "Mythology and Teratology" in a 1902 issue of the *British Medical Journal* reviews a commentary on "the idea that the birth of monstrous human infants was the origin of the deformed deities of mythology."[4] This discussion of why certain deformities are selected for gods and others are not leads the commentary's author to the conjecture that national identity must play a role in such choices. Ergo, the Greeks' love of beauty supposedly inclined them to choose the relatively more attractive deformities. For example, regarding cyclops fetuses, there is "an ugly one and one which in comparison might be termed pretty; the Greeks took the pretty (!) one for the construction of the god Polyphemus."[5] The reviewer betrays a welcome skepticism; nevertheless, there is something to be said about localizing deities and monsters — the lobster of Seriphos being one case in point. The lobstrosity of Stephen King, a lifelong Mainer or Maineiac — to use the local nickname — is another.

When he graduated from the College of Education at the University of Maine and could not find work teaching, King took a job at a commercial laundry. "The greatest part of what I loaded and pulled were motel sheets from Maine's coastal towns and table linens from Maine's coastal restaurants. The table linen was desperately nasty. When tourists go out to dinner in Maine, they usually want clams and lobster. Mostly lobster," King wrote. "By the time the tablecloths upon which these delicacies had been served reached me, they stank to high heaven and were often boiling with maggots. The maggots would try to crawl up your arms as you loaded the washers; it was as if the little fuckers knew you were planning to cook them."[6] Given that association, it is less surprising that King wreaked revenge through Roland's brutal pulverization of the first lobstrosity he encountered.

There's a different variety of lobster monster in King's earlier horror novella, *The Mist*, published in 1980. This work is set in a small Maine town, where — in the wake of a violent storm — a thick mist shrouds everything. A group of people is trapped inside the local supermarket. Outside the store a collection of human-killing monstrosities has assembled, including some with tentacles on which suction cups serve as mouths; a six-legged whale-size behemoth that carries hundreds of those creatures on its legs; black, spiderlike insects that make deadly acidic webs; and one with our familiar segmented shell, resembling both a scorpion and a lobster, with claws that rip a man in half—a preview of horrors to come.

The Drawing of the Three is a fantasy of nearly five hundred pages that plays out in parallel worlds—Mid-World is where the story begins, with Roland's first encounter with the lobster monstrosity; its parallel is the drug- and crime-infested streets of New York City. Passage between the two worlds is through large wooden doors that appear on the beach. When Roland first falls through the door to New York, he meets and enters the mind and body of Eddie, a heroin addict and thereafter his companion in commutes between worlds. Violence, evil, blood, broken bones, blown-up faces, the horrendous scenes of Eddie's suffering from drug withdrawal, and Roland's poisoned fevers caused by the lobstrosity's bites move us through the pages. The armies of monsters—lobstrosities in Mid-World and drug-dealing human killers in New York—are always present. At one point, when Roland is comatose and near death, Eddie takes the gunslinger's weapon and begins shooting lobstrosities from a distance beyond the shore where they do not trespass. Eddie cooks and eats them, and he serves them to Roland during periods when the gunslinger shuffles back to consciousness. It is the only food they have and quite tasty. Then:

> Suddenly, in an utter blast of horror, Roland realizes what the whitish-pink chunks of meat Eddie has been feeding him have been. He cannot speak; revulsion robs him of what little voice he has managed to get back . . .
>
> "What did you think I was doing?" [Eddie] nearly snarls. "Calling Red Lobster for takeout?"[7]

Humor is a momentary antidote against the fear of monsters. But the monsters persist. They continue attacking members of the cast when they can, tearing and eating faces and limbs, cracking and crunching on bones. Killing and questioning. Moaning. Stopping to beseech the heavens.

Roland regains his health; Eddie falls in love with a woman named Susannah; and the book ends with the promise that three gunslingers will continue the quest for the Dark Tower.

Appendix 4 of the first volume of Robin Furth's concordance to The Dark Tower series has a map of Roland's Mid-World.[8] Covering roughly the northern third is the Great West Woods, populated by cone-shaped pines interspersed with a few mushroomlike deciduous trees. South of the woods is the barren Mohane Desert, and in the southernmost third of the map are the rounded peaks of the Cyclopean Mountains and their foothills. Running along the left edge and widening toward the bottom of the page is the Western Sea. Lobstrosity Beach and the three doors to the other world are labeled along its shore. The last thing to catch our eye — it makes us do a double take — is the small writing inside two lines representing the wash of tide: *"Dud-a-chum? Dod-a-chock? Dud-a-chum? Dod-a-chock? Dud-a-chum? Dod-a-chok."*

Imaginary monsters have a long, vivid history. An early example is the hordes of them reported to have been battled by Alexander the Great and his army during their campaign in India in 326 BCE. There were hippopotamuses larger than elephants, serpents, scorpions, dragons, giant crabs, and crocodiles, all followed by enormous white lions and pigs of many colors. Large bats flew in the soldiers' faces, and a beast bigger than an elephant and having three horns killed seventy-six of Alexander's men.[9]

In principle monsters serve us in diverse ways.

First, as in Alexander's example, they make heroes of those who prevail over — or in spite of — them.

Second, with their ability to wreak fear, death, and destruction, they can keep potentially unruly, rebellious, or otherwise disobedient members of society in thrall to their supernatural and usually unpredictable powers.

The third way is still more portentous. An August 2011 review by Terence Rafferty in the *New York Times Book Review* questioned the current popularity of books about zombies: "With every fashion in horror, it's worth asking, Why do we choose to fear this, and why now?" Rafferty speculates that because we live in a world with dwindling resources and an expanding population of starving people, we fear that their "urgent needs . . . will simply consume us." Worse still, zombies "might be serving as metaphors for actual people—undocumented immigrants, say, or the entire populations of developing nations—whose only offense, in most cases, is that their mouths and bellies demand to be filled." Rafferty continues: "Fear is a primitive impulse, brainless as hunger, and because the aim of horror fiction is the production of the deepest kinds of fears, the genre tends to reinforce some remarkably uncivilized ideas about self-protection."[10]

There is something zombieish about lobsters. Lobstrosity mutants are even more fearsome because they combine the unknowable, unpredictable, mindless clawed lobster, supersized to boot, with the awful, venomous scorpion. Arachnophobia, the fear of spiders, is one of the most widespread phobias in the world.[11] The evil and dangerous potentials of lobsters are vastly enhanced by their scorpion hybridism.

King's lobstrosities may be a metaphor for the demon of addiction, a monster that the author himself struggled with. However, their bizarre ritualistic questioning behavior as day fades to night seems prayerful. It is as though they were in thrall to a fierce, vengeful, all-powerful god. In fact, they are characters in a tale by Stephen King, one of the world's leading writers of gothic horror fiction. Moreover, the lobster has a gothic past of its own.

The Path of the Lobster

The map of Roland's Mid-World is quite different from that of a sixteenth-century Swede, Olaus Magnus (1490–1557), who published a geographic masterpiece known as the *Carta Marina* (the full title of this amazing work in English is *A Marine Chart and Description of the Northern Countries and the Wonders They Contain, Meticulously Made in the Year 1539*).[12] One rationale for the creation of this map, although not the foremost, was to correct inaccuracies of Ptolemy's second-century representation of the same northern region. Based on later voyagers' reports and his own travels, Olaus knew that Ptolemy had made some errors. However, his *Geographia* was still Olaus's primary source, and under its influence he mistakenly believed that Scandinavia reached almost up to the North Pole.[13]

Olaus's map was printed from nine separate wood blocks arranged in rows of three and labeled from A to I.[14] The map is approximately four feet high by five and a half feet wide. In section G is a key to many, though not all, of the numerous illustrations. Besides Norway and Sweden, the map includes Iceland; part of Greenland; Lapland; and parts of Russia, Germany, England, and Scotland—all washed by seas where monsters lurk.

The map truly is full of wonders. Both land and sea are packed with characters and events like an antique version of one of Richard Scarry's "busy, busy" worlds. The crowded nature of the sections brings to mind the medieval *horror vacui*, a fear that empty spaces on an illustrated surface, usually of a religious manuscript, leaves an opening for evil to sneak in. Indeed, one of the characters in Olaus's map is a devil-like figure sweeping out a hallway. (According to the key, it is a demon indentured to humans.) More appealing are a flock of reindeer marching off to milking and a single reindeer enjoying being milked (with the notation that domesticated reindeer give excellent milk); a man and a horse trekking over a mountain, both with plates on their feet to keep them from sinking into the snow; a shepherd fighting snakes; tamed otters that are trained to bring fish to the cook; the kings of Norway and Sweden on their thrones; and opposing armies on either side of a river, with the notation: "During the winter fighting takes place on the ice as during summer it does at sea."

The sea is also where monsters rule: "Sea monsters huge as mountains capsize the ships if they are not frightened away by the sounds of trumpets or by throwing empty barrels into the sea." One ship rocking on the waves has a sailor at the rail blowing his trumpet and another sailor dumping barrels into the water. Two behemoths watch nearby. The map also shows seamen who find themselves in mortal danger when they inadvertently anchor on the backs of monsters in the belief that they are islands.

There are lobsters. One is a gargantuan individual in section D (the western islands) balancing on its tail in what Stephen King would call the honor stance. Gripped in one raised claw is a fully dressed man, flailing his arms. The victim is just a little longer than the claw that grips him. The ratio is about the same as that of Eddie Murphy's Larry to Robert Wholey's Bubba (see chapter 4). Then, in section E, off the coast of Norway, is a polka-dotted

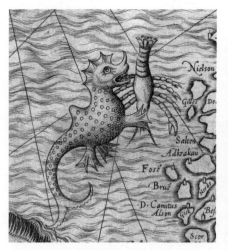

GEOGRAPHIAE STVD
TYPOGRAPHVS.

Olaus Magnus, *Carta Marina*, two lobster details, 1539. From the James Ford Bell Library, University of Minnesota, Minneapolis, Minnesota.

monster that looks like a rhinoceros, according to Olaus. Though it does have a horn on its nose, it also has webbed feet, a forked tail, and a head rather like that of a dragon. A dragonoceros? Whatever it is, it is at least two times bigger than the lobster it is about to devour, and the lobster, Olaus notes, is twelve feet long. Olaus must have had "shock and awe" in mind: the intention to "affect the will, perception, and understanding of the adversary to fit or respond to [one's] strategic policy ends."[15] In this Olaus's purpose resembles that of Stephen King: both mount challenges to their adversaries with missionary zeal.

Olaus's adversary was the Protestant revolution.

A surprisingly short time after Martin Luther published his ninety-five theses, Europe divided into hostile camps for and against the Reformation. In 1518 a young Swedish priest returned home from Wittenberg, Germany, and began to preach Luther's ideas. In 1523, after successfully battling a Danish king and troops who had been installed in his country, Gustav Vasa was elected regent of Sweden. Olaus Magnus and his elder brother, Johannes, emissaries to the papal court at the Vatican, returned home, and Johannes was appointed Catholic archbishop of Uppsala. Though the Lutheran reform movement was only coincidental with his rise to power, it was very convenient for Gustav. He was in dire financial straits, and the independent and powerful bishops controlled enormous wealth. He concentrated on subordinating the church to the state and directed the reformist clergyman, Olaus Petri, "to build an entirely new church in Sweden."[16] Gustav became increasingly mistrustful of Johannes Magnus, who — with his brother, Olaus — left Sweden for Poland and then Italy. They never returned home.[17]

The Magnus brothers were devoted to their country and their church. In exile they extolled what was marvelous about their land, its traditions, and its history. They argued and wrote in the hope that the Roman Catholic Church would be moved by admiration for their country and compassion for the plight of Swedish Catholics to support the Counter Reformation in Sweden and other northern countries. "On October 5, 1537, the brothers Magnus arrived in Rome. As an exiled bishop from an unknown country on the periphery of the European struggle for power, Johannes Magnus's task was to break the wall of indifference and reach the inner circle around the cardinals and the pope," writes Kurt Johannesson.[18] To that end, Johannes wrote a history of the Goths, claiming that they had originated in Sweden. Though not thoroughly documented, that belief has a long tradition. The importance of the Goths, who invaded vast territories and established powerful kingdoms throughout Europe, is unchallenged. Just as the Goths had conquered Rome by force in 410, Johannes hoped to conquer Rome with rhetoric in the sixteenth century. Olaus had the same motivation: "Olaus Magnus's Counter-reformation zeal could build on his pride in the glorious Gothic past of his nation and his confidence in the character of his 'Gothic' countrymen. His 'Gothicism' was not merely antiquarian: he could see it as the destiny of the modern Goths of Sweden to turn back the tide of Lutheran corruption that had flooded into the universal Church."[19]

Though his map came to be called *Carta Marina*, Olaus himself called it *Carta Gothica*.[20] The map text, including the key, is in Latin and — significantly for his political purposes — Olaus had the key printed separately, in both Italian and German. Olaus followed the map with a multivolume *Description of the Northern People*. It was a reversal of the usual order, in which pictures evolve to illustrate a text—Olaus's *Description* was conceived as a textual extension of the map. One vignette in the book is a picture of a lobster dragging a man out of a boat. Nearby is this commentary: "Let princes take note, as I have said earlier: do not lead out dissolute men to make war, for they are fit for nothing on the battlefield."[21] *Description*, too, is wonderfully illustrated. Both book and map were designed as inspirational works of political propaganda that used fear—as in the second principle of monster power—to try to overcome the enemy.

The Goths whom the Magnus brothers strove to glorify gave their names to everything from medieval art and architecture to our era's "dark" subculture that is obsessed with both suffering and death. And of course the Goths also gave their name to a literary genre, gothic fiction, so named by Horace Walpole in reference to his novel *The Castle of Otranto*, published in 1764. Though not founded on any original or specific Gothic artifacts, since none had been found, the term "gothic" refers more particularly to an approach that is purposefully anticlassical, no doubt because the Goths overran the Romans of classical antiquity.

Also known as gothic horror, the literary genre launched by Walpole unites romanticism and terror, the sublime and the melodramatic, good and evil. Among contemporary writers of gothic horror, Stephen King is preeminent. It is a long stretch in time, distance, style, philosophy, and subject matter between the heroic Swedish tribe of Goths that the Magnus brothers believed in and the demon world of horror that King explores. But the brothers and King share the idea of employing man-eating monsters to express their warning of danger, the notion that fear will keep people from straying from the righteous path.

The Magnus brothers' religious and political dreams were never realized. However, Olaus's *Carta Marina* did influence other mapmakers. One of his contemporary followers was Sebastian Münster, a German Franciscan monk, mathematician, and professor of Hebrew who left the Franciscan order when he became a friend and follower of Martin Luther. Münster produced a woodcut of the North Atlantic in his *Cosmographiae Universalis*, first issued in 1544. Münster's iconography resembles that of Olaus, although the victim in the grip of the lobster's deadly claw is lying face down in the water instead of struggling frantically in the air. Nearby is the polka-dotted dragonoceros, still about to chomp off a lobster's tail. Münster and Olaus used the same imagery despite their opposed religious convictions. Monsters cross such boundaries with impunity, it seems. In fact, the Gothic spirit is continuously reinvented to transcend not only religious differences, but those of time, history, and artistic medium as well.

Maps are great vehicles for rhetoric. A map proclaims boundaries and denotes ownership. It may also warn of dangers or be an invitation to or prohibition against colonization. The very gesture of making a map is an assertion of power, a statement of organization, like naming things and places. The point isn't just that monsters threaten the unwary or unworthy on Olaus's map; it also has something to do with the excoriating idea that, as Jean-Paul Sartre wrote, "the European has only been able to become a man through creating slaves and monsters."[22] Those slaves include a devil with a broom to serve him, and lobsters and other sea monsters. All of Olaus's sea monsters are strange composites of imaginary creatures, except for the lobsters. Though his lobsters are huge, they look like real-life lobsters. Just lobsters. Why is that?

The (In)Compleat Angler
Axel Boeck, a Norwegian fisheries researcher and historian suggests an answer in an article published in 1876:

> In our Sagas, especially in their poetical portions, [the lobster] is often mentioned. In Snorre's Edda, in the song of Skàldskaparsmål (chapter 75 of the Copenhagen edition), it is mentioned among fish and other marine animals. In Olaf de Helliges Saga, it is mentioned in a song of Björn Heldölekaempe, where the sea is poetically described as "the path of the lobster." In a similar poetical sense, the word is used in Olaf Trygvesens Saga, chapter 88, by the Skjald Thord Kolbeinsson, where he says that "the wave-horses run over the fields of the lobster," meaning the ships that sail on the waves of the sea. In a song by Snigly Holle, in Harald Haardraades Saga, chapter 105, the expression "to be at the bottom with the lobster" is used for drowning. In the Selkolle Songs of Einar Gilson, in Bishop Gudumunds

Saga the term "the light of the lobster," equivalent to the fire of the sea, or gold, is used. In the same place the expression "the horse of the lobster mountain," meaning the ship, is used. Finally there is found in the poem of Liknar-braut, the expression "land lobster," meaning a serpent or dragon.[23]

The whole sea, then, is the path of the lobster, and ships sail on fields of lobster. To drown is to join the lobsters. The lobster is gold from the sea. Such are saga metaphors for lobsters. And these are "real" lobsters, not teratological reconstructions. Except if they wander onto land—that is, off course—and become serpents, dragons, and lobstrosities!

Though Boeck doesn't specifically make the case in his recitation, reading between the lines we see that lobsters, unmediated and not hybridized, do appear to be part of the foundational mythology of the Gothic/Viking/Nordic peoples. Boeck also brings to light additional information that deepens consideration of the lobster's mythic attributes. He reports the "well known" information that the coast of Norway supports the largest of all fisheries, on which a great percentage of the country's population depends for a living. These fisheries have been carried out "from time immemorial, their origin being so much enveloped in obscurity that our ancestors supposed that the gods themselves had taught men fishing."[24]

With one exception: the fishing syllabus of the gods did not include lobsters. Fishing for lobster did not then exist—in fact, it did not begin until a good deal later than the time of the sagas, which were written in roughly the ninth to the eleventh centuries. "Although . . . the lobster had been known even in olden times," Boeck continues, "it had during the Middle Ages scarcely ever been used as an article of food in the northern countries. Lobster-fisheries are not spoken of in the Sagas or in the Old Laws; and even now, although the lobster has been caught on our coast for several centuries, it is but rarely, if ever, eaten by our fishermen, and only the higher classes seem to like its flavor."[25]

Boeck wrote that in the 1870s. In 2010 I repeated his comment to my friend Herdis Eriksson. Herdis lives in Massachusetts, but she was born in Iceland and has vivid recollections of her homeland, to which she returns periodically. Among her memories are piles of lobsters rotting on the docks after the fishermen came home and emptied their nets, leaving the unwanted portion of the catch behind. "We never ate them," Herdis said.

Possibly the gods did not teach men to fish for lobster.

Possibly for reasons now also "enveloped in obscurity," the gods may have instructed men not to fish for lobster, as they did also on the island of Seriphos.

Or were the gods even more purposeful? In that case, they would have forbid fishing for lobsters.

At the very least, the cultural significance of lobsters in those northern lands probably inhibited Olaus Magnus from hybridizing them in any way that would have interfered with their profound allegorical and spiritual significance.

6 SF

Are We All Lobsters Yet?

Horror and SF (the abbreviation that writers and readers of science fiction prefer to "sci fi") are not mutually exclusive. The American philosopher Noel Carroll narrows the gap between them, writing: "We shall not respect the notion that horror and science fiction are discrete genres. Much science fiction of the bug-eyed monster school, for instance, is really a species of horror, substituting supernatural forces with futuristic technologies."[1]

There is no doubt that Stephen King is a full-fledged horror writer, and his relation with his lobstrosities reflects Carroll's distinction that "in works of horror, the humans regard the monsters that they encounter as abnormal, as disturbances of the natural order," rather than — as in fairy tales, for example — "monsters [that] are part of the everyday furniture of the universe."[2]

The bug-eyed monster category in science fiction refers to a concept of extraterrestrials popularized in the 1930s, peculiar creatures with saucer-shaped eyes. Neither those monsters nor the abject types of horror's monsters, such as King's lobstrosities, resembles the strange creatures that inhabit the text of the world's pioneer SF writer.

His name was Lucian. He was born around 125 CE in the ancient Assyrian city of Samosata, which was on the banks of the Euphrates but has been submerged beneath its waters since the construction of the Atatürk Dam. The lobster, which seems increasingly omnipresent in one shape or another, plays a part in history's very first science fiction adventure, Lucian's *True Story*. Not a leading part, it's true, for the author himself takes that role.

Lucian's amazing journey began "once upon a time" when he set out from the Pillars of Hercules with fifty of his equally adventurous acquaintances to discover where the ocean ended. Carrying weapons and well provisioned with water and nourishment,

Lucian anticipated "a long and difficult voyage."[3] After enduring a storm that lasted seventy-nine days, he and his colleagues escape from an island with mortally dangerous sirens — only to have their ship spun around by what must have been a tornado and lifted into the air on a waterspout. They sailed through space for seven days and nights and then landed on the moon.

During their lunar visit they engaged in intragalactic warfare before happily returning to the ocean. "It would seem, however, that a change for the better often proves a prelude to greater ills," Lucian wrote. "The third day was breaking when toward sunrise we suddenly saw a number of sea-monsters, whales."[4] The largest whale — 150 miles long — came toward them with open mouth and swallowed them, ship and all, in a single gulp. Inside the whale they found a forest, islands, a barking dog, and a farmhouse — where they met a man and his son who had been swallowed twenty-seven years earlier. Their current life, they explained, was tolerable except for some "neighbours and fellow-countrymen [who] are extremely quarrelsome and unpleasant, being unsociable and savage."[5] Those foes were named the Broilers, the Mergoats, the Crabclaws, the Codheads, Clan Crawfish, and Solefeet. The Mergoats, men on top and fish below, were the least wicked. The worst were the Broilers, people with faces like lobsters and eyes like eels — bold and cannibalistic.

With Lucian in command, war was declared. Thousands of the enemy faced Lucian and his fellow adventurers, but they were armed — with swords, shields, perhaps javelins, bows and arrows, helmets, and armor — whereas the enemy's only weapons were fish bones. Our hero and his men routed all their foes.

Faces like lobsters and eyes like eels — it is curious that Lucian combined the lobster with a fish that is its prey. Even so, the result seems to be a prototype for several thousand years of hybrid monstrosities. Whereas King's lobstrosities provoke deep-seated fear and disgust and are never thoroughly conquered, Lucian's Broilers are almost benign, quickly and easily dispatched with superior hardware, and soon forgotten.

Besides lobsterlike foes, another thing that King and Lucian share is humor. As abject as they are, lobstrosities are paradoxically funny when lifting their claws and singing their ditties.

Lucian prefaces his story by describing parody, satire, and amusement as his intention. The war inside the whale, for example, may be a Homeric send-up with reference to the tale of Odysseus and Telemachus conquering the suitors.[6] I suspected the combination of the eel and lobster as a Broiler might be Lucian's answer to Oppian's description of the battle between the two (see chapter 1), but *True Story* may have preceded Oppian's *Halieuticks*. More likely Lucian had Aristotle's *History of Animals* in mind: "The spiny lobsters ... overcome large fishes. [They] overcome the congers [eels], for their roughness prevents them from falling off."[7]

Lucian was disdainful of philosophers and historians because they presume to know the truth. The very title of his book, *True Story*, concerns the question of truth versus fiction: The one dogmatic statement Lucian makes is that since he "had nothing true to tell, not having had any adventures of significance, I took to lying. But my lying is far more honest than theirs, for though I tell the truth in nothing else, I shall at least be truthful in saying that I am a liar."[8]

In the worlds of interstellar and inner-whale travel and colonization, Broilers and all the other monstrous creatures in *True Story* are not out of character, but neither are they everyday or ordinary. Lucian's imaginary voyage is not the fairy tale that Carroll describes. It is a science fiction as defined in the *Oxford English Dictionary*: "Imaginative fiction based on postulated scientific discoveries or spectacular environmental changes, freq[uently] set in the future or on other planets and involving space or time travel." Not necessarily seen, experienced, or heard of, the voyage is conjecture and projection based upon as much as one can possibly imagine, given the world in which one lives.

Space Lobster

Juhl Din is a space pilot on interstellar patrol in *Outside the Universe*, by Edmond Hamilton. In 1929 this adventure ran as a series in the magazine *Weird Tales*. Founded in 1923 and still published today, *Weird Tales* promotes itself as a magazine of "The Unique, Fantastic & Bizarre." Its mission is "to showcase writers trying to publish stories so bizarre and far out, no one else would publish them — stories of unearthly dimensions and dark possibilities, gothic seductresses and cosmic monstrosities."[9]

As *Outside the Universe* begins, a spaceship is tumbling crazily. When the whirling relents, Captain Dur Nal, an earthman and the narrator of the story, stumbles into the "pilot room," where his "two strange lieutenants stood at the ship's controls." One, Korus Kan, is a mentally and physically tireless metal man from the constellation Antares (also known as Alpha Scorpii). The other is the lobster-man, Juhl Din. He is "patently of Spica, of the crustacean peoples of that sun's planets, with his big, erect body armored in [a] hard black shell, his two mighty upper arms and two lower legs short and thick and stiff, while from his shiny black conical head protruded his twin round eyes."[10]

Spica is the most luminous star in the large constellation Virgo (the Virgin). Among the hottest of the first magnitude stars, Spica is actually not one star, but two: a dwarf star with a mass nearly eleven times that of our sun orbits the lesser star. The two are so close that they raise tides in each other. Their winds slam together to create X-rays. Spica is regularly covered, or occulted, by its moon — a marvelous sight. It was policy that the patrol crews were made up of members from every inhabited star in the galaxy and, according to the captain, none were stranger than Korus Kan and Juhl Din.

The world in which Edmond Hamilton lived and wrote *Outside the Universe* gave him more information to build upon than Lucian could possibly have had, but Lucian could have known how to find Spica since the Greek astronomer Hipparchus had discovered it some two hundred years before Lucian wrote *True Story*. Hipparchus's accomplishments included the compilation of the western world's first star catalog.

Jhul Din speaks: "This squadron is supposed to have the easiest section of the whole Interstellar Patrol, but we're no sooner clear of one cursed current than we're into another."[11] He is perfectly cogent. Throughout the story, in fact, he is entirely rational; rigorously, militarily polite; physically quick and competent; and exceptionally brave. A lobster-man as hero, piloting a spaceship: once the premises of space travels and wars are accepted, then something as bizarre as a lobster spaceman becomes, as Carroll says, everyday.

There is, in addition, a highly utilitarian logic in the crustacean identification of space warrior Juhl Din: he comes pre-accessorized with a "hard black shell" of body armor.

Recognition of lobster shells as armor and as beneficial to warriors goes as far back as the thirteenth century BCE, when Egyptian images show the so-called Sea Peoples of the Mediterranean wearing torso armor known as the lobster corselet. It was made up of overlapping bands — like those that cover the lobster's tail — of metal or leather.[12] It seems also to have been worn by Agamemnon, of Homer's *Odyssey*.[13] By the seventeenth century CE, elaborately ornamented metal helmets, or burgonets, had bands covering the neck that gave them the name "lobster tail helmets." These became popular in Europe, especially with the cavalry, and most particularly with a British unit called the London Lobsters.

This helmet reference leads to an evocative twentieth-century association that has more peaceful connotations. The sculptor Henry Moore used the theme of helmets in his work, and he explained the idea in a 1967 interview:

> I think it may be the interest I had early on in armour, in places like the Victoria and Albert Museum where one used to wander round as a student in the lunch hours . . . And it may be that I remembered reading stories that impressed me and [the painter and author] Wyndham Lewis talking about the shell of a lobster covering the soft flesh inside. This became an established idea with me — that of an outer protection to an inner form, and it may have something to do with the mother and child idea; that is where there is the relation of the big thing to the little thing, and the protection idea. The helmet is a kind of protection thing too, and it became a recording of things inside other things. The mystery of semiobscurity where one can only half distinguish something. In the helmet you do not quite know what is inside.[14]

This commentary accompanies a photograph of Moore's gleaming, polished black lead sculpture, *The Helmet* (1939–40), which is only eleven and a half inches high but nevertheless appears epic in both size and meaning. The enclosing shape is both a helmet and a mother wrapped around a standing child. It reminds me of luminous Spica, orbiting her smaller star so closely that they raise tides in each other.

Punchinellos

When Lucian wrote, there was nothing of what we call science, let alone science fiction, though there was other conjectural writing about the sun and moon and planets. Today there are several synonyms for science fiction including scientific novels, scientific fiction, scientific-marvelous fiction, hypothesis novels, wonder tales, realistic romances, socioscientific novels, fantastic novels, supernatural science, and the term H. G. Wells used: scientific romances.[15]

In 1884 Wells began his studies in biology with Thomas Henry Huxley at what would become the Royal College of Science. In 1901 Wells wrote: "I believed then that he was the greatest man I was ever likely to meet, and I believe that even more firmly today."[16] That was also the year in which Wells's *The First Men in the Moon* was published. There are allusions to the lobster, or a lobster likeness, in several of Wells's books, and he was surely aware of Huxley's famous 1861 lecture on the lobster (see chapter 3), but the lobster association in *The First Men in the Moon* is very strange and far removed from the specimen Huxley exhibited.

In Wells's book, Mr. Bedford, a businessman, and Dr. Cavor, a scientist, undertake a space voyage. They name the creatures they find on the moon Selenites.[17] It is Cavor who makes the point that the moon's weaker gravitational field allows ordinarily small creatures like insects to achieve human and superhuman dimensions. He also comments that Selenites exceed humans in their intelligence, morality, and wisdom. When he finds himself among a large number of them, he notes how they jostle one another in order to see him. Here is his description of them:

> It was an incredible crowd. Suddenly and violently there was forced upon my attention the vast amount of difference there is amongst these beings of the moon.
>
> Indeed, there seemed not two alike in all that jostling multitude. They differed in shape, they differed in size! Some bulged and over-hung, some ran about among the feet of their fellows,

some twined and interlaced like snakes. All of them had the grotesque and disquieting suggestion of an insect that has somehow contrived to burlesque humanity; all seemed to present an incredible exaggeration of some particular feature; one had a vast right forelimb, an enormous antenna arm, as it were; one seemed all leg, poised, as it were, on stilts; another protruded an enormous nose-like organ beside a sharply speculative eye that made him startlingly human until one saw his expressionless mouth. One has seen Punchinellos made of lobster claws — he was like that. The strange and (except for the want of mandibles and palps [mouthparts of lobsters and other arthropods]) most insect like head . . . And oddest of all, as it seemed to me at the moment, two or three of these weird inhabitants of a subterranean world, a world sheltered by innumerable miles of rock from sun or rain, *carried umbrellas* in their tentaculate hands! — real terrestrial-looking umbrellas![18]

Punchinellos are funny commedia dell'arte characters, often puppets, with humped backs, long noses, and pointed hats. The Italian commedia was founded in the fifteenth century and evolved over the years in Europe, with the mischievous Punchinello in the role of satirist, highlighting contemporary issues. In 1649 Punchinello (Polichinelle, in French) proclaimed audaciously to a French audience that he was more popular among the people than the diplomat and politician who was at the time chief minister of France: "How often with my own ears have I not heard them say: 'Let us go and see Polichinelle,' but who has ever heard any of the people say: 'Let us go and see [Cardinal] Mazarin!'"[19] The English version of Punchinello, dating back to 1661, was the Punch and Judy show. The British humor magazine *Punch*, founded in 1841, was inspired by Punchinello and carried on that character's name and mission until 2002.

Wells's Selenites seem to "burlesque humanity," but they cooperate with each other and live together in harmony. "Only at the very end, after the fundamentally inoffensive Selenites finally understand just how dangerous Earthlings can be, does the tale abandon its light touch and its satirical Swiftian sheen," writes Warren Wagar.[20] Did Wells intend to portray the Selenite community as utopian or dystopian? "The likeliest answer is that Wells — at least at this time [1901] — was taking himself only half seriously. If Selenite civilization had its virtues, *The First Men in the Moon* was also meant, as he wrote in 1934, to 'burlesque the effects of specialisation.' It is neither utopia nor dystopia, but an engaging cross between the two."[21]

There is a long tradition of imaginary cosmic travel, from Lucian's Broilers through Wells's lobster-clawed Punchinellos toting umbrellas, and into the twenty-first century. Much of the literature, and of SF in general, has undercurrents of social criticism aimed at the time and place in which it is written.

The phrase "science fiction" was first used in 1881 by William Wilson in *A Little Earnest Book upon A Great Old Subject*, in which he wrote that fiction might create an interest in science that science will not create by itself. "He does good work who leads us thus seductively, along the pleasant road of fiction to such thought-inducing glimpses of the 'Poetry of Science,'"[22] Wilson comments on a work he considers a science fiction exemplar. That work, R. H. Horne's *The Poor Artist; or, Seven Eyesights and One Object*, is a sort of natural science *Rashomon* with a bee, an ant, a spider, a fish, a cat, a robin, and an artist as interpreters of the experience of vision. All look at the same object; each sees it differently, according to his or her own biologically determined sight, and culturally or environmentally enforced perspective. "The Poet's mission," in Wilson's opinion, "is to reveal the mighty world of light within his great soul to the world without, displaying in all its magnificence, the Beauty of the Universe."[23]

The style of Wilson's argument is poetically stilted and biblically romanticized. But the idea of the "poet" communicating the fascination and beauty of science works is striking. I was a fledgling reporter at *Newsweek* when the US space program got under way — I worked in a newly founded department named "Space & the Atom — and I clearly remember discussions of what a wonderful idea it would be to send a poet on one of the missions into space. That has not yet happened, but artists and writers have continued to enter outer space in their imagination. SF writers from Lucian on have aimed to go beyond the constraints of what is scientifically, experientially known, especially in matters of biology, anatomy, and gravity. It took almost two thousand years for Neil Armstrong to follow in Lucian's footsteps.

Weird Medicine

Science fiction is not only about outer space. It includes everything from brain surgery to robotic inventions. And when lobsters appear, it is not necessarily they who are the deviants, monsters, or caricatures. Sometimes the human being is the villain, as is the case with the evil doctor in the next science fiction tale.

A short medical mystery that bridges horror and SF appeared in *Weird Tales* in 1924. Romeo Poole's "A Hand from the Deep" is narrated by a medical intern who answers an ambulance call after an explosion at the home run by the disreputable Dr. Whitby. Though suspected of malpractice, Whitby had never been convicted. He and all but one of the home's residents have died in the explosion. The only survivor, Simon Glaze, was staying on the ground floor. Glaze is stunned but uninjured by the blast. He was in Whitby's care because his arm had been amputated just above the elbow in a mill accident, and the doctor had taken him in.

After being rescued and taken to the hospital, Glaze insists that his bandages be kept wet and that he be allowed to bathe in cool water as Whitby had prescribed. Since it seems to do no harm, the attending physician agrees to Glaze's wishes while he and his staff try to understand Glaze's odd behavior: when startled, Glaze doubles up into a ball and moves backward, away from anyone who comes toward him. As his condition grows worse, he loses the power of speech, odd growths appear on his stump, the shape of his head changes, he spends ever more time in cold water, and at one point he nearly crushes the intern's hand.

Another intern named Lacey follows a hunch and discovers what has happened. He gathers the other doctors interested in the case and explains that Whitby had been experimenting with a theory of regeneration. He had bought thousands of small lobsters in order to extract a glandular substance from them. He saturated Glaze with that substance. Now, the intern announces to his colleagues, Glaze is turning into a gigantic lobster. After that explanation, they all hurry to Glaze's room only to find him curled up underwater, dead. "Poor devil," Lacey says. "His lobster brain taught him that the only safe place for him was under water, but he lacked the lobster's breathing apparatus. Well, it's better this way after all."[24]

Limb regeneration — especially of crustaceans — has been recognized since Aristotle. The French scientist René-Antoine Ferchault de Réaumur presented the first known paper on the topic in 1712. He described an experiment in which he used crayfish:

> I took several of them, from which I broke off a leg; placed them in one of the covered boats which the fishermen call "Boutiques," in which they keep fish alive. As I did not allow them any food, I had reason to suppose that a reproduction would occur in them like that which I had attempted to prove. My expectation was not in vain. At the end of some months I saw, and without surprise, since I had expected it — I saw, I say, new legs, which took the place of the old ones, which I had removed; except in size they were exactly like them; they had the same form in all their parts, the same joints, the same movements. A kind of regeneration like this hardly less excites our envy than our imagination; if, in the place of a lost leg or arm, another would grow out again, one would be more willing to adopt the profession of the soldier.[25]

Réaumur explored the worlds of bees and ants; the digestion of birds; and the locomotion of mollusks, starfishes, and other invertebrates. He also wrote a history of insects. He surely had some practical application of his findings in mind, at least for the crayfish experiment: he seems to have been inspired by the idea that soldiers might have missing limbs restored by the regeneration method he documented.

As opposed to reproduction by self-division, lobsters regenerate by means of autonomy: the casting off of an injured or discarded part. An American, Thomas Hunt Morgan, coined the term "epimorphosis" to describe the process, and wrote a book called *Regeneration* that was published in 1901. It is said that when he couldn't solve the problem of regeneration, Morgan moved on to an easier problem — genetics — for which he won a Nobel Prize. The findings of Morgan and Réaumur are among the sources that were a rich feeding ground for the imagination of such SF writers as Romeo Poole.

In the preceding commentaries, scientific hypotheses and studies seed the endeavors of writers. To what extent do writers of science fiction blaze a trail that straight science follows?

In 1989 Erica van Dommelen — assistant editor at the journal *BioScience*, published by the American Institute of Biological Sciences, and president of the Washington Science Fiction Association — wrote a literature review titled "Biology in Science Fiction." She commented that "science fiction has always invented, or at least predicted, biological as well as other sciences."[26] Cases cited:

- The remote manipulator arms used in laboratories, called waldoes, were invented in 1942 by Robert Heinlein in his SF story "Waldo." The good news is that the man who designed the invention, used in biohazard labs, credited Heinlein.
- Edgar Pangborn wrote a story set in the future, in which a twenty-minute-long nuclear war caused the condition that is now a worldwide concern: global warming. Collected posthumously, his descriptions of the resulting changes to the Atlantic seaboard are consistent with what is now called the greenhouse effect.
- Research later conducted by wiring the pleasure centers of the brain was predicted, in a way, by two SF authors who wrote about human "wireheads" who were voluntary addicts to household current.[27]

"Homefaring"

Robert Silverberg, born in Brooklyn in 1935, has been writing and publishing for over fifty years, most prolifically and gratifyingly, in the science fiction genre. Silverberg has been nominated for more of the top SF awards — the Hugo and the Nebula — than any other writer, and he has won many of both. His eighty-eight-page novella "Homefaring" first appeared in the magazine *Amazing Stories* in 1983 and was anthologized the same year in the *World's Best SF*, and at least two times after that. In his introduction to "Homefaring" in a collection of his own novellas, Silverberg begins, "I had always had a sneaking desire to write the definitive giant-lobster story."[28]

Silverberg's lobster story is extra-extraordinary, from its very first words: "McCulloch was beginning to molt."[29] Silverberg turns the giant lobster story upside down, reinventing the lobster. I always thought that Buffon had written a strong literary description of the process of molting, but Silverberg's several pages about the process follows it moment by moment from McCulloch's point of view, from the first dreadful sensation that his body is going to split apart to the actual cracking of his shell, his soft inner body's struggle, the feeling that it will burst, the convulsions, and the final release. Each claw pulls through too-narrow passages and "wrists" through what feel like "handcuffs." Then follow McCulloch's naked vulnerability and his urgent need to seek shelter to hide from predators. And we don't yet know who he is.

McCulloch is a time traveler who was supposed to be launched a few hundred years into the future but is accidently blasted millions of years ahead, when the land is again under the sea. His experience as a human and a lobster takes place in a fabulous underwater landscape, among a community of intelligent creatures that is more like a congregation of meditative Buddhist monks than aggressive lobsters. They believe his arrival to be an omen that the Molting of the World is coming, and that a New World will follow. With McCulloch as their herald, they will start a long pilgrimage. "Homefaring"—as in seafaring or wayfaring—refers to the journey of McCulloch and the lobsters.

Before the pilgrimage, realizing that he is shares a lobster's body and persona, McCulloch contemplates his circumstances: "The entire human race, he thought, has migrated into the bodies of lobsters, and here we are on the ocean floor, scutting about, waving our claws and feelers."[30]

Scuttling about on the ocean floor—the image calls to mind T. S. Eliot's "The Love Song of J. Alfred Prufrock": "I should have been a pair of ragged claws / Scuttling across the floors of silent seas." That's just the first time in "Homefaring" that Silverberg alludes to the poem. Later, when McCulloch and the lobsters are on their pilgrimage—a fictional procession that mirrors the actual migratory marches of Caribbean spiny lobsters (see chapter 7)—Silverberg invokes Eliot more directly: "an endless line of yellow-robed holy men singing a great Om as they made their way up some Tibetan slope. He was awed and humbled by it—by the intensity, and by the wholeheartedness of the devotion. It was getting hard for him to remember that these were crustaceans, nor more than ragged claws scuttling across the floors of silent seas."[31]

Posthuman

Cyberpunk is a darker side of sf, and if you're not a fan, it's not easy to catch up. You may have to have one finger on Google looking up definitions, maybe of "teledesic satellite cluster" (the Teledesic company was formed to build a satellite constellation for broadband Internet access, but the project fell through). Or you may stumble over "You know anyone who can use a Warpac [Warsaw Pact] surplus espionage bot [robot]? Recent model, one careful owner, slightly paranoid but basically sound — I mean, claims to be a general purpose AI [artificial intelligence]?" or "Extropian investment fields" ("extropian" refers to principles developed by Max More that emphasize rational thinking and practical optimism)." Even so, it's possible to get caught up in the energy, negative as it often is.

Charles Stross writes like that, and the protagonist of his story called "Lobsters" is Manfred Macx, whose profession is patenting inventions that make other people rich; he is a venture altruist. He receives no money, only gifts (such as accommodations, travel tickets, and clothing) that free him from the evils of finance. Soon after we meet him, he receives a prepaid, Fed-Exed untraceable phone that rings as soon as he gets it. The speaker on the other end has a thick Russian accent, wants to defect, and is seeking asylum. Macx hangs up on him.

Macx later reads the news on his eyeglasses. Among other breaking stories is this one: "In San Diego researchers are uploading lobsters into cyberspace, starting with stomatogastric ganglion, one neuron at a time."[32] The next day the man with the Russian accent calls back, and it turns that out he represents the aforementioned lobsters. "Can you help us?" ask the lobsters. "Let me think about it," says Macx.[33]

He reflects: "Some day he, too, is going to be a lobster, swimming around and waving his pincers in a cyberspace so confusingly elaborate that his uploaded identity is cryptozoic [relating to invertebrates, like lobsters, that hide in places like crevices]: a living fossil from the depths of geological time, when mass was dumb and space was unstructured. He has to help them, he realizes — the Golden Rule demands it, and as a player in the agalmic economy [the economy of nonscarce goods], he thrives or falls by the Golden Rule."[34]

Not as daunting as the monsters in horror fiction, SF lobsters range from admirable to passing strange and perversely inappropriate experimental objects that pose the as yet unresolved question of regeneration. Silverberg's "Homefaring" suggests that in the very distant future, lobsters will survive humankind. They preceded *Homo sapiens* by millions of years, and they may survive us by as long a time. In Silverberg's future, we would be better off as lobsters. Alternately, the point Stross makes is that someday we may all be uploaded into cyberspace as lobsters. We will all be lobsters then.

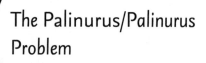

7 The Palinurus/Palinurus Problem

Palinurus is a lobster, a person, and a mythic messenger.

In its taxonomic classification, *Palinurus* is a genus of lobster in the Palinuridae family, also known as spiny or rock lobster, and sometimes called langouste.

Palinurus is also the pen name that Cyril Connolly — the English writer, editor, and influential intellectual — used to write *The Unquiet Grave*. Naming *Palinurus* his "ancestor" and "old incarnation" he writes: "O *Palinurus Vulgaris* . . . whether feeding on the spumy Mauretanian Banks or undulating — southward to Teneriffe, northward to Scilly — in the systole and diastole of the wave: free me from guilt and fear, free me from guilt and fear, dapple-plated scavenger of the resounding sea!"[1]

Connolly wrote *The Unquiet Grave* from the fall of 1942 to the fall of 1943, years when France was occupied, the European culture he loved seemed doomed, and his own marriage had failed. His prayerlike plea expresses doubts and despair about his own time and the past. *The Unquiet Grave* was first published in December 1944 in *Horizon*, the literary magazine founded by Connolly in 1940 and edited by him until it ceased publication in 1949.[2] Later published independently, *The Unquiet Grave* is a strange book, seasoned by aphorisms from and appreciations of other writers.

The references in the excerpt brought the past to bear on the current war's immediacy. Mauretania was an ancient kingdom on the Mediterranean coast of North Africa, part of the Roman Empire until the fifth century CE, when the Vandals invaded it. The first British ocean liner named after Mauretania was launched in September 1906; at the time, it was the largest and fastest ship in the world, sleek and beautiful. The second liner, named to honor the glory of her predecessor, was launched and christened in July 1938, three years after the old ship had been sent to the scrap yard.

Each of the seaworthy *Mauretanias* was called to military service during the world war of its era. The second one was still carrying troops as Connolly wrote.

Both the *Homarus* and *Palinurus* lobsters are found in the seas that wash the Scilly Isles, off the coast of Cornwall. Perhaps Connolly knew the story of a vessel named *Palinurus* that was wrecked on the Scilly rocks in December of 1848. Seventeen bodies were recovered, but there were no survivors to tell what happened or how many more had died.

Systolic and diastolic, the heartbeat of past and present, of seasonal migrations, departures and returns, doublings and repetitions: "free me from guilt and fear, free me from guilt and fear," Connolly pleads. Filled with depression and self-doubt, he considered opium and suicide, but he chose life and literature, and Palinurus as his alter ego — both the lobster *Palinurus vulgaris*, the "dapple-plated scavenger," and the man, described below. Perhaps he took the lobster's name to express his doubt and dejection. Connolly knew and admired T. S. Eliot, so he may have been thinking of that disturbing phrase from "The Love Song of J. Alfred Prufrock" (quoted in the last chapter), "I should have been a pair of ragged claws / Scuttling across the floors of silent seas." Scuttling suggests uncertainty. Their isolation and combativeness implies loneliness. The fact that they are dark-hued searchers on the bottom of the ocean projects an aura of despondency.

Palinurus the man was an ancient Roman character with few appearances but of lingering importance in Virgil's *Aeneid*. After the battle at Troy, when Aeneas is telling his story to Dido, he introduces Palinurus, as the helmsman of his own ship and leader of his fleet. Connolly uses John Dryden's translation of the *Aeneid*, first published in 1697:

And in redoubled peals the roaring thunder flies.
Cast from our course, we wander in the dark.
No stars to guide, no point of land to mark.
Ev'n Palinurus no distinction found
Betwixt the night and day; such darkness reign'd around.[3]

That phrase "ev'n Palinurus" suggests that, despite the lack of navigational aids — stars, horizon, or landmarks — the skilled Palinurus could have found his way, but that he was vulnerable because, as we will soon discover, the will of the gods opposed him.

Having won the love of Dido, Aeneas abandons her. Distraught, she throws herself onto her funeral pyre. As Aeneas's fleet departs, the sailors can see the glow from the funereal fire on shore. Soon the fleet is battered by a terrible storm, but the excellent Palinurus, knowing that they cannot ride it out, is able to steer the ships to Sicily and safety. Connolly comments that the pilot knew not only the awful reason for the fire's glow but also that the current storm (another punishment from the gods) was connected to Aeneas's betrayal of Dido. Palinurus "realized that Aeneas was guilty of hubris and impiety; he was 'not the Messiah.'"[4]

In an effort to prevent the men from leaving Sicily, a group of women sets the ships on fire and five of the galleys are lost. Also on Sicily, Palinurus's fate is sealed: when Venus implored Neptune to guarantee that Aeneas, her son, and all his men would henceforth voyage safely, Neptune agreed on the condition that one life must be sacrificed for the many.[5] That one life was Palinurus's. The sacrifice begins when the disguised god of sleep, Somnus, tries to persuade Palinurus to leave his post and rest for just an hour. Palinurus refuses, and the furious god not only puts him to sleep but then throws him overboard, with part of the stern and the rudder still in his grasp. Palinurus survives three days at sea, but no sooner does he reach shore than the savage inhabitants of the land murder him. His ghost is doomed to wander the banks of the Styx until he is properly buried. Aeneas, later visiting Hades, finds Palinurus there, hears his story, and takes care of his burial. Now Palinurus may rest in peace.

His appearances in the *Aeneid* may be rare, but Palinurus makes a strong impression and stirs deep emotions. Is he an innocent victim of the willful, unruly gods, or is he one way or another complicit in his fate? Does he somehow deserve it? Was Palinurus without guilt? Connolly suggests that he

> was tired of the fruitless voyage, horrified by the callousness of Aeneas, by the disasters which he seemed to attract . . . In Virgil's account, the God of Sleep is angry when Palinurus refuses the first temptation. But surely the clue we should no-

tice is that, although the sea is calm, Palinurus when he falls takes with him tiller, rudder and a section of the poop [deck]. Tillers may come off easily but not part of the stern! Thus he provides himself not only with a raft but inflicts a kind of castration on Aeneas by removing both his chief pilot and his means of steering, and this within the dangerous orbit of the Sirens! Surely this is a typical example of anti-social hysteroid resentment![6]

In Connolly's reading, Palinurus is responsible for — even designed — his fate. His character betrays a will to fail, to quit rather than succeed, and ultimately demonstrates self-hatred for doing so. Because Connolly has named himself Palinurus, this is not only an attack on Aeneas's pilot but also a scalding self-assessment on the writer's part. As a lobster, he is a forager in the deep. And as Palinurus? Connolly writes: "Sometimes at night I get a feeling of claustrophobia; of being smothered by my own personality, of choking through being in the world . . . It is like being pinned underneath the hull of a capsized boat, yet being afraid to dive deeper and get clear. In those moments it seems that there must be a way out, and that through sloughing off [or molting?] the personality alone can it be taken."[7]

In naming himself after both a genus of lobster and a mythical ancient pilot, Connolly bridged more than the years that separated him from Virgil, who wrote the *Aeneid* between 29 and 18 BCE. The legend of Aeneas and the tragedy of Palinurus date back to the Trojan War of the early twelfth century BCE. Aeneas's voyage would continue and lead to the founding of Rome without Palinurus, who was sacrificed to the gods in order that Aeneas might ultimately land safely.

Cape Palinuro, supposed to be the place where Virgil's helmsman was killed, is named in Palinurus's honor. A barren, rocky landmark in southeastern Italy, about forty miles southwest of Salerno, it became famous as a place of shipwrecks.

The search for an etymological explanation of Palinurus is a challenge. A note accompanying Frederick Ahl's translation of Virgil's *Aeneid* says that the name "suggests [Palinurus] should *come back* to Italy (Gk. *palin*, 'back')."[8] Another claims that "Palinurus is a hybrid formed from the Latin *palans* (wandering) and Greek δείτε (seeing)."[9] The most convincing source is "returning, favorable wind," because Philip Ambrose marshals the most persuasive arguments: (1) Virgil himself etymologizes the name that way; (2) Greek literature uses δείτε as a technical term for the wind of homecoming; (3) other Latin authors besides Virgil connect Palinurus with wind; and (4) Cape Palinuro is known for its winds.[10]

Connolly's assessment of Virgil's tragic Palinurus was not shared by others. For example, in canto 1 of *Marmion*, Sir Walter Scott calls on his countrymen to remember the great statesman William Pitt, "deep graved in every British heart":

> O think, how to his latest day,
> When Death, just hovering, claim'd his prey,
> With Palinure's unalter'd mood
> Firm at his dangerous post he stood;
> Each call for needful rest repelled,
> With dying hand the rudder held,
> Till in his fall with fateful sway
> The steerage of the realm gave way![11]

Palinurus, the heroic patriot! Or was he a resentful, castrating pilot with an Oedipal complex?

Both, perhaps. It depends on whose alter ego or avatar he is: *I, Palinurus.*

The figure of Virgil's Palinurus continuously preoccupied the worlds of literature and politics. He has only a walk-on role in Dante's fourteenth-century *Divine Comedy*, though there he is once again a symbol of a far-reaching idea: troubled Italy as a disabled ship of state. The poet Payne Fisher also used the ship-of-state metaphor during the seventeenth century to praise Oliver Cromwell as the man who, by dissolving Parliament, had — like Palinurus — saved the rudderless government. Unlike Virgil's pilot, who was thrown overboard and later killed, Fisher had the British leader rescue the foundering ship of state and steer it to safe harbor.[12]

After Scott but before Connolly, Henry Wadsworth Longfellow summoned up the pilot's name at least three times in letters. Writing to his father from Europe in 1826, Longfellow described his passage through a cave where the head room above water was at times as little as three feet, at which point "the traveler . . . stretches himself upon his back and is propelled forward by a kind of ragged Palinurus, who navigates the boat by pushing with his feet against the roof of the cavern."[13] The following year he wrote his sister, mentioning "our Palinurus" in reference to a guide who was reluctant to accompany Longfellow and his companion after dark on what he feared was a dangerous path patrolled by robbers.[14] And to a historian friend, Longfellow jokingly wrote that he would visit in the summer "so as to give you an opportunity of drowning us in the Bay, in testimony of yr. skill as Palinurus."[15] Longfellow produced the first American translation of Dante's *Divine Comedy*, published in 1867. His Palinurus was an idiosyncratic shape-shifter, a reminder of Scott's famous lines from *Marmion*: "Oh! what a tangled web we weave / When first we practice to deceive!"[16]

Two wonderful twentieth-century writers called upon Palinurus in this long chain of connections. The sestina "Recitativo de Palinuro," by Giuseppi Ungaretti, was published in *The Promised Land* in 1950. Ungaretti's "Palinurus is an allegorical figure, who seems to stand for the steering-mechanism in life, for a combination of conscience and will, for fidelity to ideals," writes Michael Hanne. "And the 'Recitativo' is Palinurus's surprised complaint at the discovery that the unwavering pursuit of an image of perfection is not enough to ensure its attainment."[17] Hanne adds: "If we take the storm and the fury of the waves as symbolic of forces inside man (and Ungaretti encourages this interpretation . . .) then the 'Recitativo' becomes a representation not of guiltless behaviour, but of the actual process of moral corruption."[18]

Ungaretti died in 1970. Still very much alive as I write is Fernando del Paso, who published *Palinuro de Mexico* in 1977. Connolly's *Unquiet Grave* inspired and motivated his *Palinuro* in the aftershock not of a world war but of the disastrous Tlateloco massacre, which took place on October 2, 1968, when some ten thousand university and secondary school students gathered at the Plaza de las Tres Culturas in Mexico City. They assembled to protest governmental abuses of their freedom and to listen to speeches. It was supposed to be a peaceful rally, but about two hundred army tanks and trucks and five thousand troops moved in. The number of dead has never been confirmed. The government insisted that the students opened fire first, but about thirty years later that accusation was disproved. The final words have not been written.

The Palinuro in this layered book is both a first-person narrator and an individual referred to in the third person. He is a medical student who is having an affair with his first cousin. Set in that cataclysmic historical context, it is said that del Paso is trying to find a language that will in some way express if not explain the massacre.[19]

The multiplicity of the literary Palinurus's identities is matched by the complication of names given to lobsters in the Palinuridae suborder or family. In 1958, for example, the International Commission on Zoological Nomenclature issued Opinion 519 as an addition to the Official List of Generic Names in Zoology regarding the spelling of Palinurus. The problem was that the first naming of this genus in 1795 had been spelled with a double "l": Pallinurus. The opinion concludes:

> As, however, the spelling Palinurus has been consistently employed by practically every carcinologist [a scientist who studies crustaceans] from 1798 to the present day . . . it would be very awkward to change the spelling to Pallinurus. This is the more true since the name Pallinurus has, as far as I am aware, no sensible meaning, while Palinurus is the name of a mythical figure, viz., the steersman of Aeneas's ship. The Commission is therefore asked to use its Plenary Powers to approve the emendation of the spelling of the generic name Pallinurus Weber, 1795 [Weber being the first person to name the genus, and 1795 the date he did so] to Palinurus.[20]

Did the first person to name this lobster have Aeneas's pilot in mind but misspell his name? Whether he did or not, the name has taken on that association over the centuries. And if etymological possession is nine-tenths of the law, then Palinurus lobsters (in all their anagrammatic spellings) are named for the legendary pilot of Aeneas's fleet.

"Intelligent of Seasons"

There are some fifty-eight members of the *Palinurus* genus (popularly known as spiny lobsters), and none of them are of the clawed lobster variety. One genus has an idiosyncratic spelling for reasons unknown, but also has stunningly idiosyncratic behavioral characteristics. This is *Panulirus argus* (unregularized spellings such as this one are so far called "synonyms" for *Palinurus*), commonly known as the Caribbean spiny lobster and found in areas near Florida and the Bahamas.

William Herrnkind, of the Biological Sciences Department of Florida State University, has studied the autumnal migration of *Panulirus argus* both in the field and in laboratory pools for over three decades. Herrnkind and Paul Kanciruk report that there is a strong correlation between increased wind speed, which brings storms as well as cooler weather, and the lobster's migration.[21] So when the temperature goes down and the winds blow fast and hard, these lobsters form long chains on their migratory parade along the ocean floor, a fact that would appear to further connect this particular group to Panilurus the pilot, whose name is related to wind. However, the link is unsupportable since no one has known of their migration behavior until recently.

Be that as it may, when John Milton wrote of migratory geese that "Part loosely wing the region, part more wise / In common, rang'd in figure wedge their way, / Intelligent of seasons, and set forth / Their airy caravan high over sea's flying,"[22] he might as well have written of migrating Caribbean spiny lobsters. They too, "intelligent of seasons," rally their "caravan," but under the sea, and ranged head-to-tail in parallel rather than in V-shaped lines.

In the autumn, thousands of these lobsters form long, marching columns, often in daytime. This is curious because under ordinary circumstances, they tend to hide in solitary confinement in crevices or dens during the day and come out to hunt for food at night. Ethologists — scientists who study animal behavior — coined the term *zugunruhe* to describe the migratory anxiety that takes hold in the animals when a migration period is approaching. In this mood, it may require nothing more than one lobster passing another to start a queue. Mood and movement seem to be important stimuli. Herrnkind and his colleagues have even attached a mock lobster to a glass rod and moved it around in the research pool. Sure enough, a line started forming. Leadership of the queue does not depend on size, shape, or gender, and leaders change as the journey proceeds. The queue may be established visually or, if visual clues are not available because the water is murky, by tactile and chemical stimuli, but once in line, each lobster remains in antennal contact with the individual ahead of it. Thus they stay in alignment and can continue their migratory journey day and night, and in all weather. We might imagine them as members of a fleet of lobsters like the fleet of vessels guided by Palinurus the pilot.

This community-based migration of the achelate (clawless) *Panulirus argus* is very different from the behavior of homarid (clawed) lobsters. Homarids, such as *Homarus americanus*, are far more aggressive and far less sociable, and they migrate as individuals rather than in groups. It's entirely rational that lobsters without claws are sociable rather than aggressive. However, they are not entirely defenseless: when the need arises, they use their long antennae as whips.

Panuliris is one of various anagrammatic adaptations of the pilot's name. The second part of its binomial nomenclature, *argus*, refers to a specific characteristic: the four large spots on its tail reminded someone of the Argus in Greek mythology, a monster with a hundred eyes.

Herrnkind introduced Jacques Cousteau to the migration of the spiny lobster and joined him on the *Calypso* for the filming of "Incredible March of the Spiny Lobsters," which was aired on ABC in 1976 as number 27 of the Undersea World of Jacques Cousteau series.

Cousteau describes how he and his crew waited off the coast of Mexico's Yucatan Peninsula for the winter wind that would inspire the migration. He'd been told that after the first winter storm of the year, the migratory parade would begin. To watch it, he organized an underwater "night patrol": "We were right on time: Below, we saw thousands of lobsters, each reaching toward another with its antennae, assembling into groups. Suddenly, the leaders all moved out, as if in response to a silent gunshot to 'be off,' with queues of lobsters following behind."[23]

When the lights of the *Calypso* crew bothered them, the lobsters "circled like wagon trains" and waited until the disturbance was gone. Cousteau guessed there were more than a million lobsters, moving at almost one mile per hour. Where did they go? They disappeared "too deep and too far to be followed, heading for a destination no one has located for reasons no one has fathomed."[24]

On the downside, the crew also filmed what seems a profane act: fishing boats, taking advantage of the animals' mass migration, netted an estimated 7,000 lobsters during a four-day period.

Cosmic Messenger

The Cousteau patrol watched the lobster parade underwater until it went deeper than they could see or follow. Someday an ersatz "lobster eye" may scan the universe from higher above the earth than anyone can travel.

Considering the low light and often murky water on the ocean floor, lobsters would find twenty-twenty vision a needless extravagance. However, even though they can't see very clearly, or in color, lobsters' eyes are remarkable enough that they have been investigated over the past thirty years as a model for use in outer space. Rather than being set into their heads, lobsters' eyes are raised on stalks, allowing them access to a wider panorama than that of ordinary inset eyes. And the stalks can move, which adds to the animals' visual flexibility.

The great distinction of the lobster eyeball is that it is a compound system that works by reflection, not by refraction. When light rays enter a human eye, the cornea bends them and directs them through the pupil, the lens, and the retina to the back wall of the eye, where photoreceptor nerve cells change the light into electrical impulses and send them through the optic nerve to the brain. In the brain, the impulses are perceived as an image.

There's no lens behind a lobster's cornea. Instead, there is an array of minute tubes, square at the surface of the cornea where they receive light, and tapering toward the retina. The tube interiors are coated with a substance that reflects incoming light onto the retina. These minute tubes are optical units called ommatidia, and they make up the lobster's compound eye. Each eye has around thirty thousand ommatidia.

Roger Angel, of the University of Arizona, first proposed the lobster-eye model for use as an X-ray monitor of the sky in 1977. It took more than thirty years to perfect the optic technology. An almost unlimited field of view is its most significant recommendation. It is anticipated that when it finds a platform in space, the lobster telescope will be a major breakthrough in X-ray astronomy.

Work on the Lobster Eye Telescope is proceeding at the University of Leicester, in Great Britain, where a recent status update noted: "The sky viewed at X-ray wavelengths is a violent and unpredictable place. Many sources brighten without warning, then vanish just as suddenly. Others vary cyclically over a period that can range from minutes to years. The ideal X-ray telescope, therefore, would observe 'all the sky, all of the time' an ideal which might seem unattainable, but which is approached by the Lobster concept."[25]

Professor George Fraser, Director of the Space Research Centre at Leicester, describes the mission enthusiastically:

The scientific impact of Lobster will span all of astronomy— from studies of the X-ray emission of comets to stars and quasars, from regular X-ray binaries to the catastrophic events of supernovae and the enigmatic gamma-ray bursts. Through frequent re-observation of each point in the sky during the lifetime of the mission, Lobster offers the opportunity to perform deep, sensitive surveys of both galactic and extra-galactic sources. This will lead to the collation of a 'Lobster All-Sky Catalogue' containing hundreds of thousands of sources, including a significant population of objects for which photometry on approximately 1 day timescales will be available.

Such a rich catalogue of sources offers an unprecedented opportunity to study the large-scale distribution of matter in the Universe, probing possible links between supercluster filamentary structures and the purported existence of dark matter in the cosmos.[26]

The intended placement of the Lobster Eye Telescope was on the International Space Station, but scientists are currently contemplating a free-flying satellite platform instead.

Rock Lobster

The play *Cowboy Mouth* was written by Sam Shepard and Patti Smith over two days (they reportedly passed the typewriter back and forth in their room at the Hotel Chelsea) toward the end of their affair. *Cowboy Mouth* was staged at the American Place Theater in New York City in 1971, but only once. Its cast of three consisted of Slim (played by Shepard), Cavale (Smith), and Lobster Man (Robert Glaudini). Shepard literally fled the scene just before the second night's performance — deciding, it's said, to keep his inner torment and identity crisis more private than performing it allowed.

Cowboy Mouth is a raw and messy situation in character with the messed-up lives Smith and Shepard had been leading. The script calls for "a fucked-up bed center stage," a dead crow, and lots of junk on the floor. Cavale, we learn, has kidnapped Slim in order to turn him into the rock-and-roll Jesus she urgently seeks. Deciding to leave, Slim persuades the Lobster Man to take his part. Lobster Man's shell cracks open. The rock and roll savior emerges, puts his gun to his head, and pulls the trigger — but the chamber is empty. The lights fade, and the curtain comes down.

It was over.

But it was omniscient.

Lobster rock was in the wings.

It stepped onstage again with the 1978 release of "Rock Lobster," by the New Wave band, the B-52's. The band was inspired by the avant-garde music of John Cage and Yoko Ono. "Rock Lobster" was the first single from the B-52's. It was on their first album, released in 1979, and it was soon their signature tune and a huge success. The band's members were Cindy Wilson (vocals); Ricky Wilson (guitar), her brother; Kate Pierson (vocals and keyboards); Keith Strickland (drums); and Fred Schneider (vocals and cowbell).

The lyrics of "Rock Lobster" don't make much sense. The song starts at a beach party, where someone's earlobe falls into the deep and turns out to be a rock lobster; everyone is having fun "rockin'" and "fruggin'," and the music is twangy with a *Twilight Zone* feeling. The performance is wacky and jumpy; the lyrics are cryptic; and it's all confusing and maybe fun.

A new kind of lobster metaphor was in the air, and—like the *zugunruhe* Herrnkind describes—it was rocking another generation. Palinurus began life as a tragic hero of ancient mythology and loaned his name to a lobster that has, in its own way, become an obsession for generations of writers and, more recently, musicians, who have all recreated *Palinurus* in the image of their own personal and cultural obsessions.

8 "Secrets of the Sea"

Lobsters are everywhere — under the ocean, obviously, and there are freshwater varieties too. There are lobsters, and then there are more lobsters, and the way they live their lives in their natural habitat has very little to do with how they live their lives in our world. This is about the most important thing you can understand about them. Their reproductive behavior has been studied to the extent possible, which is limited by our inability to follow them in their natural habitat. Nevertheless, enough is known to describe how and when they mate. But no matter how much information is gathered, their character beyond the domain of research is corrupted by human morality, fear, pleasure, and pain. Especially in reference to their sex life.

Among our cultural history's most famous lobsters was one attached — whether literally or in a figurative sense — to the French poet Gérard de Nerval, who allegedly walked his pet lobster at the end of a blue ribbon. A few other well-known lobsters belong to Salvador Dalí. And one is connected — imaginatively — to Lewis Carroll, the author of *Alice in Wonderland*, where we discover what the lobster quadrille is about. These are the international celebrities. They will take their bows in this chapter, but I will begin with a relatively unknown lobster and the man who invented him.

Lobster is the title — and the name of the main character — of a book by Guillaume Lecasble that was published in 2003 in French and in 2005 by Dedalus in an English translation. According to the publisher's website, "Dedalus has invented its own distinctive genre, which we term distorted reality, where the bizarre, the unusual, the grotesque and the surreal meld in a kind of intellectual fiction which is very European."[1] Among its current top ten titles are *Memoirs of a Gnostic Dwarf* and *The Arabian Nightmare* ("In a city of sultans, seductresses and apes, Ballan of Norwich is pursued through a maze of streets by the Father of Cats.").[2] *Lobster* is a Dedalus "Euro Short": short—or long—enough to be read during the Eurostar trip between London and Paris, which takes two hours and thirty minutes.

Whichever direction you're traveling when you read *Lobster*, reviewers suggest that you will be reeling when you step off the train. Nicholas Lezard wrote: "All I know is this: by the time you stumble out into the Gare du Nord, you will be a different person to the one who boarded the Eurostar. You may also find yourself with a most unsettling craving for lobster."[3] Lezard's review was in the *Guardian*, a newspaper that was founded in Manchester, England, in May 1821 with a commitment to civil and religious freedom and to reform. During the *Guardian*'s centenary, in 1921, it was reaffirmed that the paper has a "moral as well as a material existence." That phrase was quoted in a May 2011 editorial that looked forward to the paper's 200th anniversary, a mere decade away, and reported its largest ever circulation, of forty-nine million.[4] This is a better than average readership for a newspaper, one from which Dedalus may draw those who enjoy "intellectual fiction which is very European."

Lecasble's story begins "Lobster didn't want to go," as lobsters are being caught, crated, transported, and so forth.[5] Deceptively, the plot and language of *Lobster* seem to have the forthright simplicity of children's books, and Lecasble has written books for children. He's also a painter and filmmaker. *Lobster* is his first novel for adults.

It is very definitely not for children. Lobster and his parents end up on the *Titanic*—in the dining room's aquarium, which people circle to choose the lobster they want to eat. Lobster sees a beautiful young woman, Angelina, select his dad; his mother goes into the pot two days later, and the next day Lobster himself is chosen. Just as he's thrown into boiling water, the ship's collision with an iceberg topples the pot and he comes out red, but not dead. He finds himself with beautiful Angelina, a suicidal opium addict who has never achieved sexual gratification. But with Lobster's gentle manipulations, she does. They fall passionately in love and then are dreadfully parted. And this is just the beginning of a troubling and terrible sexual fantasy: Angelina substitutes another of his species for her beloved Lobster, and instead of gratification she suffers a clictoridectomy. During his Atlantic wanderings, floating like a red beacon among communities of naturally dark lobsters, Lobster becomes a totem for all lobsters, and for men, too.

It has been suggested—ironically, I hope—that Lecasble means this story to be an allegory for the way people build shells around themselves when they are unable to relate to the one to whom they want most to relate. I demur. It reminds me most of the Lobster Boy, the decadent, violent, circus "freak" (see chapter 4). He bragged about his sexual exploits, in particular with one woman: "This teacher, she really liked my claws . . . and she just kept coming back and back and back because of this. Everyone I have sex with wants to have sex with my claws. They love it when I use my claws."[6]

The best I can offer is that *Lobster* might be a good book for a train ride, as long as you have no serious work to do at the end of the line. And I must add that the last thing I wanted to eat when I closed the book was lobster.

All I know is this: *chacun à son goût*—to each, her own.

The *Titanic* crashed into an iceberg on the evening of April 14, 1912, and sank early the next morning. On August 9, 1996, during filming in Nova Scotia of the movie *Titanic*—which cost $100 million to make—about fifty members of the cast and crew were rushed to the hospital. Someone had seasoned the lobster chowder with phencyclidine, also known as PCP and angel dust. Shades of the opium addict, Angelina.

Lobster Erotica

The seductive lobster dinner in the movie *Tom Jones* and the lobsters consumed during the lobster palace era highlight the lobster as an aphrodisiac, but never before Lecasble's book, to my knowledge, was the lobster active or complicit in the seduction itself. It's true that in Robert Silverberg's "Homefaring," while co-inhabiting a lobster body, McCulloch does have sex with a female lobster. But McCulloch is a lobster at the time of his mating. Angelina is not and never had been a lobster—only her seducer is. The difference is not just science fiction versus erotic fiction: as far as I can tell, these erotic fantasies flow from male imaginations, not female — the Lobster Boy's boast notwithstanding. As Dedalus's website observes, the company publishes books that, like Lecasble's, are surreal.

We can trace Lecasble's lobster eroticism to Salvador Dalí, whose work fits the Dedalus criteria for this genre: bizarre, unusual, grotesque, and surreal — a very peculiar mix of reality and imagination. Indeed, Dalí was in the forefront of the Surrealism movement of the 1920s as well as a manic inventor in the field of sex, lobsters, and the unconscious.

Dalí's *Aphrodisiac Telephone*, first exhibited in 1936, was made of plaster, plastic, and metal: it had a conventional black base (vintage 1930s), a rotary dial, and what would be an ordinary black handset were it not covered by a bright red lobster. Maybe it's humorous. But in fact it is an assault on sanity and perverse to combine a familiar object designed for personal communication with a fearsome-looking, aggressive creature. There is madness in the very idea of holding a lobster close to the face as a telephone receiver, its claws to the ear and "tail" — really the underside of the stomach that, on its surface, contains the male lobster's sexual organs — to the mouth. Though a cooked red lobster is a food, and in fact the tail meat is especially succulent, the idea of Dalí's *Aphrodisiac Telephone* in the context of sexual stimulation may be disturbing enough for some people to be the reason that numerous versions of it in museum collections (colored white as well as red) are now generally known as *Lobster Telephone* rather than *Aphrodisiac Telephone*.[7]

To tell the truth, "aphrodisiac" is only a modest introduction to the ideas about lobsters that erupted in Dalí's mind. He was a follower of Sigmund Freud. He read Freud's complete works in Spanish and talked about Freud "like a Christian talks about the New Testament," according to Julien Green, a writer and one of Dalí's patrons.[8] Dalí believed in the significance of dreams and of childhood memories, the Oedipus complex, castration anxiety, and incestuous desire. He defined his own theory of "critical paranoia" as a "spontaneous method of irrational knowledge based upon the interpretative-critical association of delirious phenomena."[9] Dalí's paranoia and delirium were voluntary; in fact, they were cultivated.

Freud provided a language for Dalí's attack on reality as well as for Dalí's personal fears and obsessions, from which he suffered mightily. Castration was one of his deepest anxieties, and the lobster became a symbolic implement for performing castration. Consider the lobster's serrated claws — the smaller and sharper of which is known as the slicer — and imagine, as Dalí probably did, it slicing off his testicles. Then consider that if one combines the concept of the lobster as sexual stimulant (that is, an aphrodisiac) with the idea of employing a lobster to punish the event resulting from that sexual stimulation by castrating the perpetrator — well, perverse or not, it makes some kind of sense. The provocateur causes the misdeed and then carries out its punishment.

In a 1933 painting he named *Gala and the Angelus of Millet Preceding the Imminent Arrival of the Conical Anamorphoses*[10] Dalí placed a lobster on the bald head of Maxim Gorky — the revolutionary Russian activist, writer, and founder of social realism — who stands in shadow behind an open door. Gorky is eavesdropping on a conversation in an overlit room where Gala (Dalí's wife) sits talking to Vladimir Ilyich Lenin. According to an exhibition catalog entry for the painting, "although the ultimate meaning of this mysterious work remains unfathomable, the presence of Gala, Lenin, Gorky, and [André] Breton [the founder of surrealism, whose bust is on a shelf in the painting] under the sign of Millet's *Angelus* suggests the painting was intended as an allegory of the artist's deepest anxieties and obsessions centered around mothers devouring their sons in a form of engulfing sexual cannibalism."[11] Gala is a stand-in for the cannibalistic mother.

In Millet's *Angelus*, which Dalí reproduces above the doorframe in his painting, a peasant and his wife stand praying, heads bowed, in the field where they have been working. The man holds his hat in front of his genitals. In Dalí's interpretation, the scene has "the sinister connotations of the bizarre mating ritual of the praying mantis, in which the husband is about to be devoured by his sexually aggressive mate after copulation."[12]

In the introduction I wrote about a Dalí drawing brought to me by someone who learned of my lobster project. Among the mysterious details of that drawing is a man with a handlebar moustache and a lobster holding onto his bald head. I wonder now if it might

Salvador Dalí, Gala and the Angelus of Millet Preceding the Imminent Arrival of the Conical Anamorphoses, 1933. © National Gallery of Canada, Ottawa, Ontario, Canada. Salvador Dalí, Fundació Gala — Salvador Dalí, Artists Rights Society (ARS), New York 2011. Photo: Bridgeman-Giraudon / Art Resource, NY.

have been a study for Gorky as he appears in the equally strange, provocative *Gala* painting. (The drawing, which was framed, was not visibly titled or dated.)

Dalí also interpreted the legend of William Tell shooting an apple off his son's head with an arrow as a metaphor for castration. One such apple appears in the curly mop of hair on Harpo Marx's head, balanced on the tail of a lobster, in Dalí's *Harpo Marx*, from 1937.[13] This is a delicately drawn portrait of Marx in graphite and ink, sitting at his harp, and nothing about the lobster looks threatening. Until, as with the telephone—where, following Dalí's chain of associations, even an ordinary receiver may bring a lobster to mind—the sight of a lobster on anyone's head becomes a metonymy for castration. Thus the apple and lobster on Marx's head point with a doubled association to the theme of castration anxiety. And once you see it, you can't get rid of the association.

Dalí's most attractive if incongruous lobster was the one he created in 1937 in collaboration with Elsa Schiaparelli, the clothes designer and follower of surrealism. The full-length ball gown of white silk organza is filmy and sleek but shocking because, below its lobster-red cummerbund is a large red silk lobster in the soft ripples of the skirt—its tail fins fanning out in the vicinity of the wearer's mons veneris, and its claws hanging down around her calves. Without the lobster, any young lady would have loved the dress for a prom gown. With the lobster, it took the audacity of a Wallis Simpson to wear it—she bought the gown for her trousseau shortly before she married the Duke of Windsor in 1937. She also modeled it for a photograph that appeared in *Vogue*. The photograph was taken by Cecil Beaton, the photographer of society's crème de la crème.

Dalí's most outrageous lobster invention was a costume he designed himself for *The Dream of Venus*, a midway fun house at the New York World's Fair of 1939 with an erotic, aquatic theme. Women were to swim around nearly naked in enormous fish tanks wearing a kind of thong with a whole, live-looking lobster that stretched from their pudenda to their navels. Penis envy was the idea behind this cannibalistic motif.

The production process of *The Dream of Venus* was a nightmare for Dalí—the sponsors were, he thought, intent on sabotaging his

George Platt Lynes, photograph of Salvador Dalí, 1939. © Estate of
George Platt Lynes. The Metropolitan Museum of Art, New York. David
Hunter McAlpin Fund, 1941. Image copyright © The Metropolitan
Museum of Art / Art Resource, NY.

designs, substituting what he called "siren fish tails" for his costumes.
In retaliation he went to the workshop with scissors, and "the first
thing I did was to cut open . . . the dozen sirens' tails intended for
the swimming girls, thus making them totally unusable." [14]

What would Sigmund Freud have said about that? He and

Dalí were contemporaries, but Freud paid little attention to Dalí or surrealism. Yet most of Dalí's creative energy, especially when using lobster imagery, derives from his interpretation of Freud.

The fantasies of Lecasble and Dalí reveal a scary side of the lobster in sexual fiction. There are also examples of its participation in gentler fantasies.

Joseph Cornell, who lived from 1903 to 1972, was an American artist known for his assemblages, usually shadow boxes filled with very small found objects. He did not join the surrealist movement, but during the 1930s and 1940s, he worked "at the edge of its orbit," as William Rubin, head of the Museum of Modern Art's Department of Painting and Sculpture, once put it: "Related on one side to the American tradition of an art that celebrated memorabilia — the *trompe l'oeil* painting of Harnett and Peto — his style and iconography are unthinkable without surrealism."[15] Cornell's boxes served simultaneously as little cabinets of curiosity and as stage settings. He filled them with photographs, cutlery, doilies, and toys that he might find at a dime store — he was, as one writer put it, a "dime store connoisseur."[16]

In one of Cornell's boxes — *Pantry Ballet (For Jacques Offenbach)*, from 1943, ten and a half inches high by eighteen inches long and six inches deep — the artist arranged ten small red plastic lobsters dressed in white tutus as a chorus line. They stood in front of delicately detailed wallpaper, and in the foreground were cutouts of lacy white doilies representing stage curtains.

This lobster chorus line paid homage to the art of ballet, for which Cornell had a passion; to Offenbach, a composer he greatly admired; and to Lewis Carroll's lobster quadrille as well.[17] Though shy and reclusive, Cornell was in tune with the roughly fifty thousand people who flocked to the New York Museum of Modern Art's show called "Fantastic Art, Dada, Surrealism" during 1936–37, to say nothing of the people who saw the exhibition when it traveled to other cities. Lewis Carroll inspired not only surrealist artists but also enthusiasts of high society who went to costume parties where they danced a lobster quadrille.[18]

Cornell's love of ballet extended to the ballerinas who captured his romantic imagination and sometimes obsessed him. Cornell met Renée Zizi Jeanmarie—who danced with Roland Petit's Les Ballets de Paris and was married to Petit—backstage when the troupe performed *Carmen* in New York. He expressed his admiration by dedicating several boxes to her. The *Zizi Jeanmarie Lobster Ballet Box* of 1949 includes more jaunty red lobsters in tutus, but now they are outshone by a stunning prima ballerina: a cutout photograph of Zizi Jeanmarie dressed in a costume from *Carmen*, which resembles a toreador's jacket. Her balancing leg is on point, while the other is raised in an extraordinary grand battement, at an angle of about 135 degrees. She is the epitome of elegance and grace, with a smile on her face. The lobster corps de ballet is smiling, too.[19] As Cornell's work reveals, sublimated erotic fantasies may revolve around lobsters in charming rather than calamitous ways.

*L*obsters are so bizarre, unreal, and in many ways nightmarish that it is not surprising they found an enthusiastic audience among surrealists' explorations of the irrational and subconscious mind. In the portfolio of Salvador Dalí, the creature stands for the artist's worst fears. A smile in a painting of Dalí's, such as that on the face of Gala in the painting discussed above, is more like a predatory grin. In contrast, a wistful heart beats in the work of Joseph Cornell. His lobsters, projections of something more like romantic fantasy than libidinous violence, are smiling because they are happy, albeit for reasons only Cornell knows (and perhaps only in his subconscious).

Lobster on a Leash

The following description of the Palais-Royal and the incident of mischief that may or may not have occurred there sets the stage for another current of idiosyncratic madness with a lobster at its center.

One of the most formidable buildings in Paris was the Palais-Cardinal, named for Armand Jean du Plessis, Cardinal Richelieu, and built between 1629 and 1634. Richelieu bequeathed the property to Louis XIII, and after the cardinal's death in 1642 it became known as the Palais-Royal. Behind the palace was a large garden that came to be surrounded by arcaded shops and was opened to the public in 1784. It was a vibrant gathering place where news and rumors circulated, drinking and gaming were enjoyed, and speeches were made. On July 12, 1789, Camille Desmoulins stood on a table at one of the cafes there and cried out the revolutionary words "Aux armes, citoyens!"[20]

A notable feature of the garden at the Palais-Royal is a cannon that was set on the prime meridian (before the prime meridian was moved to Greenwich, in 1884) so that the sun's noon rays, passing through a lens, lit the cannon's fuse and caused it to fire at midday. It was said that just about everyone in earshot set his watch to the cannon's blast. An article in the 1854 edition of *Chambers's Pocket Miscellany* — a publication that advertised its offerings as choice selections of interesting and instructive reading — reported that a few years earlier a young rogue had climbed over the railing, stealthily crawled up to the cannon, and lit a match that fired the cannon at 11:30 a.m. Among the resulting troubles was a missed appointment of great consequence between a banker in dire straits and a man who, insisting on promptness, would arrive before noon if he were able to bail the banker out of his financial difficulties. When the false noon alarm sounded, the distraught banker awaiting salvation left the park — compelled, he thought, to confess his insolvency: "That little ragged rascal of the streets had caused an important bankruptcy — in fact, a pretty serious commercial crisis."[21]

I can't vouch for the authenticity of this story, but if it happened, it is also entirely possible that Gérard de Nerval (1808–55) was walking his pet lobster, attached to a blue ribbon, in the garden of the Palais-Royal on the same day.

Nerval was a French symbolist poet,[22] a "mad poet" to his admirers and detractors alike, whose distractions, periods of gloom, and nervous breakdowns were not welcome or of his own making, as Dalí's tended to be. Nerval previewed many surrealist beliefs. "Our dreams are a second life. I have never been able to penetrate without a shudder those ivory or horned gates which separate us from the invisible world," he wrote.[23] For his attention to the dream world and his embrace of supernaturalism, the Surrealists embraced him. In 1924 André Breton proclaimed: "I believe that there is no point today in dwelling any further on this word [surrealism] . . . [W]e could probably have taken over the word SUPERNATURALISM employed by Gérard de Nerval . . . It appears, in fact, that Nerval possessed to a tee the spirit with which we claim kinship."[24]

De Nerval was the poet's pen name; his given name was Gérard Labrunie. In 1855, before his forty-seventh birthday and after his third breakdown, he committed suicide. That was long before Breton was born, in 1896, let alone before he wrote his *Manifestoes of Surrealism.*

Nerval explained his lobster to his longtime friend Théophile Gautier: "I have a liking for lobsters. They are peaceful, serious creatures. They know the secrets of the sea, they don't bark, and they don't gnaw upon one's monadic privacy like dogs."[25]

What "secrets of the sea" did Nerval imagine that lobsters were privy to? Are they secrets as shadowed as those of people? Where shipwrecks' bodies are to be found, perhaps? And what does Nerval mean by "one's monadic privacy"? A philosophical term, "monadic" refers to singular entities, like individual people, each of them self-sufficient and unique. But Nerval is mistaken about lobsters on this account: as carnivorous bottom feeders, they would, indeed, happily gnaw on one's monadic privacy given half a chance.

Still, the concept of Nerval's lobster on a leash has been an irresistible magnet to other poets. In 1996, for example, the *Antioch Review* published "The Lobster Sestinas," by Angela J. Davis. A sestina is a poem of six stanzas, each containing six lines, and a final triplet. Its rigidly designed structure also specifies a repetition sequence of words that end certain lines. Davis's lobster poem contains a total of six sestinas, and it is in the first, titled "Confession," that she speaks of Nerval leading his lobster on a leash. She contemplates what Nerval might have thought of tossing the live lobster into boiling water. That, she confesses, is what she is about to do.

While awaiting the moment when the water reaches a full boil, Davis remarks that, were God a lobster, she would be in serious trouble. Yet death on the cold ocean bottom seems preferable to being scalded: she describes her body first numbed, then her flesh torn and her bones crushed by lobster claws. Her marrow hisses, and her blood flows an "irresistible" red.[26] This image of a lobster, or lobsters, shredding her limbs resembles the violence of Dalí's castrating lobster. Can a case be made that Davis is the first woman to present the lobster in the context of erotic sadomasochism?

Yet another question is, could emasculation or its female equivalent be on a lobster's agenda? Perhaps that is why lobsters release odors that control other lobsters' aggressive behavior. But according to the philosopher and cognitive scientist Daniel Dennett, a lobster's sense of self (which relates to its sense of others) is limited to an automatic response wired into its nervous system, like blinking at something, or shivering when it's cold. The lobster, Dennett writes, "might well eat another lobster's claws, but the prospect of eating one of its own claws is conveniently unthinkable to it. Its options are limited, and when it 'thinks of' moving a claw, its 'thinker' is directly and appropriately wired to the very claw it thinks of moving. With human beings . . . on the other hand, there are more options, and hence more sources of confusion."[27] Those options and confusions involve investing lobsters with human fears, frailties, and desires. Emasculation and other acts of violence are in the self-absorbed eyes of the human beholder, from Dalí to Lecasble to Davis. These are visions that confound fact and fantasy — that are, in other words, surreal.

Did Nerval really have a pet lobster — or was it a Parisian conceit? An urban legend? In addition to the letter he wrote to Gautier about his fondness for lobsters, the discovery of a letter he wrote to a childhood friend — describing how, at the seashore, he stole a lobster from a fishing net to save it from being cooked and named it Thibault — might seem to confirm that he did. Moreover, the reason for Nerval's adopting a lobster links him to Angela Davis, David Foster Wallace, and many others who commiserate with the lobster's suffering at the hands of people including . . . Charles Kingsley and Samuel Beckett.

But did he really walk a lobster at the end of leash?

Frankly, I can't imagine anyone who likes lobsters, as Nerval professed to have done, subjecting one to a promenade on dry ground. Just picture how they react to being lifted out of the water — flailing all their legs as if in panic — and remind yourself how they lumber more like drunken sailors than like dogs on a leash, and the likelihood dwindles. Moreover, just how long can a lobster live out of water? Perhaps as long as twenty-four hours, if kept under refrigeration. But walking one on the end of a ribbon out of its element seems a self-serving aberration. If Nerval did it once under mistaken expectations, I can forgive him. If he tried it more than once, I can't. The very idea reeks of surrealist recklessness, even before the advent of surrealism.

Water Babies

In an 1857 speech at the Linnaean Society, Richard Owen — an English biologist, anatomist, paleontologist, and outspoken foe of Darwin — said that three sections of the human brain, one being the hippocampus minor, differentiated humans from apes enough to warrant separating them into two distinct subclasses. Later studies showed, however, that humans and apes had the same brain structures, which led, as Thomas Henry Huxley argued, to "the impossibility of erecting any cerebral barrier between man and the apes." [28] And that, in turn, led to the great spoof in Charles Kingsley's 1863 children's book, *The Water Babies: A Fairy Tale for a Land-Baby*, in which the naturalist Professor Ptthmlln-sprts declares: "You may think that there are other more important differences between you and an ape, such as being able to speak, and make machines, and know right from wrong, and say your prayers ... but that is a child's fancy ... Nothing is to be depended on but the great hippopotamus test. If you have a hippopotamus major in your brain, you are no ape." [29] That is something of an aside to demonstrate that, in its true Victorian clothing, this fantasy for children is morally instructive, containing some science-related politics as well as a talking lobster that plays an important part.

While the professor was speaking those words to a young lady named Ellie, who was anxious to see some water babies no matter how loudly he insisted there were no such beings, the professor dropped his net in the water and, to his dismay, hauled up Tom — who looked to Ellie exactly like a water baby.

Tom, the ten-year-old hero of the story, had been a chimney sweep. He was cruelly used by his employer and had recently escaped a band of pursuers who believed him responsible for a crime that hadn't even been committed. He was now living underwater with a lobster he had befriended. Like Ellie, Tom, too, was anxious to find the legendary water babies. The professor, wondering what this specimen was, poked at Tom "for want of anything better to do,"[30] and frightened him so much that he bit the professor's finger. The professor dropped the boy, who quickly dove back into the water.

Traveling among the rocks, Tom soon discovered a lobster trap with his friend inside. He tried to pull the lobster out through the hole by which he'd entered, but Tom was mistakenly pulled into the pot by the lobster. A vengeful otter, "all eyes and teeth," then squeezed herself in through the hole to get at Tom, and the lobster seized it by the nose. This trio thumped and tumbled over and over each other until Tom was able to climb on the otter's back and crawl back out through the hole. He was now free, but Tom wouldn't desert his friend the lobster. He would have struggled to pull him out, except that the lobster would not let go of the otter. Only when fishermen came by and raised the trap to the boat did the lobster give "a furious and tremendous snap" and escape, though he left a claw behind.

The unexpected outcome of this last adventure was that Tom's greatest wish came true—he suddenly saw a water baby. "Now was not that very odd?" the narrator asks. "So odd, indeed, that you will, no doubt, want to know how it happened, and why Tom could never find a water-baby till after he had got the lobster out of the pot. And, if you will read this story nine times over, and then think for yourself, you will find out why."[31]

If you haven't time for nine readings here is the answer: It was Tom's selfless and virtuous deed of saving the lobster from being served at someone's dinner table—following in Nerval's footsteps (and at certain risk to himself)—that allowed Tom's wish to come true.

How many young minds did reading *The Water Babies*, or having it read to them, influence? It first appeared serialized in a magazine, and when published in book form, it became one of the foundational didactic morality lessons for children right through the 1920s. Samuel Beckett probably read it.

Death and Dying

Kingsley died in 1875. When Beckett was born in 1906, *The Water Babies* was still very popular. It is clear that Beckett was aware of Kingsley's writings because in 1983 Beckett wrote *Worstward Ho!* — a parody of Kingsley's 1855 novel, *Westward Ho!*

Kingsley touches on the lobster problem, or question, by having Tom release one from captivity and thereby save it from human consumption. The problem occurs in Beckett's story of 1934, "Dante and the Lobster," in which he leads up to the question slowly and then jumps right in. That is, the question of whether is it wrong to boil live lobsters in a pot.

When "Dante and the Lobster" begins, Belacqua — named after a character who appears in Dante's *Purgatorio* as well the Bible — is reading Dante's *Paradiso* and finding himself puzzled and frustrated, "running his brain" against an impenetrable passage.[32] During the course of his day Belacqua's agenda includes: (1) eat lunch (black toast and Gorgonzola cheese); (2) fetch a lobster for dinner with his aunt; and (3) have an Italian lesson. He accomplishes the first two tasks and arrives at his aunt's house, where he passes the parcel to her. She opens it and puts the lobster on the oilcloth-covered table. He sees it move:

> His hand flew to his mouth.
> "Christ!" he said. "It's alive."
> . . . They stood above it, looking down on it, exposed cruciform on the oilcloth. It shuddered again. Belacqua felt he would be sick.
> "My God," he whined, "it's alive, what'll we do?"

His aunt laughs and goes about her business. Finally he cries out, asking what she's going to do.

> "Boil the beast," she said, "what else?"
> "But it's not dead," protested Belacqua, "you can't boil it like that."
> She looked at him in astonishment. Had he taken leave of his senses?
> "Have sense," she said sharply, "lobsters are always boiled alive. They must be."

She caught up the lobster and laid it on its back. It trembled. "They feel nothing," she said . . .

She lifted the lobster clear of the table. It had about thirty seconds to live.

Well, thought Belacqua, it's a quick death, God help us all.

It is not.[33]

What a downpour of image and emotion! Christ, cruciform on the oilcloth. Lobster upside down, trembling. Quick death. God help us all. It is not.

Does that mean it is a long and painful death? What can a quick death mean? "The quick and the dead" is a biblical phrase in which "quick" means "alive," not "fast." So the phrase becomes self-contradictory, at least in terms of being alive and dead at the same time. Michael Shapiro zeros in on this oxymoron, as he calls it, and its Christian extension as salvation, which denies death. "The 'God help us all' coupled with the 'quick death' no longer seems to be just an exclamation but rather a recognition that the idea of God is connected to the idea that death is not really death." And then, "'No, it's not' . . . is a response to the contradictory notion that death is not death."[34]

But death is real. And it is a recurrent theme in reference to lobsters.

The boiling of lobsters alive is as obsessive a problem as the lobster itself proves to be. The question of whether the lobster feels the pain of the boiling water cannot be determined, as discussed in chapter 1 and again in this chapter. Even neurological studies of lobsters cannot tell us. To repeat Dennett's assessment, the lobster's reactions are automatic, like blinks and shivers: "Its 'thinker' is directly and appropriately wired to the very claw it thinks of moving." That's not "thinking" as we know it, or feeling pain as we feel it, because to recognize pain takes a level of self-consciousness that a lobster does not have.

So considering what we can know, the question of whether or not boiling lobsters alive is justifiable is a specious question. The valid question each individual has to answer is whether he or she thinks it is right to eat lobsters at all. We can't make a decision based on something we can't know — what the animal feels.

We have to come to grips with how *we* feel, which is something each of us, individually, can explore and hope to understand. I am fond of dogs and cats, cows and horses, and sheep and goats, and I wouldn't want to eat any of them—not even if they were humanely euthanized before cooking and tasted better than lobsters. I submit that arguing about cooking a lobster before or after it has died is playing an irrelevant, pseudo-intellectual game. The question is whether to eat lobster or not. I do, but to tell the truth I'm beginning to feel ambivalent about it.

In the poem "Lobsters," Howard Nemerov, twice appointed US poet laureate, returns us to a setting ironically reminiscent of the aquarium in Lecasble's *Titanic* and Woody Allen's fantasy/nightmare in the *New Yorker* (see chapter 10). It is the glass lobster tank in a Super Duper supermarket before which we stand with Nemerov, watching the "herd" of these somnambulant creatures, an unsettling word that usually refers to much larger animals. We contemplate the strange beauty of their slow-motion movements, meditating and "bemused" until we sink into a sense of identification with the lobsters and realize what we have in common. It is death: "The flame beneath the pot that boils the water."[35]

Death is real, for those lobsters and for us.

Alice and Others

Surrealists and their followers mined the work of Lewis Carroll for its humor, fantasies, and insights masquerading as nonsense. In Wonderland with Alice and her friends, as a child I enjoyed what seemed silly: old father William standing on his head, Tweedledee and Tweedledum, and all the earnest and comical characters. As an adult I discovered what a marvelous scoundrel Carroll was: a master of parody, puns, satires, and jokes on everyone. The book that makes Alice that extra treat for me is Martin Gardner's *Annotated Alice*, the latest edition of which was published in 2000.[36] This despite G. K. Chesterton's upbraiding of scholars and annotators for turning Alice into a pedagogue. On the contrary, as Gardner explains, Carroll's book was written in another century, when its readers were au courant with the author's references. We aren't. So many jokes in *Alice* fall flat if we don't get them. With Gardner's help, we do.

In chapter 10 of Carroll's book, we are introduced to the lobster quadrille. In Gardner's text we learn that the quadrille was a fashionable dance from the eighteenth century on, still popular at the time Carroll was composing *Alice*, around 1865. It was a lively dance for four couples arranged in a square, and it is a direct predecessor of the modern square dance. The Mock Turtle and the Gryphon start their dance with two lines of "seals, turtles, salmon, and so on" at the seashore. Each dancer has a lobster as a partner. Once the jelly fish are cleared away, the lines "advance" two times, face their lobsters, hop first on one foot and then on the other, change lobsters, and then . . . throw the lobsters "as far out to sea as you can."[37]

Why?

Gardner speculates that this particular dance might be based on a variant known as the Lancers quadrille. The Lancers were a cavalry regiment armed with lances that had long shafts and pointed metal heads, and Gardner speculates that tossing the lobsters into the sea may have been related to the Lancers' throwing their weapons.

Once the lobsters in Carroll's quadrille have been launched, the other dancers are meant to swim after them, somersault, change lobsters, and return to the land.

Carroll's wordplays sound like something from Groucho Marx: "No wise fish would go anywhere without a porpoise," the Mock Turtle tells Alice. "Wouldn't it really?" she asks. "Of course not," he answers. "Why, if a fish came to *me*, and told me he was going on a journey I should say, 'With what porpoise?'"

"Don't you mean 'purpose'?" says Alice.

"I mean what I say," the offended Mock Turtle answers.[38]

It's but a slight digression from lobsters. We are soon back on topic, and the Gryphon tells Alice to recite "'Tis the Voice of the Sluggard." As Gardner notes, the first thing that usually comes to the reader's mind is the biblical phrase "voice of the turtle" from the Song of Songs—referring to the turtle dove, not the hard-shelled reptile known for moving slowly and tucking its head in

Sir John Tenniel, a lobster primping for the lobster quadrille, illustration for Lewis Carroll's *Alice's Adventures in Wonderland*, 1865.

when danger threatens. But there really is a poem by Isaac Watts that begins with a sluggard, and that is what Carroll parodies when Alice, whose head is still ringing with the lobster quadrille, recites a verse that begins:

> 'Tis the voice of the Lobster: I heard him declare,
> "You have baked me too brown, I must sugar my hair."
> As a duck with its eyelids, so he with his nose
> Trims his belt and his buttons, and turns out his toes.[39]

The Mock Turtle calls it nonsense, and it may be—but not entirely. I puzzled a long time over "I must sugar my hair" and eventually connected some dots when I came across the mention of a portrait of Sir Walter Scott with "powdered hair." It would be in character for Carroll to make fun of the powdered hair conceit, and maybe even of Scott.[40]

The verse, with or without allusion to Scott, was illustrated with a wood engraving by Sir John Tenniel — a black-and-white drawing of a lobster primping in front of a dressing table with a mirror. He stands upright on dancing slippers that cover his two tail fans and that are turned out in the first ballet position. In one of his claws, he holds a large hairbrush.[41]

This is the perfect illustration for the lobster quadrille. That a lobster has no hair really doesn't matter at all.

9 A Metaphor for People

In December 2008, the artist Jeff Koons installed a lobster in the Mars Salon at the Palace of Versailles, in France. Made of aluminum, steel, and vinyl; decoratively painted red, of course; and detailed in yellow and black, the lobster measured eight feet long, from tail to nose. It was strung upside down, with its tail toward the ceiling and nose pointed at the floor, at the end of a red chain. Nearby glittered baroque two-tiered crystal chandeliers, true to the building's seventeenth-century origins — except for the electrified faux candles.[1]

Koons's installation was cool, in the paradoxical sense of calmly audacious. Most surprising is the fact that, after the first shock of seeing a lobster displayed so out of context, it seemed to belong there. Wherever the animal is found, from a lobster palace to the top of someone's head (à la Salvador Dalí) or Versailles, its character evolves into a conceptual interpretation of the situation in which it is set. In other words, it seems infinitely adaptable to the human environment. Not incidentally Jeff Koons's life and art, like those of Dalí (whom Koons admired and visited), are purposefully outrageous.

In reference to his work, on several occasions Koons has described the objects he creates as metaphors for people.

What does he mean? When I look at his lobster, I see a very large, blimplike, amusing, decorative creation. It resembles an inflatable pool toy rather than a lobster, and indeed pool toys inspired this and Koons's other large, colorful sculptures. Its impact is due primarily to its dimensions; were it five inches long, I'd expect to find it at a toy counter. (It would be fun — if it had legs — as a tin wind-up toy, shuffling along on its eight back legs and bumping the claws of its two forelegs.) Hanging at Versailles, it is absurd, ironic, even oxymoronic . . . but metaphorical?

Before Louis XIV, known as the Sun King, remade the palace into his grandiose château, it was his father's hunting lodge in the little country village of Versailles, some twelve miles from Paris. Louis XIV transformed and expanded the palace and moved the court and government of France to Versailles in 1682. Conjure up the famous 1701 portrait of this king by Hyacinthe Rigaud, in which he looks quite as inflated as a pool accessory as well as elaborately gaudy — with his huge, curled wig and flowing blue coronation robe embroidered with gold fleurs-de-lis and folded back to reveal, in Hollywood cheesecake style, Louis's shapely, white-stockinged and gartered legs. Yet he looks directly down at us from the portrait, and the bejeweled hilt of his sword rests upright at his side, bespeaking aggression and virility. Might Koons's lobster be a metaphor for the Sun King himself?

Koons doesn't say. The lobster was but one of his objects on view at Versailles as part of a retrospective of his works, which included his infamous bare-breasted beautiful blonde woman hugging a wide-eyed pink panther (1988) and *Michael Jackson and Bubbles* (1998). The Salon of Mars, where *Lobster* (2003) was exhibited, is named for the god of war, and at Koons's suggestion, the red, yellow, and black colors of the lobster might be thought of as flames of battle.[2] Perhaps the artist was exploring the imagery of war, royalty, and power and contemplating where he fits into it. His marble self-portrait was installed in the salon where portraits of French kings hang. That might be considered hubris, or it might simply reflect the fact that Koons, a member of the art world's ruling class, is widely known as the king of kitsch.

Still Life

In 1770 Louis-Auguste was married to Marie Antoinette, the fifteenth of sixteen children born to the Hapsburg Empress Maria Theresa and Emperor Francis. Four years later Louis-Auguste ascended the French throne as Louis XVI.

Looking back on the previous century from their vantage point in the nineteenth, the brothers Jules and Edmond de Goncourt wrote: "Woman in the eighteenth century is the principle that governs, the reason that directs, the voice that commands. She is the universal and fatal cause, the origin of events, the source of things . . . Nothing escapes her, she holds within her grasp the King, France . . .—everything."[3] That is an interesting slant on the court of Marie Antoinette, who was admirable for her encouragement of women artists. The three most renowned were Elisabeth Vigée Le Brun, the queen's own portraitist; Adelaide Labille-Guiard, and Anne Vallayer-Coster. Le Brun and Labille-Guiard were both portrait painters. Little has been written about Anne Vallayer-Coster, and even in Whitney Chadwick's pioneering study *Women, Art, and Society* she is hardly mentioned, in comparison to Le Brun and Labille-Guiard. But the most breathtaking of all the images reproduced in Chadwick's well-illustrated book is Vallayer-Coster's *Still Life with Lobster* (1781), an amazing two-page spread, with a deep, dark background and a bold, richly red lobster in the front of the picture, reaching over the edge of the platform on which it rests.[4]

For many centuries, the hierarchical class system of art history ranked still-life paintings at the bottom of its three academic categories, below history painting and portraiture. History painting was often based on mythical, literary, and biblical stories or classical themes. Although portraits are undeniably historical documents—they often reveal as much contemporary history as any dramatic battle scene or passage of the Bible—portraiture nonetheless was in second place. As for still lifes, though they are texts in and of themselves, the best of them holding secrets that can draw a person into a canvas as into a literary tour de force, they still get less than their fair share of attention. Moreover, those academic classifications don't even consider style, skill, technique, and composition. The prejudice was intact during the eighteenth century, but Vallayer-Coster was nevertheless celebrated and well known as one of the very best still-life painters of her era. Perhaps her rediscovery by feminist art historians of the twentieth century was late in coming because of both the lingering academic discrimination against still lifes and the historical lack of regard for women artists.

Marie Antoinette actively supported Vallayer-Coster by helping to secure her lodgings at the Louvre, a great financial as well as professional advantage, since at the Louvre she worked close to the major artists of her time. In fact, she was the first female artist so honored. She was also one of only four women permitted to become members of the Académie Royale before the French Revolution. When she married Jean-Pierre-Silvestre Coster — a lawyer and collector of tobacco taxes at Versailles — the queen was present and signed the wedding contract.

Still, Vallayer-Coster was not so closely bound to the royal family that she felt she must flee the country during the revolution. She stayed in France and was able to keep working. Nearly twenty years later, during the restoration of the monarchy, she presented Louis XVIII with another *Still Life with Lobster* (1817), a portrait that has endured considerably longer than the reconstituted French monarchy did. The background here is unlike that of the earlier work; it has a lighter tone throughout, and different objects surround the star of the show, which is the same lobster Vallayer-Coster had painted in 1781. It isn't unusual for an artist to repeat a well-received theme in either the same or, as in this instance, a different context.

Her first lobster still life is twenty-seven and three-quarter inches high by thirty-five and one-quarter inches wide. As mentioned earlier, the background is dark, but not uniformly so — there are tonal variations that lend it depth and texture. The composition is lighted from the left, and the objects on the stone surface of what is either a table or a counter rise in height from left to right. Although those two techniques — lighting and grading — move the eye from the showstopper in the foreground to the vanishing point at the upper righthand corner of the canvas, let us save the best for last by moving the eye backward.

Looking, then, from right to left, we see a woven basket full of lustrous green grapes, with one stalk and a leaf disappearing toward the top of the canvas. In front of the basket are two small loaves of bread, one propped against the other. Behind the loaves, a rounded glass jar filled with something dark is covered with fabric fixed in place by twine. To the left of the jar is a curvaceous, highly polished silver tureen with handles; its delicately ornamented cover leans against it. To the left of the tureen are two crystal and gold cruets, and in front of them is a small but heavy-looking silver container.

In the lighted foreground, occupying about two-thirds of the

Anne Vallayer-Coster, *Still Life with Lobster*, 1781. Toledo Museum of Art (Toledo, Ohio), purchased with funds from the Libbey Endowment. Gift of Edward Drummond Libbey, 1968. Photo: Photography Incorporated, Toledo.

width of the stage, the lobster rests on top of a white cloth that covers a silver platter. Its two big claws extend beyond the platter, and the larger of the two extends even beyond the stone surface, as if gaining control of our attention isn't enough and it also intends to invade our space. Also, juxtaposed with the claw angled off the platform from the front of the tray, toward the back is a silver knife with the tip of its blade beneath the tray and its shaft angled off the platform in the other direction. The entire composition plays with the balancing of objects, colors, movement, and light.

And there is still another extravaganza, though this one — as far as an extravaganza can be — is discreet: the polished curve of the tureen serves as a convex mirror showing a reflection of the lobster just in front of it, including the subtle glow of the animal's red tint.

The tureen also reflects the room that is in front of the still-life arrangement, where the artist would be working. It is smaller, being a more distant image, distorted by the curve of the tureen's surface and difficult to see, but alluring. Do we detect windows? A door? The tiny figure of the artist?

The role of the tureen is second in importance only to the lobster splayed out commandingly in front of it. A convex mirror that is a reflecting surface, as the art historian Craig Harbison has pointed out, goes back to pilgrimages during the fifteenth century. When the pilgrims reached their destinations, they bought mementos, especially religious medals: "Set into some pilgrims' medals were small convex mirrors, the magic device for capturing and taking home the rays emanating from the miraculous object [they expected to see]." The Dutch painter Jan van Eyck (1390–1441) went on a pilgrimage, and he recognized the convex mirror as "the perfect way to capture a vast interior on a small surface; the curve of the mirror had the effect of drastically condensing the space it recorded as well as reflected."[5] Van Eyck used a convex mirror as the centerpiece of one of his most famous paintings, the *Arnolfini Double Portrait* (1434). The mirror is mounted on the wall behind the man and woman whose portrait it is; it reflects their backs and the frontal views of two men who would have been standing there, looking at them. One of the men is van Eyck himself. It is a record of the artist's presence and a visual claim, along with his large, eloquent signature above the mirror, of his proud authorship. Numerous artists followed van Eyck in using various convex reflecting surfaces in their paintings, not only mirrors but also glass vases and various polished metal surfaces and vessels.

Vallayer-Coster's reflection in the silver tureen is also a record of her presence, though without a flourishing signature, it is a more modest claim than van Eyck's. However, there is nothing modest about the lobster. It is by far the largest object in the picture, and it is more carefully detailed than most still-life lobsters, including the sharp points of the slicer claw reaching toward us. A most unusual detail in terms of art history, though known among lobster fishermen, is the clusters of barnacles on this lobster's shell. The large size of the lobster plus the presence of barnacles suggests the lobster's advanced age. Though both are crustaceans, lobsters are predators and barnacles are parasites. The type of barnacle on Vallayer-Coster's lobster has "one of the most extraordinary and persistent myths of medieval natural history, dating back to the 12th century at least" attached to it.[6] The myth was that a type of bird that came to be called the barnacle goose emerged from this barnacle's shell. The myth was still current during the eighteenth century when Vallayer-Coster painted her barnacled lobster. Whether she thought of it or not, the combination could suggest a sort of poetic unification of a creature that crawls along the ocean's floor with another one that flies across the sky. Since that association hasn't been made so far as I know, it is only conjecture, but it does demonstrate that there are many expressive connections possible about apparently uninspired things, such as barnacles on a lobster's back.

Laughing Girl

The northern Italian city of Cremona is famous in music history as the birthplace and home of Antonio Stradivari (1644–1737), who made various stringed instruments there, including at least one harp and, most glorious of all, violins.

Before Stradivari, Cremona was known for several outstanding painters who worked there during the Renaissance, including Bernardino Campi (1522–91) and his student Sofonisba Anguissola. She was born in 1532 and lived to the age of ninety-three.

Sofonisba was one of the six daughters of Amilcare and Bianca Anguissola, parents who were unusual for that era in that they encouraged and supported their daughters' education in the arts. Sofonisba had a successful career as a painter in Italy and, for a time, at the Spanish court. Before she left for Madrid in the winter of 1559, she painted a curious and complicated double portrait of herself and her teacher—the usual title is *Bernardino Campi Painting Sofonisba Anguissola*, though like many such titles it was probably not chosen by the artist herself but invented as a convenient identification for the painting, perhaps well after her death.

At about forty-three inches square, it's a good-sized canvas in a time when size correlated with importance. The idea of an artist painting another artist painting a portrait of her or him was original. In this case the subject-object dynamic is further distinguished and complicated by the student-teacher and female-male relationships. Art historical and philosophical questions about this painting by Sofonisba are bound up with ideas of gender, authority, autonomy, and self-promotion.[7] What seems to be missing from the discussion is the notion of a sense of humor behind the situation portrayed. The fact that both subjects — Sofonisba on the canvas that Bernardino is ostensibly working on and Bernardino himself — are looking out at us, the audience, with bemused expressions as if to ask, "What do you make of this?" It is a stage setting as surely as Vallayer-Coster's still life is, and if the lobster could speak, wouldn't it ask the same question?

There is no denying that Sofonisba was exceptionally talented and ambitious, but we also have evidence of her streak of naughty playfulness. One story is that Michelangelo was given a picture she had made of a girl laughing, and he answered with a challenge to the effect that it would be more interesting to see a boy crying. Fulfilling her assignment, she sent him another picture, drawn with charcoal on paper, that has accumulated several titles — including *Portrait of a Young Boy and Girl, Boy Being Pinched* [or *Boy Bitten*] *by a Lobster* [or *Crab, Crayfish*, and even *Lizard*]. The boy, seated at the left, must be about two years old and the girl next to him holding a basket about ten. The creature(s) in the basket are impossible to identify, as suggested by the different titles, but whatever it is has got the boy's finger in its claw, and the boy is crying. Michelangelo liked it very much. Mission accomplished.

Bernardino Campi was a member of a large family with many well-known practicing painters in Cremona. Among them was Vincenzo Campi, who — along with the Bolognese Bartolomeo Passarotti and Annibale Carracci — began to paint scenes from everyday life, known as genre paintings, around 1580. Many of their works are market scenes that have a bawdy, comic character, poking fun at the peasants tending their stalls: pictures for upperclass patrons that make fun of the lower classes. A number of fish markets are included, and three of Vincenzo Campi's fish market scenes include a baby whose finger is being nipped by a crab, crayfish, or lobster, as if in reference to Sofonisba Anguissola. The ambiguity regarding the type of crustacean involved is pertinent.

As was true of northern European genre paintings, the themes of these market paintings may be linked to popular proverbs. Sheila McTighe writes:

> There is an affinity between the vogue among *virtuosi* or *letterati* for textual collections of proverbs in the sixteenth and seventeenth centuries and the contemporaneous vogue for collections of marvels and wonders of nature and art. A number of published proverb collections state their interest in the curios or marvelous ubiquity of such folk sayings, which seemed to transcend their local origins and take on the character of a universal, if crude, form of wisdom.[8]

McTighe also warned that the terms *granchio*, *gambero*, and *gamberelli* (crab, lobster, and crayfish) could be interchanged in these proverbs.[9] This partly alleviates our frustration about the various names for what was nipping the little boy's finger in Anguissola's drawing. And as to the related proverb, it plays on the well-known information that shellfish don't have much in the way of brains and comments to the effect that a little of the lobster's brain would improve the intelligence of the individual being bitten. That shouldn't be a laughing matter, but—as Anguissola may have been the first to demonstrate—sometimes it was. For better or for worse, in or out of character, lobsters punctuate art history, as they do all the arts, carrying someone's message related not to lobsters but to the artist, in Anguissola's case, the desire to please a higher authority.

Sturm und Drang

Between 1824 and 1830, Eugène Delacroix painted three pictures for which he is famous. The first is *Massacre at Chios* (1824), portraying the genocide that had taken place on the Greek island of Chios two years earlier. Though just a few Greek revolutionaries had demanded freedom from the Ottoman Empire, the retaliation by the Turks was wholesale mayhem: twenty thousand Greek islanders were tortured, butchered, hung, or starved to death; fifty thousand were enslaved; and twenty-three thousand were exiled. Delacroix's dead and dying mothers, children, and men—all strewn across the canvas—summon up the waves of sympathetic horror felt throughout Europe. The canvas is monumental, over thirteen feet high and eleven feet wide; the colors are morbid; and the impact is powerful.

Byron's *Sardanapalus, a Tragedy*, was published in December 1821, dedicated "to the Illustrious Goethe." Delacroix's *Death of Sardanapalus* (1827) was inspired by Byron's poetic drama. It is another massacre, with the Delacroix touch and monumentality —a little over twelve by sixteen feet—but there is a great difference in tone and setting, compared to the 1824 painting. Where the landscape of Chios is sere, *Sardanapalus* is set indoors, in the pink-toned, palatial bedroom of Sardanapalus, according to legend the last Assyrian king. Facing defeat, he ordered and oversaw the death of all his possessions, women, and slaves as a preamble to his own suicide. It is an erotic, orgiastic scene, overflowing with the storm and stress of the Romantic era.

The third painting, *Liberty Leading the People* (1830), commemorates the July Revolution that overthrew Charles X of France. Thirteen by eleven feet, it is more exciting than the other paintings despite the bodies underfoot. This is because of the personification of Liberty, bare-breasted, waving the tricolor in one hand, gripping a musket with a bayonet in the other, and soldiering forward despite the dead and dying bodies all around her.

During this period of his preoccupation with cruelty and violence, Delacroix painted a picture that he sent to the artists' salon of 1827 along with *Death of Sardanapalus*. It is more veiled than the three well-known works, but it is connected not only chronologically but also thematically. It is known as *Still Life with Lobsters* and is dated 1826–27.

At two and a half by three and a half feet, *Still Life with Lobsters* is a good deal smaller than the associated works. Two important influences become apparent. The easy one has to do with the importance, after Delacroix's trip to England in 1825, of John Constable's landscapes and skies. If ever you want a metaphor for a human emotion (attention, Jeff Koons), you will find it in Constable's sky studies and paintings. The weather, expressed by the advance of darkening clouds in *Still Life with Lobsters*, is fair warning that you are witnessing an ominous event. The grouping of dead animals in the foreground of what we call "still life" but the French call *nature morte* (dead nature) is — as were the bodies in *Chios*, *Sardanapalus*, and *Liberty* — evidence of a massacre.

Still lifes are usually painted and arranged indoors, even when wild game is included. Delacroix's *Still Life with Lobsters* is set outdoors, and in the distance he painted tiny, red-coated hunters responsible — figuratively at least — for the kills, including the lobsters. Finding a lobster in a painting devoted primarily to more conventional targets of the hunt, as in Snyders's still life described the introduction to this book, is an occasional but interesting theme. The correlation of fisherman and hunter is to be found in Plato's late dialogues: "An angler has a humble profession, familiar to everyone . . . : an angler hunts water creatures using a special sort of hook [or trap]."[10]

Was Delacroix thinking of Plato? Curiously, though inconclusively, while he was at work on *Chios* in 1824, Delacroix wrote in his diary, "I must try to live austerely, as Plato did. . . . I need to live a more solitary life."[11] Instead, he went to England the next year. And while there he painted *Still Life with Lobsters* for a Scottish patron, so there is a plaid fabric included with the game bag and large musket that are part of the composition. In the foreground are two red lobsters, a hare, and a pheasant, all of which are twisted into the unnatural contortions of those who have had a violent, unnatural death, as in Delacroix's large masterpieces. Set within the context of his other paintings and his contemporary frame of reference, this still life too is a picture of the consequence of violence. I believe it may be the only lobster still life in which the killing of lobsters can be associated with the slaughter of human beings.

Picasso and Others

In 1935 Picasso wrote: "I can no longer bear this miracle that of knowing nothing of this world and to have learnt nothing but to love things and eat them alive and to listen to their farewells when the hours strike in the distance."[12] It sounds like brutal cannibalism but is characteristic of Picasso, whose visual appetite is often so savage. His grotesque portrayals of women, for example, seem prompted by hatred, though he had a succession of passionate relationships, friendships, marriages, and love affairs, in addition to several children.

Pablo Picasso, *Le homard et le chat* (Lobster and Cat), 1965.
Solomon R. Guggenheim Museum, New York. Thannhauser
Collection, Bequest, Hilde Thannhauser, 1991.

As experimental and outrageous as his works are, they also express suffering and rage and, in his later years, the angry pain of a
man who is driven too hard by desires that the infirmities of age
prevent him from satisfying. It was in this late period, when he
was in his eighties, that Picasso painted *Lobster and Cat* (1965).[13]
The animals are almost cartoon characters: Stage left is the blue
lobster, patterned with darker blue stripes and dots, waving its
claws in the modified honor stance of one of Stephen King's lobstrosities. At the right is the brownish cat with — *dear God* — its
fur standing up as jagged as a bread knife, its mouth wide open, its
claws curled under. Is it a standoff? Which of them is paralyzed
with fear?

A Metaphor for People ⁂ 139

If you visit the website of the Guggenheim museum, which now owns this painting, please consider this descriptive sentence: "The painting demonstrates Picasso's ability to derive serious implications from what is essentially humorous."[14] True, there are serious implications to this imaginary confrontation—fear and impotence on the cat's part, since it has no possibility whatsoever of fending off the lobster, and in that tight spot it has nowhere to run. This scene is about as humorous as the babies and little children whose fingers were nipped by lobsters (or other creatures) described above. Like beauty, humor is in the eye of the beholder.

There are few instances when Picasso needs our compassion. There is no defense against age, impotence, and impending death. The Guggenheim's Fred Licht may be right in saying that "Lobster and Cat attests to the artist's unbroken creative energy [that is, his art] during the last years of his life,"[15] but apart from that, to me this is a sad picture—a furious memento mori.

In the 1950s Willem de Kooning began a series of paintings named *Woman*. The women characteristically have enormous breasts; huge, all-seeing eyes; horse-like teeth; and often hands or feet that look like claws. Could anything look more like misogyny? It is tortured and torturous. *Woman 1* is at the Museum of Modern Art in New York City.[16] One is more than enough. (The others in the series are not any nicer.) That, too, is in the eyes of the beholder—in this case, me.

Then, in 1965, something happened. De Kooning took a piece of tracing paper just shy of nineteen by twenty-four inches and some red oil paint. With about fifty distinct brush strokes, he created *Lobster Woman*.[17] It is an amazing swirl of evocative lines, and in contrast to the rage implied and evoked by the images in the *Woman* series, this composition of curvaceous, abstract lines results in a surprising and appealing image that even seems to be an affectionate portrayal.

Homarus americanus

There are some handsome and some exotic lobster still lifes by American artists, but the real innovations in this country are works that represent, explore, imagine, and document the occupation of fishing for lobsters. Some of these works portray scenes around other coastal waters, but the Gulf of Maine has always been the chief fishing ground for American lobsters, as well as a place where a great number of great American artists worked.

Rockwell Kent was born in Tarrytown, New York, in 1882 and went to visit Monhegan Island, Maine, when he was about twenty-five. Monhegan — the name is an adaptation of the Algonquin phrase for "out-to-sea island" — is an often rough ferry ride more than ten miles from the mainland. The island is famous for many things, including the artists who return every year to experience and paint its sheer cliffs and tough but vibrant lobster fishing community. The season for lobster fishing off Monhegan runs from January 1 to June 25. Kent was so taken with the island in 1907 that he stayed through its treacherous winter to learn about lobstering as well digging ditches and to spend time "painting, painting, painting with a fervor born . . . of my close contact with the sea and soil, and deepened by the reverence that the whole universe imposed."[18]

It is chill daylight, and snow lies on top of one of the island's sheer, high cliffs in Kent's *Toilers of the Sea*. In a small boat below the cliff, a man holding the oars steadies the boat, while another hauls up a trap. The large round barrel between the men looks like it is full of lobsters. A blue and white buoy and another red one bob in the rough, icy cold water. On the horizon line in the background, another small boat bucks the waves in a nearly upright position: it is a reference to a boat painted by Albert Pinkham Ryder in the early 1880s in a work also named *Toilers of the Sea* — which depicts an eerie, moonlit night scene with a single boat fighting the waves. Ryder was a strong influence on Kent and his generation, and Kent's painting is a paean to his predecessor.[19]

It was Robert Henri, Kent's teacher at the New York School of Art, whose enthusiasm for Monhegan inspired not only Kent but also other American artists, including Edward Hopper and George Bellows. "Why do we love the sea? It is because it has some potent power to make us think things we like to think," Henri said.[20] Bellows, also Henri's student, is best known for his paintings of the teeming street life of New York City: boxing matches, the low life, seamy and muscular. And he put that same raw emotional energy into his paintings of Maine. He wrote: "It seems to me that an artist must be a spectator of life; a reverential enthusiastic, emotional spectator . . . There are only three things demanded of a painter: to see things, to feel them and to dope them out for the public."[21]

Matinicus Island, two miles long and one mile wide, is about twenty miles south of Rockland and is the most remote of the Maine islands that are inhabited year-round. At last count, it has some sixty-six permanent residents. The harbor at Matinicus serves mainly working vessels, which is how we see it in Bellows's *Fish Wharf, Matinicus Island* (1916).[22] The canvas seems incredibly crowded. It really isn't — the few fishermen are in the distance — but the thick, fleshy brush strokes make the rocks, water, lobster traps, boats, structures, and all kinds of miscellany seem alive, noisy, and kinetic.

Edward Hopper did not seem drawn to lobster themes — fishing, eating, or otherwise. In his inimitable way, however, he did paint the cliffs of Monhegan, Maine's lighthouses, and a road and trawler and dories and other things in one of Maine's premier lobster fishing grounds, and he made them all unforgettably Hopperesque — frozen in time, still, silent, sad, and ambiguous. It says as much about Hopper and about lobsters that he did *not* paint them, for Hopper expresses ideas of isolation, distances between people, and the coldness of things. He shows people *not* doing things: *not* fishing, *not* eating, and probably *not* even thinking of lobsters, especially in the midst of a community devoted to those very things. I believe it is an example of commission by omission.

I was walking along the main street of Rockland several years ago when a glance down a side street — Union Street — caught me by surprise. If you happened to be out walking in Rockland, Maine, between May and November of 2009, you too would surely have spied the enormous banner hanging from the Wyeth Center at the Farnsworth Museum, showing a large seagull standing tall, with a blast of red running from its beak down its snowy white throat and chest. The banner announced an exhibition of a series of Jamie Wyeth's paintings, and what was dangling from the bird's beak was a lobster. Nowhere in Maine is a picture of a lobster (with or without seagull) ever unexpected. But this one was very surprising.

The white clapboard building that houses the Wyeth Center was formerly a church, so there was a certain synchronicity between the site and the exhibition: the series of paintings being shown was named the Seven Deadly Sins. Seagulls are here stand-ins for human transgressors, and the specific sin represented in the painting with the seagull and lobster is pride: the seagull's boastful pride in capturing a dangerous and prize sea creature — though one does have to wonder who cooked the lobster. Irony and humor help palliate the consequences of deadly sins.

Jamie is in the youngest of the three generations of the Wyeth family represented at the museum. N. C. (Newell Convers Wyeth, 1882–1945) was the patriarch, a brilliant and successful illustrator of magazines and books — especially children's books, from *Treasure Island* to *The Yearling*. In 1930 N. C. bought and restored an old captain's house in Port Clyde, Maine, and began painting seascapes. *Deep Cove Lobster Man* (ca. 1938) looks down, as if painted from a cliff above the cove, on the lobsterman in his slicker and rain hat pulling a heavy trap into his dory.[23] The perspective plus the rocky coast right behind him makes the viewer conscious not only of the physical challenge of the lobsterman's work, but also of its danger.

Andrew Wyeth (1917–2006), N. C.'s son, painted similar scenes of lobstermen but also some extraordinarily strange paintings. *Night Hauling* (1944) is a scene that haunts some of my sleepless hours in the very early morning, when I hear the sound of a motor on the Medomak River. I look out the window when the motor stops, and the only thing visible is a flashlight shining from the boat and splitting the dark. Wyeth has seen this more closely than I have: *Night Hauling* looks like a record of poaching by flashlight in the black of night. Bright light emanates as if from the inside of the lobster trap and bounces off the spray of white spume. *Embers* (2000) is another of Andrew Wyeth's unsettling pictures, showing the debris remaining on the beach after a lobster cookout: charred wooden boards, with scattered pieces of bright red lobster shell strewn about.[24]

Jamie Wyeth, Pride (Seven Deadly Sins), 2008.
Private collection. © Jamie Wyeth.

Both N. C. and Andrew Wyeth were tremendously influenced by Winslow Homer's work. In fact, N. C. named his house in Maine after Homer's famous painting of 1886, *Eight Bells*. Jamie was influenced by his father, grandfather, other artists in his family, and Homer.

Homer

In 1873 Winslow Homer painted *A Fisherman's Daughter*, also called *Three Girls with a Lobster*. The three young girls are sitting on large rocks, an upturned boat on the mound behind them and the shoreline somewhere off canvas in front of them. The middle girl is holding the focus of their rapt attention—a lobster. The following year Homer combined the three girls with a group of boys on a seesaw (inserted in place of the boat) and made other adaptations such as covering the rocks with fishnets. The object of the girls' awe was transformed from a lobster into an innocuous game of cat's cradle. The ever-changing lobster is here taken to the nth degree of separation from itself—into a pattern of strings held by children's fingers. Thus *Three Girls with a Lobster* reappeared as *See-Saw—Gloucester, Massachusetts* in *Harper's Weekly* on September 12, 1874.[25]

A humorous illustration by Homer had appeared in *Harper's Weekly* on August 17, 1859. The title of this work is *August in the Country—The Sea-Shore*. It is a wood engraving of a beach scene that is extremely crowded with people who—in the high Victorian manner—are overdressed in their city clothes, including shoes and hats. The engraving is equally packed with details, including a lady on top of the sand dune sketching beneath an umbrella, children misbehaving, and every kind of hustle and bustle. The protagonist is a young man who is brandishing a lobster, intending to surprise or scare three lovely young ladies. Or perhaps invite them to a cookout.

During the 1870s, Homer painted men fishing. An especially touching work is a watercolor of a man and three boys fishing for lobsters. It is serene in mood and has sherbet-colored tints of sunset on the water. The sea was always an inspiration for Homer, especially after he left the social and public world behind. He lived first in the English fishing village of Cullercoats for two years; then, returning to America in 1883, he settled on the coast of Maine. That is when the sea changed for him from a background for amusing leisure and idyllic activities to an all-powerful, all-absorbing force in its own right. The ocean was now everything to Homer.

In his transcendent history of American art, Robert Hughes wrote of Homer:

> He understood the structure of waves, currents, surges, loops of foam; the sheer power of water, its relentlessness, and its strange, fickle, maternal beauty . . . [He] moved to Prout's Neck, which is remote enough from New York now but in the 1880s — especially in the winter — would have been intolerable for anyone without a marked taste for solitude. It perfectly suited a man whose four favorite words, as one of his friends recalled, were "mind your own business."[26]

Homer painted many views of waves crashing against rocks, sending up blossoms and cataclysms of spume. He painted fishing boats, too, some in rough weather, but he did not paint lobster fishermen or their boats. His primary subject in Maine became the ocean itself.

Why did Homer's interests change so much? What might have turned him away from the life around him? Perhaps, it was simply his increasing fascination with the seacoast. But another possibility is that he became disgruntled by economic and social changes taking place along the Maine coast: the development of canneries, the industrialization of fisheries, and the expansion of tourism. After removing himself from the culture and commerce of the city for a solitary way of life, he must have been appalled by such new challenges to his hopes for peace in the retreat he had chosen. And needless to say, he would have despised the waves of summer tourists (artists or not).

If lobsters were metaphors for people, as Koons maintains, we would have to recognize that every person creates a different lobster, lobster boat, lobster fisherman, and situation, depending on where and when he or she lives and what is going on at the time, not to mention that individual's emotional and political state of mind. One can't quote Heinrich Wölfflin often enough: "Not everything is possible in every period."[27]

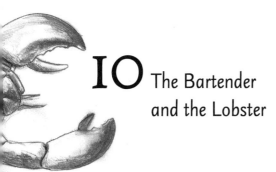

IO The Bartender and the Lobster

You can tell whether a lobster is male or female by turning it upside down and looking at the underside of its stomach (which most people call the tail). The first pair of pleopods or swimmerets on a male lobster are hard, whereas on a female lobster they are soft and feathery. (Females store fertilized eggs on the underside of the stomach until they are released.)

Fishermen who bring up a female lobster that is carrying eggs cut a V-shaped notch in the end of her tail and throw her back in the water to protect her and her eggs until they hatch: others who catch her later will recognize the notch and also set her free. The notch identifies her as a "breeder," and her return promotes lobster conservation for now and the future. In *The Secret Life of Lobsters*, Trevor Corson tells a story about the time one of the lobstermen he wrote about hauled up his trap to discover a lobster dressed in a Barbie-doll outfit, including high-heeled sandals. In order to find out if she was a breeder, he had to lift her skirt to see the notch. About a week later another lobsterman brought her up again. She had, Corson reports, walked three miles in her high heels (though he doesn't say how many — high heels, that is).[1]

That is one example of a lobsterman's sense of humor. Here is another.

Ellen Ruppel Shell, a correspondent for the *Atlantic* magazine wrote a personal essay for the *New York Times* about a kayak trip that almost ended badly. She and her husband went out for a paddle on a "gorgeous" November Saturday morning. They were not surprised to be the only small craft heading out because, as she knows (and as the promotional ads point out), "Maine is a state of mind," and they were in good spirits. But the weather quickly changed, and a gust of wind dumped Shell head first in forty-seven-degree water. The hypothermia countdown gave her about forty minutes before her body temperature would fall below the critical ninety-five degrees Fahrenheit, resulting in probable heart and respiratory failure and death. Her husband managed to help her back into her kayak and handed her the water pump. But he lost his paddle in the process. And they were being blown out to sea.

Either calculating or panicking, Shell got back into the water to swim to an island she figured was a hundred yards away. Then re-calculating — not the distance, but the decision — she chose not to leave her husband, who wasn't a swimmer. "And then I heard a motor," she reports.[2] It was a skiff with five lobstermen, who had been out hunting, lobster fishing season being over. There was a deer in the bottom of the boat, and Mr. and Ms. Shell soon joined it there. She continues:

> One guy laughed — my shivers, he said, were strong enough to power the boat, which was good because they were almost out of fuel. Another guy, also laughing, said, "We've got enough to get these fools home."
>
> A joint was lighted, and offered, as were bottles of Twisted Tea.[3]

Both stories have a pedagogic punch line, the first having to do with conservation (a good fisherman will respect what he finds under a lady lobster's skirt) and the second with caution (as in discretion is the better part of valor). Both stories are contenders for being added to the Maine folklore chronicles.

Those chronicles were launched in 1956, when Richard Dorson took a tape recorder large enough to need transportation by car to the northern Maine coastal town of Jonesport and nearby Beals Island — a fifteen-minute ride on a ferry that could carry four autos. Dorson collected narratives and anecdotes from the residents, "pure-bred Yankee fishermen" who made their living mainly from catching lobsters, clams, and herring.[4] The stories ranged from ghost tales to the exploits of a renowned hometown giant, who took shelter from a storm in a blacksmith's shop. There, fearful that the metal of a plough would attract lightning, he picked the five- or six-hundred-pound machine up by the handle, swung it around his head a few times, and threw it a safe distance away.

Dorson heard about several local séances, or "calling the spirits."

Each one would start with a hymn before all hands were placed on the table and a spirit made itself known by moving the table. One of Dorson's informants described the following séance:

> Now my wife and I was there one time, and a feller lost his trawl, he had a lobster trawl setting right there and they stole it. And he come over there and wanted him [the medium] to call up the spirits and find out who done it. Well they thought they would, for him. So my wife and I was there in the room and I put my hands under my mother's and she put hers under father's, to see if he bore down on the table, see. But they didn't — they just laid their hands right on top of yours, called the spirits up. And it was twice for yes, and once for no. See. And they told him who took the trawls, and where they put it, and they told him they'd never get it. They went after it, but they never got it. They lost it right out. And it was proved that it was the same people took that trawl that they said took it.[5]

Fate is so often out of human hands that some account or illusion of taking charge is needed. Such is provided by this eyewitness story about a four-masted schooner, the *Abbie Stubbs*, which, upon setting sail, "all at once she hove to." That night it was discovered that a crewman had been lost overboard. Recognizing a bad omen, the captain abandoned the ship. Another captain came and "took her over in the bay there to clean her bottom and paint up a little bit, and ground her on a damned ledge, and she broke in two. And her old frame ribs is right there now." Bad luck at the beginning, or any time, damns the whole fishing season. The only conclusion possible: once jinxed, give up on the sea and go back to "making hay" for the rest of the year.[6]

So here are some rules to avoid bad luck:

+ "Oh, if you come out on deck and you forget your plug of tobacco you never turn around and go back after it . . . Oh no, never turn around if you forget anything. It's bad luck. Oh, yes, and there's so many things that's bad luck. Oh, hundreds of 'em."[7]
+ Don't turn your boat around against the sun. If you have to, take her right back to the mooring because if you don't, you'll have bad luck all day long.[8]

- Never launch a boat "dry" — that is, without a big party. If you do, "You'll have hard luck with her from the day she goes afloat … La'nch 'em wet, no matter what it costs you, la'nch 'em wet."[9]
- A captain named Paris Kaler was becalmed and decided to buy a quarter's worth of wind, so he threw his quarter overboard: "So … it commenced to blow, it blowed till it blowed the sails off her, and he was three or four days off his course; he was three or four days getting back again. He said if he knew it was as cheap as that he wouldn't have bought half as much."

This story was told to Dorson by a third person, who put it in context when Dorson asked, "Well is that a bad thing to do, to buy wind?" "Yes," his informant said, "never buy wind when you're on a boat. You're daring God Almighty, and he won't stand for that. You'll get all the wind you want." Dorson then asked, "This Paris Kaler was a kind of bad man?" The informant replied: "Yes, he was a wicked man. Paris was swearing, ripping tearing, a wicked man."[10]

Seventy-year-old Curt Morse, a retired lobsterman and party boat captain who lived in the township of Kennebec, was another of Richard Dorson's storytellers. Curt was an outgoing man with a great sense of humor, often directed at himself. One of his stories begins: "Well, it was a kind of slack time in the lobster fishing. There wasn't many lobsters anyhow. Fellow lived just a little ways from me had an old Model T Ford. He wanted me to go up to Aroostook County with him and pick up potatoes. Well, I didn't think much of it, but after a while he talked so much I told him we'd start."[11]

Curt's saga is a true shaggy dog story of one mishap after another, mainly automotive: What he thought was the sound of someone firing at a partridge turned out to be a flat tire. On instructions from his friend, Marston, he lifted the wheel with a cedar pole, and Marston pulled out a piece of rubber he'd laid by from his wife's old shoes and used it to patch the tire. At a place called "Fresh Air, Free Air" they pumped the tires so full that all four burst. And so misfortune accumulated.

"I guess the moral of that story is, a lobster fisherman should never go picking potatoes," Dorson commented. Curt agreed: "Oh no, no, never never leave your job and start something new."[12]

Each of these stories defers to superstition. Calling the spirits, knowing a bad omen, changing course unwisely, running against the sun, launching "dry," bargaining for wind, picking potatoes or doing anything else when you're supposed to be fishing — all are bad omens. Superstitions and omens have been called upon since ancient times to deal with shades of the dead, magic, curses, and human frailty. In their effort to survive bad luck (or foolishness or stupidity), people keep trying to break the code of superhuman powers.

Just Joking

I have accumulated a small collection of lobster jokes to go along with my lobster galoshes, lobster socks, necklace of red lobsters on hemp, and my white T-shirt and baseball cap with the logo of the Boston Lobsters — a professional tennis team located in Middleton, Massachusetts. (Sometimes I wonder if it's bad luck to wear all your lobsters at the same time.) The following is a joke that always makes me laugh:

> So a man goes into a bar with the gift of a lobster for the bartender, who had helped him out by serving his dog the day before.
>
> Pleased, the bartender says, "I'll take the lobster home for supper."
>
> "Don't bother," the man says. "He's eaten. Take him to a movie."

This joke shares the basic quality of misunderstanding that fuels another story Dorson tells:

> Curt recounted a visit to the insane asylum at Bangor to see a committed friend. Some of the inmates were cutting grass with pruning shears and sickles under the supervision of guards when a big, black-whiskered, wild-looking fellow carrying a sickle looked at Curt and started after him on the run. Scared, Curt began running too, but stubbed his toe and fell down. The chap with the lethal instrument touched Curt and said, "tag."[13]

Dorson categorizes the "tag, you're it" story as belonging to the canon of comic American folktales.[14] A variant reported in a folk-lore journal has a ranchero in Brownsville, Texas, telling the story, in Spanish, about going to Guadalajara to see the sights when he realized he was being followed by a "big, ugly-looking *pelado*." The faster he walked, the faster the *pelado* walked. Then he started running down the street, but the other man ran, too, and caught up with him. "*Tú la tráis!*" (Tag, you're it!), the pursuer called out, and then he skipped off as if inviting a chase.[15]

Whoever or whatever the protagonist is in such stories, the plot evolves from misunderstanding or oblivion leading to fear and being resolved, tenuously at best, by comedy. The faded photo-graph at the Rockland Cafe in which a lobster fisherman is un-aware of the gargantuan lobster claws looming over his head is an example of this genre.

Here are a few gems from a category I'll call miscellany. Most of them float around anonymously in the great humor firmament.

> There was a young person named Ned,
> Who dined before going to bed
> On lobster and ham
> And salad and jam,
> And when he awoke he was dead.

> Diner: Do you have lobster tails?
> Waiter: Certainly, sir: Once upon a time there was a little lobster . . .

> After a day fishing at sea, a man is walking from the pier car-rying two lobsters in a bucket. A game warden spots him and asks for his lobster fishing license.
> The man tells the warden, "I didn't catch these lobsters, they are my pets. Every afternoon I come down to the water and whistle, and these lobsters jump right out and I take them for a walk. Then I return them at the end of the day."
> The warden expresses his doubts and reminds the man that it is illegal to take lobsters without a license. Turning to the war-den, the man says, "If you don't believe me, then watch," and he throws the lobsters back into the water.

A fellow goes into a restaurant and orders a two-pound lobster.

"Waiter, this lobster only has one claw," he complains, when the waiter brings his order.

"I'm sorry, sir. Sometimes lobsters fight in the tank," answers the waiter.

"Well, if that's the case," the customer says, "take this one back and bring me the winner."

A Scotchman was strolling through the marketplace in Glasgow one day, and close at his heels followed his faithful collie. Attracted by a fine display of shell and other fish, the Scot stopped to admire, perhaps to purchase. The dog stood by, gently wagging its tail while its master engaged the fishmonger in conversation.

Unfortunately for the beastie, its tail dropped for a moment over a big basketful of fine live lobsters. Instantly one of the largest lobsters snapped its claws on the tail, and the surprised collie dashed off through the market, yelping with pain, while the lobster hung on grimly, though dashed violently from side to side. The fishmonger for a moment was speechless with indignation. Then, turning to his prospective customer, he bawled: "Mon! Mon! whustle to yer dog; whustle to yer dog!"

"Hoot, mon!" returned the other complacently, "whustle to yer lobster!"

So Jake goes to Hackney's Sea Food Restaurant on the Boardwalk in Atlantic City and orders a lobster. When the waiter brings it, the lobster looks at Jake with such a sad expression that Jake sends it back. The next day he tries again, and the same thing happens. The third day, it happens again.

The fourth day he goes to another restaurant, Kornblau's, and orders lobster. When it gets to his table, the lobster looks at him and says, "Hey, Jake, you're not eating at Hackney's any more?"

Richard Dorson calls Jake's lobster dilemma a Jewish dialect story. Given that the Bible forbids Jews to eat lobster, it is funny how often lobsters figure in Jewish humor. The joke about Jake and the lobster does have the cadence of a much-parodied Yiddish accent.

There really was a Hackney's Sea Food Restaurant in Atlantic City. Harry W. Hackney went into business in 1912 with a small lunch wagon, and by 1929 his restaurant was a landmark on the Atlantic City Boardwalk, large enough to seat 3,200 people. There was also a Kornblau's in Atlantic City. Both featured lobster and clams prominently on their menus.

They Lost It at the Movies

In the movie *Funny Girl*, when Fannie Brice, the famous Jewish comedian portrayed by Barbra Streisand, loses her virginity, the celebration takes place over a lobster dinner. "You don't know how proud I am to be the man who introduced you to your first lobster," says her lover, played by Omar Sharif. With a naughty look, she gleefully points out that lobster's not all he introduced her to. Losing her virginity and eating lobster are clearly connected.

In addition to making sexual problems and being nerdy into comedy, Woody Allen raises paranoia about being Jewish to the comedic stratosphere. Allen made a career out of playing a smart, neurotic nebbish who was hopeless with women and paranoid about his Jewishness, especially (as a group of aliens confides to him in *Stardust Memories*) in his "early, funny" movies. In *Annie Hall*, he quotes Groucho Marx about not wanting to belong to any club that would have someone like him as a member, and a moment later he plays the funniest lobster scene ever on the silver screen. Allen as Alfie and Diane Keaton playing Annie are at a rustic beach house in the Hamptons. Five or six lobsters have escaped from a paper bag and are crawling around on the floor of a tiny kitchen. Alfie is hyper-squeamish, and both he and Annie are nearly hysterical.

"Just call the police. Dial 911, it's the lobster squad," he shouts.

She picks one of the lobsters up and taunts Alfie with it. They both yell and laugh at the same time. A lobster disappears behind the refrigerator.

"Talk to him! You speak shellfish," he cries, cringing between the fridge and the wall.

"We shoulda' gotten steaks," he whines, "They don't have legs. They don't crawl around."

Slapstick Freud. Broadway burlesque. A low-down situation turns into a raucous send-up. It is a brilliant parody of a parody of a stereotype.

Woody Allen collaborated with Marshall Brickman on the script of *Annie Hall* and directed it himself. The movie was released in April 1977 and won four Oscars.

"In my experience directing comedies," Mel Brooks wrote in 1983, "I've found that timing for laughs is critical." He goes on to discuss the rhythm of jokes and laughter. "After a while I can judge within a few seconds either way just how much laughter we can get," he boasts. Then he adds (after the built-in pause between one sentence and the next), "Sometimes I'm dead wrong."[16] His case in point:

> In *Silent Movie* there was a sequence that no one will ever see; it's on the cutting-room floor. The sequence is called "Lobsters in New York." It starts with a shot of a neon sign that reads "Chez Lobster." The camera drops down to restaurant doors and pulls back. The doors open, the camera goes inside, and we see greeting us a huge well-dressed lobster with claws and tails; around the camera come two other very well-dressed lobsters in evening clothes. The maitre d' lobster leads them to a waiter lobster in a white jacket, who leads them to a table. They order, then follow the waiter lobster to a huge tank. In the tank, little people are swimming around. We thought this was hysterical. The lobsters choose some people, pick them up squirming around, and the sequence ends. Every time we saw this sequence we were on the floor laughing.[17]

Then they showed the hilarious bit to Brooks's preferred preview audience of secretaries, who stared at one another, seemed embarrassed, and yawned. Not a single laugh. "That," Brooks wrote, "was one of the surprises that comedy screenwriters get from time to time."[18] And that is why no one has ever seen "Lobsters in New York."

But in 2009, thirty-three years after *Silent Movie* and thirty-two years after *Annie Hall*, the concept that ended up on the cutting room floor came back to life in a short fantasy/nightmare written by Woody Allen in the *New Yorker's* "Shouts and Murmurs" section.

The first sentence is: "Two weeks ago, Abe Moscowitz dropped dead of a heart attack and was reincarnated as a lobster." From Groucho Marx (humor) to Ovid (metamorphosis). Pretty soon, Lobster Moscowitz is swimming around in the tank of a fancy Upper East Side seafood restaurant. Also in the tank is his old friend, Moe Silverman. They begin catching up and kvetching when in walks the evildoer Bernie Madoff, with whom both had invested their money. "He's the reason I'm here," said Abe. Because of Madoff, Moe said, "my net worth was bupkes ... When I learned I was broke, I committed suicide by jumping off the roof of our golf club in Palm Beach. I had to wait half an hour to jump, I was twelfth in line."[19]

Then lo and behold, Madoff is standing at the tank choosing Abe and Moe for dinner. Their ire explodes, they rock the tank until it falls over and shatters, and then they chase the wicked swindler. Sweet revenge! Moe clamps onto his ankle, and Abe leaps up heroically and grabs his nose. Recognizing the Ponzi punk, the restaurant's patrons cheer the lobsters on. Madoff runs out of the restaurant in the punishing grip of Abe and Moe, who extract a guilty plea and apology from the hustler. Madoff ends up in the hospital. The lobsters make it safely to Sheepshead Bay which, you should know, is in Brooklyn.[20]

"Everything human is pathetic," Mark Twain wrote. "The secret source of Humor itself is not joy but sorrow."[21] Sad, but true. It certainly applies to Woody Allen and to another wonderful moviemaker, Buster Keaton, who never smiled but invented, starred in, and directed side-splitting comedies of error composed of exquisitely timed near-misses and almost disasters. *The Navigator* (1924) was one of his own favorites and one of his best. The inspiration came when an associate of Keaton's discovered an ocean liner was being sold for salvage and found out that Keaton could have it for $25,000. Art is frequently made of found objects, though they are infrequently so big.

The find led to a plot in which Keaton and a woman who had earlier refused his marriage proposal, both exceedingly wealthy and unused to taking care of themselves, end up alone and adrift on this very large ship. They discover that they are floating toward an island populated by cannibals, at which point they run aground and spring a leak that must be fixed from the outside. But they find a 220-pound diving suit and assemble some tools. As Keaton prepares to go overboard, he takes a moment for a cigarette. Just then the woman drops the helmet over his head, and he nearly suffocates.

Once that difficulty is resolved and Keaton is fully outfitted and connected to a supply of compressed air, he climbs down the ladder to the sandy, murky ocean bottom. There he puts up a sawhorse with a sign that reads "Men at Work." The tools are useless, but when he finds a lobster attached to his leg, he has just what he needs. He grabs the lobster and uses it like a clipper to cut a wire attached to the ship.

Salvador Dalí was a great fan of Buster Keaton. It was during the decade after *The Navigator* premiered that Dalí started thinking of lobsters as agents of emasculation. Giving a lecture on paranoia in July 1936 at the International Surrealist Exhibition in London, Dalí was inspired by Keaton to appear dressed in a diving suit — for Dalí, the costume was meant as a visual expression of his descents into the subconscious. But the air supply to the helmet began to fail, and Dalí found himself in great distress. The audience, enjoying the show, thought it was all part of surrealism, even when his friends tried to pry the helmet off with a billiard cue and hammer. A Keatonesque moment: Dalí managed to avoid asphyxiation just in time.

Sometimes what seems like inspiration creates more problems than benefits. But there are times, as in the next example, when the outcome is far more satisfactory.

Lobster Killer

Julie Powell began a year of cooking her way through Julia Child's classic *Mastering the Art of French Cooking* in 2002, describing the adventure on a blog that made her a celebrity. A book, *Julie & Julia*, followed in 2005, and a movie of the same name was made by Nora Ephron and released in 2009. A chapter of Powell's book titled "Lobster Killer" appeared in *Best Food Writing 2006*.[22]

She had never cooked lobster before and was working herself into a panic in anticipation and fear of the whole procedure. That's when she awoke to the recorded sound of waves on her sleep machine and heard them as a crashing, crushing nightmare roar: "Lobster killer, lobster killer, lobster killer . . ."[23]

She struggled through the process, for the sake of Julia and Homard (lobster) Thermidor. There was an unforeseen glitch, "like the moment your car begins to skid out of control,"[24] when she found that the pot is too small and the lid wouldn't stay on. Her husband, Eric, helped her out. "When Eric and I start our crime conglomerate, he can be in charge of death; I'll take care of dismemberment," she wrote.[25]

The recipe goes well beyond boiling until done and dipping in butter: it requires splitting the lobster in half, removing the meat from the shell, and several other steps that bring to mind a wonderful Helen Hokinson cartoon that appeared in the December 4, 1948, issue of the *New Yorker*: pencil poised, a waiter in a white jacket attends four lunching ladies in hats, with their furs draped over the chair backs. The caption is a question that one of the women asks the waiter: "What do they call it when they take everything out of the lobster then put it all back again?"

Homard Thermidor is just such a dish: you take out all the meat; cut it up, sauté it, and combine it with vegetables, herbs, wine, and an elaborate sauce; and put everything back in the shell. As Julia Child writes in *Mastering the Art of French Cooking*, the reason restaurants charge a fortune for it is because it has so many steps.[26]

In her story, Powell admits that despite the dramatic murder, the lobsters "were, I must say, delicious."[27]

She has two more lobster assignments. The second "murder," for Homard aux Aromates, resembled the first. But she realizes that "cutting lobsters in half was beginning to prove eerily satisfying," and she tells Eric, "I just feel like I've got a knack for this shit." His answer: "By the end of this you'll be comfortable filleting puppies."[28]

The last assignment required cutting up a squirming live lobster, sautéing it, and serving the meat atop rice. "I've committed brutal murder for [Julia Child]," Julie writes, "why not make a rice ring?"[29]

Julie and Eric have a brief discussion about whether it's better to kill your meat yourself or have it killed in a factory. In Japan people enjoy eating live lobster, which adds another dimension to Julie and Eric's conversation. But I don't think that's quite the meaning of a bumper sticker that a friend spotted in Maine and told me about: under a picture of a lobster is the legend "Say No to Pot!"

Combining Julie's blog and book with Julia's autobiography, Ephron wrote and directed the movie, with Amy Adams in the role of Julie and Meryl Streep as Julia. Streep *really is* Julia, so much so that many (if not all) of us who grew up under the influence of "the French Chef" are still applauding her reincarnation — especially her ecstatic boast as she bisects a large, living lobster and proclaims: "I am *fearless!*"

Ephron is also fearless, at least with reference to the meal that she and her first husband, Carl Bernstein, had at the home of their good friends Sally Quinn and Ben Bradlee. It was a lobster dinner, so they were drinking white wine. The conversation innocently turned to knowing, or not knowing, when your spouse is unfaithful. As it happened Ephron, had just found out that Bernstein was cheating on her. She stood up and asked for red wine, took the bottle, and poured it over his head. That was the night they broke up.[30]

That meal offers a corrective to the illusion of the romantic lobster dinner.

This exchange with Miss Manners is another corrective:

> *Dear Miss Manners:*
> Lobster bibs make people look silly. I hate them. I have actually been ignored, however, by waiters who fasten them around my neck, without asking, when I tell them I want to eat my lobster without one, taking my own chances about soiling my clothes. Do I have to order something else at a restaurant unless I am willing to wear their bib?

> *Gentle Reader:*
> The reason that God made the lobster delicious, messy and expensive, all at once, was to reserve for humanity one treat that is better enjoyed in the privacy of the home. There is nothing better than boiled lobster with garlic butter, but you pay a

restaurant a considerable markup for something that is simple to make, and as it is impossible to eat neatly you expose yourself to public ridicule. Eat your lobster at home, wearing washable clothes, and you will not need a bib.[31]

Romance and bibs do not go together, it's true. However Miss Manners's editorial comments and solution are insulting and contrary. Why not just suggest to Gentle Reader that she take the bib off when the waiter goes away? Moreover, though it may be a messy endeavor, I've never seen anyone in a restaurant, with or without a bib, ridiculed while eating lobster. That would be even more uncouth than Miss Manners's response. If the question was silly, the answer was worse. I suppose it must take a good measure of hubris to advise people on etiquette — or ethics, for that matter.

There's a tradition that a criminal condemned to death can have anything he or she wants for a last meal. At exactly midnight on June 18, 2010, Ronnie Lee Gardner, a convicted murderer, was taken into the execution room at Utah's state prison and strapped into the chair. A target was pinned to his chest because, at his own request, he wanted to be killed by a firing squad. And so he was. Various sources reported that for his last meal, he requested steak, lobster tail, apple pie, vanilla ice cream, and 7-Up.[32]

Allen Lee Davis died in the electric chair in Florida in early July 1999. "On May 11, 1982, Davis — an ex-convict — entered the Jacksonville, Fla., home of the John Weiler family. Weiler, an executive with the Westinghouse Corp., was on a business trip in Pittsburgh," wrote a reporter for the Chicago Tribune. He then described in the murder of Weiler's pregnant wife and two young daughters in ghastly detail. There was no disguising the writer's pro–death penalty stand. He added: "As his last meal before his execution, Davis received from the State of Florida the dinner he had requested: a lobster tail, fried potatoes, a half-pound of fried shrimp, six ounces of fried clam strips, half a loaf of garlic bread and 32 ounces of A&W root beer. In 1982, Davis did not give Mrs. Weiler and her two children a choice of a last meal before he killed them."[33] In this context, Davis's last meal sounds revolting, and the menu — especially the lobster — suffers guilt by association.

There are no reliable or conclusive statistics on how often lob-

ster is ordered for a last meal. However, the last meal for the condemned was for a long time a magnet for morbid public curiosity:
"A list of death row meals for most of the killers executed since
1982 was the most popular feature on the official TDCJ [Texas Department of Criminal Justice] website for years, but was removed
in 2004 during a reorganization of the site. 'We had a ton of calls
about that ... We took it down because we had complaints — people said it was in poor taste, we shouldn't have it, we were making
a spectacle. We had it there in the first place because people always
wanted know what the last meal was,' the public information offi-
cer for the TDCJ explained."[34]

A. J. Liebling, who was very fond of lobster, mused: "I am philosophical, like a lobster-eater who knows that the total number of
lobsters in the world is on the decline, but is sure they will last
him out."[35] This observation, written two years prior to Liebling's
death in 1963, is a most unusual, very provocative, and strangely
interesting way to count the remainder of one's days, especially if
one is particularly interested in lobsters.

In the July 7, 1958, issue of *Life* magazine, the movie *Indiscreet* was
called "one of the happiest movies to come along this year." The story
unfolds in London, where Cary Grant is an American diplomat.
Ingrid Bergman plays a famous actress who says, according to *The
Movie Queen Quiz Book*, "I don't want a lobster, I want a man."[36]

One of the saddest characters in the history of the theater is Pierrot, a clown who appeared first in the seventeenth-century Italian
commedia dell'arte. His place in theatrical and artistic produc-
tions lasted through the nineteenth century, when — especially in
France — he was often used to caricature the shortcomings of the
bourgeoisie. The French artist Gavarni is known for his carnival
illustrations and was much admired by the Goncourt brothers,
writers who commented on French culture during the late nineteenth century (see their comment on eighteenth-century women
in chapter 9). Gavarni made a lithograph for one Pierrot's scenes:
appearing with his bushy black beard, large spectacles, and a
floppy, peaked and pompommed hat, Pierrot invites an alluring

female to dinner. She dismisses him, saying, "Yes! I love lobster well enough but I do not love Pierrot."[37] Alas.

The grand prize for the lobster dinner *manqué* is a cover of the *New Yorker* by Peter de Sève that appeared on July 28, 2008, at the peak of the lobster season. It shows the corner of a shingled beach cottage and end of the porch, where four people are drinking beer and wine and laughing heartily. Out of their sight behind them is an open window to the kitchen, where a large lobster pot is steaming away. Stealthily climbing out of the kitchen window and using a twisted tablecloth for their get-away are the escaping lobsters.

Though this cover needs no caption, the aforementioned bumper sticker works here: "Say No to Pot!"

What do lobster anecdotes, folklore, jokes, cartoons, and humor from various classes and national, social, professional, and ethnic groups share? To an extent it depends on those very groups. From the philosophical musings of A. J. Liebling, a journalist who loved good food and especially lobster, to the paranoia of Salvador Dalí, and artist who saw lobsters as instruments of violence, one's outlook depends on time and place, attitude and experience. Maybe the reason why the secretaries who watched Mel Brooks "Lobsters in New York" clip, meant for *Silent Movie*, didn't laugh was because they thought it too ridiculous to be funny. Come to think of it, maybe it really isn't funny. A joke might fall flat because the person who's telling it misses a beat, as Brooks suggests. Or maybe the joke bombs because the person hearing or seeing it has no frame of reference within which to find it amusing. Or maybe the frame of reference — for example, a crime and its punishment — casts a shadow on every related thing.

The best coda to the topic of lobster humor is a straight-faced article that appeared in the magazine *Popular Mechanics* in 1952. The subject was a French restaurateur, who believed that lobsters and humans had certain traits in common. To illustrate his point of view, he began to assemble portraits of individuals — Harry Truman, Winston Churchill, and Charles De Gaulle included — using lobster shells. The most bizarre feature of these portraits is how recognizable the subjects were. The title of the article: "Lobsters Are Like People."[38]

II Welcome to the Lobster Hotel

Captain George Waymouth (the name is sometimes spelled Weymouth) of the ship *Archangel* and a few of his men took soundings near Maine's Monhegan Island in 1605. They also cast a few fishing lines to see what was there. In no time at all they caught enough codfish to feed the whole crew of twenty-nine for three days. So wrote James Rosier, a crew member who documented the voyage. The great abundance of fish along the coast of what was then known as northern Virginia and is now New England surprised early European explorers — a surprise followed by enormous optimism. Rosier wrote: "It sheweth how great a profit the fishing would be, they being so plentiful, so great, and so good, with such convenient drying as can be wished, near at hand upon the rocks."[1]

Just two years before Waymouth's exploration of the Maine coast, Bartholomew Gosnold, looking for the elusive northwest passage to the Pacific, made his way to that great curlicue of a peninsula named Pallavisino by Giovanni da Verrazano. While at anchor, Gosnold's crew caught so many codfish in just a few hours that the men were "pestered" by them and threw many back overboard. That inspired Gosnold to change the name of Pallavisino to Cape Cod.[2]

How many cod Gosnold's men took is not known, but here's a pertinent statistic: three hundred years later, at the beginning of the nineteenth century, it was recorded that in the waters of Newfoundland's banks, the predominant cod fishery in the world for centuries, it was routine for a single fisherman to take over 500 codfish in ten or eleven hours.[3] That would average about 33 fish per hour.

Rosier was the first person to describe Europeans landing lobster on the Maine coast. Drawing a small net close to shore some twenty fathoms deep, his shipmates' haul included "about thirty very good and great lobsters."[4] He gives no specific length or weight for the lobsters, but he marvels at the size of the pipes made from the short claws of lobsters by Indians who shared a smoke with the sailors: the Indian pipes held ten times as much tobacco as the European pipes.

John Josselyn, writing about his two voyages to New England later in the seventeenth century, described how Indians fished for lobsters. He watched them paddle their birch canoes into a large bay at low tide when the wind was still. They carried spears two or three yards long, notched at the point, and when they spotted a lobster crawling on the bottom — twelve feet deep, more or less — they "stick him towards the head and bring him up." Josselyn saw an Indian lad take thirty lobsters in an hour and a half.[5] As for the size of these lobsters, Josselyn himself had seen them as large as twenty pounds, but he heard others tell of lobsters weighing twenty-five pounds.

Rosier's account, written after the *Archangel*'s return to England, describes trees, fowl, beasts (including reindeer, bears, beaver, "wild greatcat," and "Dogs; some like wolves some like spaniels"), fruits, plants, herbs, and fishes. Under fishes, Rosier lists whales, crabs, cockles, tortoises, and oysters. Singled out are cod ("very great") and lobster ("great"). He says cod were plentiful and huge, some as long as five feet and as wide as three feet.[6]

Cod and lobster were the marvels of the North American coastline in the eyes of explorers, who were dazzled by their commercial possibilities. Rosier makes this point, or pitch, relentlessly. Upon their "farewell from the land" of Maine, Rosier wrote, "it pleased God in continuance of his blessings" to reveal more of Maine's great fishing grounds, "the abundant profit whereof should be alone sufficient cause to draw men again" to those shores. He declares that fisheries there would be more rewarding than those of Newfoundland, "the fish being so much greater, better fed, and abundant."[7]

Besides tidings of great economic promise, the *Archangel* carried five kidnapped Indians to England. Waymouth gave three of his captives to Sir Ferdinando Gorges, the military governor of the port of Plymouth, in England. Gorges had a strong desire to participate in the settlement of America, encouraged no doubt by the ships traveling between Plymouth and the New World, and especially by Waymouth's and Rosier's glowing reports — as well as by the Indians, with whom he learned to communicate. With a financial stake in the settlements, Gorges hoped that what he could learn from the Indian captives would allow him to find new investment opportunities and benefit financially. He also hoped that when they learned English, the Indians would help the English in their New World ventures.

Gorges threw himself wholeheartedly into the English settlement of New England. He sponsored voyages, including one by Captain John Smith, and managed to have himself officially named governor of New England. This effort took some thirty years, and in 1639, when he was in his seventies, he finally acquired his own proprietary province of Maine, though he never set foot there or anywhere else in the New World.

One after the other, the settlements that Gorges supported failed, often due to Maine's harsh winters and conflicts with the Indians. A few armed fishing outposts were established, among them two on the islands of Monhegan and Damariscove, the first permanently settled year-round fishing locations in Maine. In the winter of 1622, when the Pilgrims at Plymouth Rock were starving, they sent a boat to Damariscove. It came back home loaded with cod.

Damariscove, a 210-acre island is located six miles out to sea from Boothbay Harbor. In 1689 Captain Richard Pattishall, whose fishing fleet was stationed there, was attacked in his sloop while asleep, beheaded, and tossed overboard by Indians. His dog jumped in after him. Both washed up on the island's shores. Damariscove still has a working fishing community and a story to tell about how Pattishall's headless ghost, accompanied by his dog, haunt the island to this day.

Less tragic, but still ultimately unsuccessful, Gorges wrote of his ventures: "All of our former hopes were frozen to death."[8] That sounds like surrender. The fact is that despite so much enthusiasm, the Maine fisheries for lobster, cod, and other species did not develop as anticipated for a very long time.

Lobsters could not be kept alive long enough to ship them any distance; they could not be preserved; and they went bad very quickly after dying. Lobster fisheries had no significant success until the beginning of the nineteenth century, and that was not in Maine but rather in Massachusetts, especially around Boston and Cape Cod, where there were hungry populations large enough to make the lobster enterprise pay. There were also some lobster fisheries off Long Island and the Connecticut coast. Not until around 1840 did fishing for lobster take hold in Maine. But once established, it did well; by 1889 the lobster fisheries of Maine had upstaged those of the other states.

Francis Hobart Herrick provides statistics that document Maine's lobster dominance: "The output of the New England lobster fishery in 1889 was 30,449,603 pounds, valued at $833,736; of this catch 25,001,351 pounds, worth $574,165, were taken in Maine."[9] Herrick also cites a later census of the US lobster industry, which reported that the total number of people working in the lobster fisheries in 1892 was 3,766, of whom 2,628 were in Maine and 616 in Massachusetts (leaving a balance of 522 working in other states). Including all states, the investment in lobster fisheries added up to $648,065; the quantity of lobsters taken and sold by US fishermen was 23,724,525 pounds, for which $1,062,392 was received. Roughly 75 percent by weight (17,642,677 pounds) of all those lobsters were taken in Maine.

Napoleon believed that an army marches on its stomach, which explains why he was the original impetus for the invention of canning in France early in the nineteenth century, to supply armies with food. The first process involved sealing cooked food in glass jars. The English soon began canning, too, and preserved food in airtight containers made from tinned, wrought iron. Producing food in this way was an expensive, labor-intensive process, but the end results were not without their lighter moments. While "our forces" were fighting the Indian war during the mid-nineteenth century, an English writer wrote:

A box of regimental stores belonging to our forces fell into the hands of the enemy, who thinking that a great capture of some kind of deadly and destructive ammunition had been made, rammed the painted tin cases, with goodly charges of powder behind them, into their immense guns, laid them steadily on the devoted British troops, and then with a flash and a thundering roar, preserved lobster, from Fortnum and Mason's, was scattered far and wide over the battlefield.[10]

Canning made shipping lobsters profitable. The first factory devoted to packing lobsters in cans was a venture that proceeded with equal measures of secrecy and catastrophe (due to sealing experiments) in Eastport, Maine, during the early 1840s. However, once the three entrepreneurs involved hired a "veteran Scottish canner," their assembly line rapidly turned out one-pound cans of lobster. "It was the first time anyone in the world had ever canned lobster, and the second time Americans had ever canned anything at all," writes Colin Woodard in *The Lobster Coast*, a narrative that illuminates the statistics later compiled by Herrick. Woodard continues: "The canneries spread like wildfire, and the lobster fishery followed. By the late 1870s, there were twenty-three from Portland to Eastport, engaging the service of 1,200 lobstermen."[11] Together they produced two million one-pound cans of lobster per season.

There had been numerous attempts to transport live lobsters by ship and, beginning in the late 1700s, the lobster smack — a specially constructed boat with an open holding well where sea water circulated, a kind of floating fish tank called a "wet smack" — in a "dry smack," the lobsters are carried on ice. At the end of the twentieth century, the railroads became the chief means of long-distance transportation for live lobsters. William Randolph Hearst is said to have launched the cross-country shipping of live lobsters by rail for a dinner party he hosted in Colorado. During the heyday of the lobster palace, many wealthy patrons — including Diamond Jim Brady — were railroad moguls whose trains not only carried lobsters to market but also served them in their elegant dining cars.

Who would have thought transporting live lobsters by rail could be the stuff of a romantic comedy? Starring Doris Day, no less! It was, in the movie *It Happened to Jane*, released in 1959. Innocent but strong-willed Jane is a widow with two children whom she supports by selling lobsters (except the one they keep as a pet) that she ships by rail from the small train station in her little town on the Maine coast. She is pitted against a large-scale capitalist — played by Ernie Kovacs, with a dark moustache and darker scowl — known as "the meanest man in the world." He is a railroad man who decides his train will no longer stop at Jane's station as he develops his transportation empire. They go head to head; she wins; and he not only concedes but also turns into a good guy in the end.

In 1900 John Cobb, an agent of the US Fish Commission, wrote:

> About nine-tenths of the lobsters caught in Maine waters are shipped in the live state. The principal shipping centers are Portland, Rockland, and Eastport, which have good railroad and steamship facilities with points outside of the state. Those shipped from the latter point are mainly from the British [Canadian] Provinces, the fishermen near Eastport bringing them in their own boats. A number also come in from the Provinces on the regular steamship lines. The other places get their supply from the smacks and also from the fishermen in their vicinity who run in their own catch. Portland is very favorably situated in this regard, as Casco Bay is a noted fishing center for lobsters.[12]

Refrigerated trucks and airplanes followed.

Hesiod Redux

Frank Algernon Cowperwood of Philadelphia — the central figure of Theodore Dreiser's novel *The Financier* — had an instinctive drive to make money that would be called talent had his father been anything other than a banker, and Frank's obsession with music, art, or literature instead of with wealth. At the age of about ten, when he looked everywhere for clues to the meaning of life, he found it at a fish market near his home, where fishermen from the Delaware Bay dropped off unusual specimens to be displayed in a tank in front of the store.

> One day he saw a squid and a lobster put in the tank, and in connection with them was witness to a tragedy which stayed with him all his life and cleared things up considerably intellectually. The lobster, it appeared from the talk of the idle bystanders, was offered no food, as the squid was considered his rightful

prey. He lay at the bottom of the clear glass tank on the yellow sand, apparently seeing nothing—you could not tell in which way his beady black buttons of eyes were looking—but apparently they were never off the squid.[13]

Every so often the lobster would catapult toward the squid, which fled in a plume of ink, and when next seen, the squid would be missing a small piece of its body. "Fascinated by the drama, young Cowperwood came daily to watch," and day by day the squid was diminished—until, sliced in two and "partially devoured,"[14] it finally was dead.

"That's the way it has to be, I guess," he commented to himself. "That squid wasn't quick enough." He figured it out . . .

The incident made a great impression on him. It answered in a rough way that riddle which had been annoying him so much in the past: "How is life organized?" Things lived on each other—that was it.[15]

Cowperwood applies what he learned at the fish tank to accumulate—and lose—wealth and power. He speculates on the stock market, invests in railroads, borrows and embezzles, succeeds, fails, and bounces back. This fictional biography, which evolves so vividly using the lobster's predation as its organizing principle, rings as true to the financial cataclysms of the twenty-first century as to those of the nineteenth, in which it is set.

*H*ard-shelled and mean-tempered as it is, the lobster itself is a victim of many predators besides the octopus. Rummaging on the ocean floor, sharks, skates, rays, pollock, bass, and other creatures feed on lobsters. But apart from humans, cod is the lobster's worst enemy.

The earliest transatlantic travelers to New England appraised the munificence of cod and lobster as if there were a symbiotic relationship between them. There is. Throughout the centuries, fishermen have probably noticed that after they landed a large codfish on the boat deck, it might spit up its most recent meal. That meal often included lobster, sometimes more than one. Voracious, omnivorous, and indiscriminate, a codfish, as Mark Kurlansky writes, swims around with its mouth wide open.[16] It's the adage traceable way back to Hesiod: big fish eat little fish. Of course, the first thing a fish biologist will tell you is that lobsters are not fish — they are crustaceans.

The rest of us do well to concede that right off the bat, and then find out what we can about such things as how a cod can manage to digest a lobster. Most of the time cod probably feed on juveniles, or molting or soft-shell lobsters. But what about swallowing a lobster with a hard shell?

Cristina Fox Fernandez, a fish biologist at the University of Massachusetts Amherst, explained: "Codfishes can be huge and so are their mouths. The digestion of a hard-shell would be very slow. Fish have a second pair of jaws on the back of their throats called pharyngeal jaws, to help breaking things like shells."[17]

Thoreau wrote: "The ocean is a wilderness reaching round the globe, wilder than a Bengal jungle, and fuller of monsters."[18]

Stephen King should consider codstrosities for a future novel. Granted, cod is not really a monster (any more than lobster is), and neither is it invulnerable: sharks and bluefish are among its predators. But they are insignificant when compared to human predation. And it is human predation — overfishing — that has so disastrously depleted the Atlantic cod population.

A lawsuit filed by the Conservation Law Foundation led to a consent decree that was signed in 1991 by the National Marine Fisheries Service.[19] The decree essentially aimed to end overfishing and rebuild stocks of depleted fish, such as cod, in New England waters. Instead of the progress that everyone hoped for, there have been endless arguments about regulations and at least one unintended consequence: large fishing vessels outcompeting smaller boats, making fishing for a living even harder than it already was. As of today, cod and various other groundfish are still seriously depleted in the Gulf of Maine. "It's a curious system that rewards the biggest, least conservation-oriented vessels that can roam throughout the Gulf and to the outer banks, at the expense of community based vessels that lack political representation at the decision making level on the council. But that's how the system works," wrote Philip Conkling, president of the Island Institute, in *Working Waterfront*, one of the institute's publications.[20]

Regarding that symbiotic relationship, the depletion of cod could make an increased number of lobsters available to fishermen. But there is little agreement on how significant that correlation is; some doubt that it matters at all. Nonetheless, at the end of the nineteenth century, the lobster catch was heading toward eighteen million pounds. In the year 2000, the catch in Maine was fifty-seven and a half million pounds. It peaked in 2006 at ninety-three million pounds.

The Commons

The legendary association of Maine lobstermen with Western cowboys is based on the idea that both have tough and dangerous jobs; fight territorial wars; and are by nature taciturn, independent loners. Some of that is true, though it could be added that the sea is generally more treacherous than the Western landscape, and Maine winters have sharper edges than many of those out West. "The Maine man," wrote one of them, Robert Coffin, "has to do his day's work in weather like the edge on a crosscut saw."[21]

Several years of watching Millard Creamer motor out to his lobster boat, often before dawn—sometimes with his sternman (the title of one member of a lobster boat's crew) and sometimes alone—and return late in the day has given me the impression that he is independent and maybe lonely, though he now and then pulls up alongside his brother Harlan's boat, or someone else's, to exchange greetings and information (I presume). The Creamers have been lobstering for generations, and they know what is on the unseen bottom of the Medomak River better than I know what's in my pantry.

I have often lain awake in the very early, very dark hours after midnight listening to a motorboat buzzing along the river, wondering if it's the sound of a drug smuggler, a lobster poacher, or a member of a lobster gang leaving a warning for an interloper, or cutting the lines of someone who has failed to take such a warning seriously. "The most distinctive feature of lobstering clusters or harbor gangs is that they claim and defend their fishing areas. Territoriality does not exist in any other Maine fishery," writes James Acheson.[22] He uses the term "harbor gang" to describe a group of lobstermen who use the same harbor and collectively claim and defend particular fishing areas. A professor of anthropology and marine sciences at the University of Maine, Acheson's field of study is economic anthropology. His research and writing during more than thirty years has explored the intricacies of Maine's lobster fishing business: what happens at sea, in harbor communities, and in marketplaces. In *The Lobster Gangs of Maine*, published in 1988, Acheson writes: "In this book I seek to describe the subculture and social organization of lobster fishermen and the way this organization is adapted to the social and physical environment."[23] He diagrams Maine's major fishing grounds and their currents, as well as the construction of a lobster, a lobster boat, and a trap. He provides insights into how lobstermen and women fish, organize, operate their territories, and collaborate — or not.

With the world becoming painfully conscious of the multitude of our environmental problems, including overfishing and global warming, in 2003 Acheson published *Capturing the Commons: Devising Institutions to Manage the Maine Lobster Industry*. In the introduction he writes: "The Maine lobster industry is one of the most remarkably successful fisheries in the world today." Scientists cannot explain that success, as measured in the record high catches since the late 1980s despite equivalently soaring years of exploitation, if not overfishing. Credit must be given, however, to the conservation rules and regulations about such things that local fishermen and the state government of Maine are "capturing the commons" by agreeing that:

- It is illegal to keep lobsters smaller than three and a quarter inches and larger than five inches, as measured down the center of the unsegmented body shell, or carapace, from the back of the eye sockets along to the rear of the carapace.
- It is also illegal to keep berried (egg-bearing) or V-notched (that is, noted as having been egg-bearing) lobsters, or females whose eggs have been removed by any means.
- And it is illegal to keep speared, dismembered, or mutilated lobsters — such as detached claws and tails.
- Maine has management zones that regulate lobster fisheries. In six zones, the maximum number of traps allowed per boat is 800; in the remaining two zones, 600 is the upper limit. There

are, in addition, two conservation areas: Monhegan,[24] with a maximum of 300 traps, and Swans Island, with a maximum of 475.

+ In general, lobster fishing runs from May through October.

+ There are various classes of licenses for commercial lobster fishing. For a Maine resident whose age is over eighteen and under seventy, the cost of a yearly license is $167.

+ Every trap has to be tagged. The 2012 fee for each tag is fifty cents.

+ Though permissible lobster size is limited, there is no limit on the number or total weight of lobsters that may be caught. And there is no average catch. "Some may land over 100,000 pounds. The average is around 5,000," commented Carl Wilson, chief biologist for the Maine Department of Marine Resources, when I spoke to him by telephone in September 2010.

+ Lobstermen have acted with political acumen as well as conservation farsightedness, although this did not happen without acrimony and ugly clashes of self-interest. Acheson comments: "It would not be far wrong to say that rules are byproducts of contests over who gets the lobster."[25] Regardless, the successful evolution of rules and regulations, governing the lobster industry has taken place in the context of the industry's economic success, based on lobsters' availability, and times are still relatively good — in contrast, for example, to the cod fishery.

Acheson examines the situation in depth and from many perspectives. He concludes:

> I believe the rules governing lobster fishing are working well and will prove to be very resilient. However, there is reason for caution in predicting long-term trends in this fishery and the future evolution of its governance structure. For the present, we are witnessing the unparalled success of an industry in which people are determined to capture the lobster commons for themselves and future generations.[26]

As usual, however, the only thing that's certain is that nothing is. Lobster catches might decline, for some currently unforeseen reason. For example, in 2007 the high cost of fuel created a domino effect, contributing to the cost of bait and other necessities without a compensating rise in boat price—what the lobsterman or woman gets per pound from the dealer. In addition, the catch that year was down somewhat from the previous year. And in the summer of 2008, the vicious economic crisis had a brutal effect on lobstermen.

The systems of pricing are mysterious in the lobster business, but an article by Sandra Dinsmore in *Working Waterfront* sheds some light on the subject. There are, she wrote, between four and six steps in what is called "the lobster pipeline":

> Starting with a hypothetical boat price of $4 per pound, in theory:
> * First buyer: A wharf buys product from fishermen paying $4 per lb. adds from 50 to 75 cents per lb. to boat price . . . and sells to trucker.
> * Second buyer: Trucker adds 50 to 75 cents for expenses and delivers lobster to Boston or New York and sells to . . .
> * Third buyer: large wholesaler, who grades out culls and bad lobsters [with cracked shells, for example], adds 75 cents per lb. for chix [lobsters one pound or less] and quarters [those weighing one and one-quarter pounds] and $1.25 per lb. for halves [those weighing one and a half pounds]. Sells to . . .
> * Fourth buyer: smaller wholesaler who adds 75 cents per lb. and sells to local markets and restaurants or to . . .
> * Fifth buyer: another smaller wholesaler, fish market or restaurant and adds 75 cents and up to take-home package or plate.[27]

Restaurants may charge customers three times what they pay for a lobster. Price fluctuations seem arbitrary, but hidden costs and other unforeseen expenses are unpredictable.

An alternative to the lobsterman's selling through a dealer is a fishermen's cooperative, owned by fishermen who elect a board of directors and hire someone to negotiate the best possible prices for them, from selling their lobsters to buying bait, fuel, perhaps other supplies, and maybe even insurance policies.

Mark Wallace fishes out of Friendship, Maine, on a thirty-five-foot-long fiberglass boat named after his two daughters, the *Leslie Elise*. He's a fourth-generation lobsterman. Most days Wallace leaves home at 3:30 in the morning and gets back home at 4:00 in the afternoon. His fishing season begins near Friendship; later he moves to an area twelve miles outside of Monhegan. He's a highliner—a successful lobster fisherman who works hard and devotes himself to his profession. One unexpected catch recently was a huge sea turtle about four feet long that got caught in his ropes. The turtle was too heavy to lift, so he and his crew pulled the turtle alongside the boat until they were able to cut the rope and set it free.

For the past thirteen years, Wallace has belonged to Fishermen's Heritage Lobster Co-Op—one of Friendship's two co-ops—which has about thirty members. For eight years, he was also a member of Maine's Lobster Advisory Council, made up of fishermen, wholesalers, and legislators. There are five council zones for the state—Wallace is in Zone D. Council members investigate problems that relate to the lobster industry, and advise and make recommendations to the commissioner of Maine's Department of Marine Resources and the Marine Resources Advisory Council. They also review and recommend research programs and consider disputed issues. One major problem under discussion now is the price of tags for the 800 traps a boat is allowed. "It started at a dime. Last year it was 40 cents. Now they're talking about $1.00 per trap," said Wallace in 2010 (as noted above, they settled on fifty cents for 2012). Licenses are also becoming more expensive. When his father was young, a license cost $1. When Wallace was young, it cost $10. Now his license costs $262. As for the boat price, it had improved from around $2.00 on average in 2009 to about $3.00 in 2010.[28]

The limit of 800 traps per boat has been a matter of contention, with some fishermen arguing it was too few while others said too many. Carl Wilson, of the Maine Department of Marine Resources, devised a series of experiments designed to test the hypothesis that more traps equals more lobsters caught. With the collaboration of Monhegan fishermen, his preliminary research took place during 2005 and 2007. The number of traps set was reduced, and other variables such as trap density and "soak time" (the length of time that traps were left in the water before being hauled up) were rigorously monitored. Though more experiments are needed, it is already clear that with a reduced number of traps and lower density, the catch is about the same as with more traps and higher density. So if half the traps along the coast were removed, Wilson said, the lobster catch would be about the same as before.

The correlation is interesting and complex. "There are so many variables," Wilson notes, such as the amount of time spent fishing, how hard the lobsterman works, and skill. "Skill is still very important," Wilson says. And here is some surprising information: "Eighty percent of landings are caught by twenty percent of those who go fishing."[29]

That, like lobster, is food for thought.

Flying Lobster

Arichat is a village in Richmond County, on Isle Madame, Nova Scotia. It was founded in the early 1700s, and in September 1776 it was attacked and pillaged by the American privateer John Paul Jones. I learned about Clearwater Seafoods' facility in Arichat in an article John McPhee wrote for the *New Yorker* in 2005. He described stacks of lobster compartments, thirty-four levels high, each inhabited by a single lobster (in order to prevent the animals from tearing one another apart). The dimensions of each residence depend on the size of the resident.

Imagine yourself on a very narrow New York City street, with a long line of thirty-four-story skyscrapers along canyon-like streets closing in on you. Welcome to the Lobster Hotel.

The temperature is just above freezing, "and there in the cold dark, alone, [the lobsters] use almost no energy . . . The cold water comes down from above and, in a patented way, circulates through the apartments as if they were a series of descending Moorish pools. Beguiled into thinking it is always winter, the lobsters remain hard, so do not molt when summer comes, and may repose in Arichat for half a year before departing for Kentucky."[30]

They go from Arichat to Kentucky because UPS built a hub in Louisville, and Clearwater also built a lobster residence there. It is a rest and recuperation stop on the way from Arichat to everywhere: Brooklyn, Guam, Phoenix, Tel Aviv . . . you name it.

The Lobster Hotel—Clearwater Seafoods' Dryland Storage facility at Arichat, Nova Scotia. Photo Courtesy of Clearwater Seafoods Limited Partnership.

McPhee calls Louisville the "flying lobster capital of the United States."[31] That article was published over five years ago, but it still sounds like science fiction.

Ironically, between 50 and 70 percent of Maine's lobsters are sold to purchasers in Canada, where they lose their Maine identity: US law decrees that if Maine lobsters are shipped to Canada and returned to the United States, they must be marketed as Canadian. According to McPhee, truckloads of lobsters from the Clearwater facility are sent to Maine, and not necessarily the same ones that were caught in the Gulf of Maine. According to the company, "in a typical year over eight million pounds of live premium lobster move [from its facilities] to customers across North America, Europe and Asia."[32]

In addition to being president of the Island Institute, Philip Conkling serves on the Task Force on Economic Sustainability of Maine's Lobster Industry. He writes that the group has proposed the formation of a Maine Lobster Marketing Institute to work on how the state and its residents can "capture a bigger slice of the value inherent in Maine's lobster brand that has eroded in the last decade."[33] While their report awaits attention on the governor's desk, some individuals have taken the initiative themselves. For example, Millard Creamer has opened a small store along coastal Maine's Route 1. And Linda Bean, who is now in charge of the family business L. L. Bean, is investing millions of dollars in wharves and infrastructure for a chain of lobster roll restaurants.

12 Bouillabaisse

"I loved the fishwives. They were a breed apart: big, loud, and territorial, they screamed at each other in nasal accents. 'When one of them dies, there's always another one just like her, ready to take her place,' an old *pêcheur* told me. They were a great resource for me, even though they didn't always agree with each other," Julia Child wrote in her autobiography, *My Life in France*.[1] She and her husband, Paul, had moved from Paris to Marseille with "their taste buds poised for new flavors."[2]

"So what was the Real McCoy bouillabaisse recipe?" Julia asks in the chapter titled "Bouillabaisse à la Marseillaise?" The answer is that correct, authoritative, absolutely definitive recipes for bouillabaisse are like opinions: everybody's got one. This reveals one of the things that bother her about the French: they are all so dogmatic. The other thing that bothered her was that, because she was a foreigner, they thought she knew nothing, and at first they were right. But eventually she knew more than they did, "because I had studied up on everything"[3]

How did she solve the bouillabaisse problem for her American audience? Bouillabaisse runs from page 52 to page 53 of *Mastering the Art of French Cooking*. On page 53 of my copy are a few light lines of scribbling that could only mean one thing. The book came out in 1961, and my copy was from the tenth printing, in August 1965. My daughter would have been about one and a half to two years old. There is no food stain with the light scribble. No doubt I thought of making bouillabaisse and realized that, for the time being, I just couldn't pull it off. I can picture myself paging through the book, pencil in hand to make a shopping list, and my daughter making the task impossible. Not to mention the fact that I probably couldn't have afforded to buy a lobster, let alone the time to spend on making the dish. The faint scribble is my toddler's signature.

Julia begins by saying that you can make as dramatic a production as you like, but you should keep in mind the origin of the soup: it was made as a Mediterranean fisherman's meal from the day's catch, or what part of it wasn't sold, probably combined with leftovers. Onions and leeks, garlic and tomatoes, water, parsley, bay leaf, thyme or basil, fennel, saffron, orange peel, salt, pepper, and six to eight pounds of fish and shellfish — she provides a list of more than twenty to choose from, including lobster — are called for. Even pasta is a possible ingredient.

A number of other American Francophiles have faced the bouillabaisse conundrum. One of them, Alice B. Toklas, wrote: "In France there are three different kinds of *Bouillabaisse* — the unique and authentic one of Marseille with Mediterranean fish, the one of Paris made of fish from the Atlantic, and a very false one indeed made of fresh-water fish." Toklas has no problem with French dogmatism, maybe because she has something of a proclivity for it herself. Witness the beginning of her instructions: "The fish should be more than fresh, it should be caught and cooked the same day."[4]

In the 1920s, Toklas and Gertrude Stein lived in Saint Rémy de Provence for one summer and into the winter. From Saint Rémy they drove the sixty miles to Marseille two or three times every month for bouillabaisse at the town's best restaurants.

Alice's bouillabaisse recipe is not for beginners. She calls for at least five and preferably seven or more kinds of fish, not counting the lobster, crab, and clams. The compulsory freshness is so important that she repeats it — in fact, she does not believe it can be repeated too often. What goes without saying is the fact that the cook is responsible for scaling and beheading, if not killing, the fish. "Take 5 lbs. gurnards, red snapper, red fish, mullets, pike, turbot and dory, wash, scale, cut off the fins and heads," she writes.[5] Some fifty pages earlier, she has confided that the kitchen is a scene where crime is inevitable. When she started to cook seriously, she says, is when her experience of murder in the kitchen began.

In Alice's bouillabaisse the lobster is boiled twice — first it is simply boiled, the shell is split, and the meat is removed. Later the lobster meat is "furiously" boiled along with other cooked ingredients, including fish heads. Considering the disintegration that takes place when even the sturdiest fish is boiled makes the very idea of boiling fish at all counterintuitive, and furiously boiling seems terrible. But the root of the very name of the soup refers to boiling, and the rationale emerges with a bit of research. The answer is in Harold McGee's *On Food and Cooking*:

> Bouillabaisse is a Provençal fish soup that takes advantage of gelatin's thickening and emulsifying properties. It's made by cooking a variety of whole fish and fish parts, some of them bony and gelatin-producing rather than meaty, in an aromatic broth with some olive oil. The soup is finished at a vigorous boil, which breaks the oil into tiny droplets and coats them with a stabilizing layer of gelatin. The consistency is thus a combination of gelatin's viscosity and the enriching creaminess of the emulsified oil droplets.[6]

According to Toklas, bouillabaisse was "born" in Marseille, and Marseille certainly stakes its claim. There are other contenders all along the coast of France and even in Corsica, as well as close analogues in Italy, and in the conjectured cuisines of ancient Greece and Rome. It is rumored that mortal feuds arise from arguments about who made bouillabaisse first and who makes it best. With bold one-upmanship, Marseille pulls a lobster out of its hat with this legend: Venus first cooked up bouillabaisse there for her husband, Vulcan, and she seasoned it liberally with saffron, supposedly a sedative. Vulcan ate until he was immensely satisfied and then fell into a deep sleep. While Vulcan slept, Venus slipped out for a rendezvous with her lover, Mars.

How did Venus happen to be cooking (not to mention sleeping around) in Marseille? The idea is not that far-fetched, since the city's association with the Roman gods came by way of its ancient relationships: It was first settled around 600 BCE, by Greeks who gave it the name Massalia. When Rome conquered Greece and vastly expanded its realm, the residents of Massalia allied with Rome and benefited not only from their new mercantile association but also from the transition from Greek to Roman gods. For example, Aphrodite was replaced by her Roman equivalent, Venus, goddess of love and beauty (if not fidelity) and bouillabaisse. Also note that among the three critical flavorings of bouillabaisse — saffron, fennel, and orange zest — saffron was thought to be not only a soporific but also an aphrodisiac.

Though Marseille may have hosted the original bouillabaisse, the more significant claim is that it is home to the best bouillabaisse. Julia Child did not dispute that, nor did Alice B. Toklas. In *French Provincial Cooking*, Elizabeth David lists seven things that everyone interested in the theory and the practice of cooking bouillabaisse should know, and number 1 is: "It is useless attempting to make a bouillabaisse away from the shores of the Mediterranean."[7] In *A Book of Mediterranean Food*, David evades the danger of pedantry by not offering her own recipe. Instead, she writes: "The recipe for Bouillabaisse is already widely known," and she defers to Jean-Baptiste Reboul's *La Cuisinière Provençale* of 1895, quoting his comment that "the serving of Bouillabaisse as it is done at Marseille, under perfect conditions, requires at least seven or eight guests."[8] Although she does not include the forty types of fish that Reboul listed as suitable ingredients to choose from, she does quote his remark that nine out of ten cookbooks will give incorrect information. His example of such an error is that all the fish should be cooked together rapidly for fifteen minutes. Reboul suggests: "To make a rich Bouillabaisse one can first prepare a fish *bouillon* with the heads of the fish which are to go into the Bouillabaisse."[9] Strain the liquid from that and use it to briefly cook the fish you want to serve with the soup. In many recipes, that fish is removed from the broth with a slotted spoon. After the hot broth is ladled (over bread) into individual bowls, the fish may be either arranged on top of each serving or passed around separately, along with a sauce called *rouille*.

La Rascasse

If it seems that there are as many recipes for bouillabaisse as there are fish in the sea, nonetheless there is just one fish that French connoisseurs insisted was key to an authentic brew: *rascasse*. From Reboul and the original *Larousse Gastronomique* in 1938 (in which *rascasse* is the sine qua non) to the journalist and food writer Waverley Root, it was a simple conviction. If Julia

Child did not include *rascasse* it wasn't because she didn't know she should, it was because her recipes were for Americans, and as every French chef insisted, *rascasse* was to be found only in the Mediterranean ...

Until October 27, 1962, when "The Soul of Bouillabaisse," by A. J. Liebling, appeared in the *New Yorker* — appropriately enough in the department called Onward and Upward with the Arts. "Ever since 1918, when I ate my first bouillabaisse — an event that in my mind overshadowed the end of the First World War," Liebling writes,

> I have been hearing from French waiters and cooks that it is impossible to produce the genuine article in this country, because the essential ingredient is missing. In memory, that initiatory bouillabaisse — at Mouquin's, on Sixth Avenue — remains impossible to ameliorate, but Roberto, the Mouquin waiter with the grenadier mustache, informed me that the dish, although sufficiently successful, was but a *succédané*, or substitute. "It lacks *la rascasse*," he said, "It is like a watch without a mainspring. The *rascasse* does not exist except in the Mediterranean."[10]

Much later — in fact, not long before this article appeared in print — while eating lunch at The Lobster on West 45th Street, an establishment that had taken bouillabaisse off the menu because too many clients impugned its authenticity, Liebling told his friend Samuel B. McDowell, a zoologist with ichthyologic interests, about *rascasse*. McDowell took on the challenge and attacked the subject with the deftness of Sherlock Holmes and the ferocity of a shark. First he was able to recognize it as one of the scorpion fishes, the most poisonous of which is the stonefish — which has two venom sacs attached to each of its thirteen spines. Numerous varieties of *rascasses*, including scorpion fishes, are available to the residents of North America, though if landed they are not regularly kept by fishermen. McDowell conjectured that probably all *rascasses* were somewhat poisonous, having a substance that lowers a human's blood pressure. This led to speculation that the venom rather than the saffron may have been what put Vulcan to sleep, and that it might also be why the chefs of Marseille considered *rascasse* indispensable. The most damaging information that

McDowell provided (from the perspective of Franco-American relations) was a "shocking discovery." He wrote Liebling: "It is my very painful duty to report that the French have known all the time that we have *rascasse* in America."[11] As evidence he cited an entry in the fourth volume of the monumental and authoritative *Natural History of Fish* by Georges Cuvier and Achille Valenciennes, published in Paris in 1829.

Waverley Root's *The Food of France* was originally published in 1958, before Liebling and McDowell exploded the *rascasse* myth. Root may well be one of the very few people — perhaps the only one — to have actually tasted *rascasse* by itself. He describes it as a "coarse fish, armed with spines, which lives in holes in the rocks, and would be allowed to stay there were it not for bouillabaisse."[12] Though it doesn't taste very good by itself, Root says it seems to act as a catalyst, bringing out the best of the other flavors in the pot.

Root's exploration of the cuisine of Provence, "the most magical of all the provinces of France,"[13] is appreciative, clear-eyed, and straightforward about bouillabaisse. He treats it at great length and is unafraid to confess that, though many people consider Marseille the "bouillabaisse capital of the world," he has "not personally had the good luck to encounter a particularly remarkable"[14] meal of it there: "The best bouillabaisse that I can recall eating on the Riviera I had at the Voile d'Or in Saint-Jean-Cap-Ferrat; but the best in my entire eating career was served to me, not on the Riviera, and not even in France but, however extraordinary it may seem, in New York — at the Restaurant du Midi, before society discovered it, when it was still a rendezvous for French sailors."[15]

That, too, is shocking, but then so is Liebling's elevation of the bouillabaisse at Mouquin's in New York above all others. That two widely traveled and widely respected connoisseurs of good eating suggest that New York bouillabaisse is better than any other is sacrilege (at least to the French). Still, their frankness is a kind of balm. And their plunging headfirst into the dispute has the pleasantly astringent flavor of another essential bouillabaisse ingredient, orange zest. This is so especially when Root talks about lobster in French bouillabaisse recipes: "The easiest, and least subtle, way to provoke a discussion guaranteed to end a lifelong friendship forever is to bring up the issue of lobster. There are two chief schools of thought about this. One is that a man who would put lobster in bouillabaisse would poison wells. The other is that a man who would leave it out would starve his children."[16]

Root says he's eaten it both ways, and both were excellent. But he doesn't know which one was the "real" bouillabaisse. (And I thought that lobster was the very reason for making bouillabaisse!)

Before the curtain is drawn on what sounds like the battles of bouillabaisse, there are a few important reflections about this great soup, or stew, that take it outside the sphere of culinary and other sciences. The first, William Makepeace Thackeray's poem "The Ballad of Bouillabaisse," is a sentimental work uncharacteristic of its author, who is best known for his (very long) satires, such as *Vanity Fair*. Thackeray begins by recounting the wonder of being in Paris during his youth and eating at an inn where he enjoyed a bowl of that "rich and wondrous stew." He describes his return — perhaps true, perhaps imaginary — years later to find the place outwardly the same. But the waiter tells him that the friendly innkeeper is dead: "It is the lot of saint and sinner ... What will Monsieur require for dinner?"[17]

Waiting for his bouillabaisse in the corner nook where he used to sit when he was so young he had "scarce a beard" on his face, Thackeray is now "a grizzled, grim old fogy" who calls to mind his young friends and peoples the tavern with them:

I mind me of a time that's gone,
When here I'd sit, as now I'm sitting,
In this same place — but not alone.
A fair young form was nestled near me,
A dear, dear face looked fondly up,
And sweetly spoke and smiled to cheer me
— There's no one now to share my cup.[18]

Thackeray was born in 1811 and stayed in Paris as a young man. He married in 1836, when he became the Paris correspondent for an English newspaper and lived there for a time with his new wife. He wrote "Bouillabaisse" in 1849, several years after she had been institutionalized for mental illness. Thackeray was not yet forty when he described himself as "a grizzled, grim old fogy" — if, that is, he is speaking of himself. And if so, it is not hard to imagine him mourning his wife, who, though she ultimately outlived him — he died in 1863 — could no longer be with him.

And here is a different sort of statement, quasi-lyrical, by H. L. Mencken, the sharp-eyed journalist and literary and social critic, who included bouillabaisse in his list of the best things in the world: "But all the charming and beautiful things, from the Song of Songs, to bouillabaisse, and from the nine Beethoven symphonies to the Martini cocktail, have been given to humanity by men who, when the hour came, turned from tap water to something with color in it, and more in it than mere oxygen and hydrogen."[19] It may be a bow to drinking men, but it is also an ode to bouillabaisse, which is elevated to the level of the best poetry, music, and spirits.

While as down-to-earth as anyone can be, M. F. K. Fisher goes far beyond recipes and ingredients in her writing on food. She is known as one of the greatest food writers of our time, and W. H. Auden, one of the most noteworthy poets of our time, said of her, "I do not know of anyone in the United States today who writes better prose."[20] Mary Frances Kennedy Fisher was born in Michigan in 1908 and died in California in 1992, after a lifetime of travel and writing. She adored Marseille and wrote as lovingly of its vices as of its beauties. She refers more or less in passing to a "majestic" bouillabaisse she'd eaten many years earlier and cannot say whether it was especially good or just "one more bouillabaisse." She confesses that she never became either passionate about or devoted to that stew, which she had eaten only four or five times since.[21]

But the essay in which the majesty of that earlier meal is revealed tells the story as a wash of citrus juice reveals secret writing in invisible ink. The time was 1932, when she, her husband, and her young sister were reluctantly leaving Marseille:

We ate lunch before the boat sailed at a restaurant on the Old Port in Marseille. Al and I had often been there before, and Norah, who was unusually acute about flavors, almost like a French child, was excited at the prospect of one final orgy of real bouillabaisse . . . The bouillabaisse sent up its own potent saffrony steam. We mopped and dunked at its juices, and sucked a hundred strange dead creatures from their shells. We toasted many things, and often, but ourselves most of all.[22]

It is not the authenticity or contents of bouillabaisse and other meals she eloquently describes so much as the experience of eating—in time and place and history.

Beyond Bouillabaisse

Julia Child's remark about bouillabaisse—that you can make as dramatic a production of it as you like—brings the theatricality of certain meals to mind.

As frequently demonstrated, the very act of putting a lobster in the pot is melodramatic. Once it exits the pot, eating it, however great the pleasure, falls somewhere between comedy and burlesque. Many restaurants serve it on paper placemats with graphically illustrated instructions on how to eat the beast in question. And they provide bibs. That, however, is a far cry for one of the last century's most famous lobster meals.

To the surprise and scorn of many, one of America's highly respected food authorities, the *New York Times* food writer Craig Claiborne, once had a meal that scandalized a good many of his admirers. Auctioned off on behalf of public television and sponsored by American Express, it was a "sky's the limit" dinner for two anywhere in the world. Claiborne won it for $300. He chose to eat at Chez Denis in Paris, a restaurant not well known but well thought of by those who were in the know, and he invited his colleague Pierre Franey to join him. They dined there on November 9, 1975. That meal has become notorious as the $4,000 dinner. The list and description of what was served—wines and champagne, savories, consommé and other soups, tarts and parfaits with mushrooms, truffles, sweetbreads, mousses, oysters, fish, fowls, beef and other meats, and so on—is itself a tour de force.

Staying on point, I will mention specifically that the meal included lobsters in "cardinal red sauce"[23] laden with truffles. Off point, and off-putting to me, was the *ortolans en brochettes*, explained as "small birds, which dine on berries throughout their brief lives, roasted whole on skewers with head on and without cleaning except for the feathers. The birds are fat as butter. Even the bones, except for the tiny leg bones, are chewed and swallowed. There is one bird to one bite."

Claiborne, still in Europe, was surprised to see his article on the meal run on the front page of the *New York Times*. By the time two weeks had passed, the paper had received almost five hundred letters to the editor about the story. The consensus ran four to one against Claiborne's meal. That constitutes a very bad review. The story caused indignation and outrage — which is not surprising.[24]

Craig Claiborne's *The New York Times Cook Book*, published in 1961, was the cookbook many couples of that era received as a wedding gift. It often became so tattered that it had to be replaced. For some of Claiborne's followers, it was difficult not to hold a grudge about that $4,000 meal, or to think of *ortolans*. If Claiborne had a chance, he probably wouldn't have such an extravagant meal again. At least, I hope so. Especially because, with Claiborne's help, I was able to end a wild lobster chase for lobster à la Française that began with *The Alice B. Toklas Cook Book*. The pursuit involved a lobster that, when finally found, was in an haute cuisine costume drama in which the costume *was* the drama.

Even though the most notorious entry is hashish fudge, lobsters do hold pride of place among the menus, meals, and several recipes recorded in *The Alice B. Toklas Cook Book*. On the first page of the second chapter, titled "Food in French Homes," is the menu for a lunch party at which Toklas and Stein were guests. They drank rare wines, and the table was set with the finest linens and most beautiful crystal, porcelain, and silver. The French hostess, we are told, was well known, and her food was famous, though we are not told her name — but that's not the mystery. It was in the menu:

Menu

Aspic de Foie Gras
Salmon Sauce Hollandaise
Hare à la Royale
Hearts of Artichokes à la Isman Bavaldy
Pheasants Roasted with Truffles
Lobster à la Française
Singapore Ice Cream
Cheese
Berries and Fruit[25]

The only items in this feast for which recipes are provided are the artichokes — which the writer Janet Malcolm tried heroically to follow without any luck at all — and the Singapore Ice Cream, as decadent (it is basically sugar, egg yolks, and cream flavored with vanilla, ginger, and pistachio nuts) as any decadent chocolate cake.

Why no recipe for lobster à la Française? Is it just too commonplace? But though I searched high and low — including in Julia Child, Waverley Root, *Larousse Gastronomique*, and on Google (unable to find an exact match, Google offered an astonishing substitute: *petits pois à la Française*) — I could not find it. I thought I was getting close when I discovered *Things a Lady Would Like to Know Concerning Domestic Management and Expenditure*, a book written by Henry Southgate and published in 1875. Southgate could be trussed for his patronizing adages about women, but he does have a notation about lobster *à la mode française*: "Pick the meat from the shell, and cut it up into small square pieces. Put the stock, cream, and seasoning into a stewpan, add the lobster, and let it simmer gently for six minutes. Serve it in the shell, and have a border of puff paste. Cover it with bread-crumbs, place small pieces of butter over, and brown before the fire."[26]

This could not be the classy dish that Alice and Gertrude ate, but the lobster shell as a serving container was a clue, reminding me of two vintage items in my lobster collection.

First is the aforementioned 1948 Helen Hokinson cartoon in which one of the four matronly ladies asks the waiter, who is patiently waiting to take their orders, "What do they call it when they take everything out of the lobster then put it all back again?"

And second is a book discovered at the take-it-or-leave-it book shed at our town's recycling center. From 1968 to about 1971, Time-Life Books published a series of illustrated books called Foods of the World. The one I found is *Classic French Cooking*, by Craig Claiborne and Pierre Franey, and it has a photo — spread across two eight-by-eleven-inch pages — of a platter with two surreally luminous red lobsters facing one another, as if in a tête-à-tête. Rising behind their heads, a small bouquet of lettuce holds a carved tomato containing lemon wedges, which in turn hold a cluster of what look like black olives, surmounted by a fancy, regal ornament.

Homard à la Parisienne, from Craig Claiborne and Pierre Franey,
Classic French Cooking (New York: Time-Life Books, 1970).

This, Claiborne writes, is the "stately," "classic" *homard à la Parisienne*.[27] And I believe — I'll even stake one of my next lobster claws on it — it is also the elusive lobster à la Française.

However . . . no recipe. Again.

When published, it turns out, the illustrated volume was packaged together with a smaller-format, spiral-bound recipe book. My search far and wide for the recipe book ended really luckily when I walked into a local second-hand bookstore, and there it was — tucked in the original cardboard sleeve and still paired with the illustrated narrative. Having paid nothing for the first book, I considered the pair a bargain.

The text of *Recipes: Classic French Cooking* is single-spaced and in small print, and *homard à la Parisienne* covers four full pages! The first step, designed to prevent the lobster's tail from curling under when cooked, today brings the unspeakable to mind: tie each live lobster in turn to a board the length and width of its body and lower it into boiling court bouillon.

Essentially, *homard à la Parisienne*, or Toklas's lobster à la Française, is cold poached lobster with, as the Hokinson lady says, everything taken out and put back in, though what the cut-open shell is filled with in this case is *salade russe* — finely cut vegetables in mayonnaise. Then sliced medallions of lobster are carefully arranged in overlapping discs above the salad. Next the shells and their contents are twice glazed with aspic and chilled — that explains the supernatural radiance of the dish. The platter is garnished with artichoke bottoms, tomatoes, fancy deviled eggs, and truffles. Imagine it, the Madame de Pompadour and Marie Antoinette of lobsters for Alice and Gertrude.

If you only see the photograph and read the brief description in *Classic French Cooking*, you'll never know that the lobsters were tied on a board to be cooked so their tails wouldn't curl under as they usually do, or that they were propped up on loaves of stale bread to give the conversational head-to-head effect. Or realize that the "black olives" below the crowning ornament is actually one large black truffle.

And if you only read the recipe book, you won't find yourself caught short by a whim which the step-by-step instructions fail to mention: in the photograph, those lobster medallions are decorated with a tiny black dots cut from a truffle (the photographer's editorial touch, perhaps); this creates a maddening illusion that wild lobster eyes are staring at you — a subversive *trompe l'oeil* that would have called forth Gertrude Stein's well-known hearty roar of laughter.

But when Toklas sat down for lunch and contemplated this theatrical and time-consuming production — this lavishly, vastly overdressed lobster set before her — I believe that she would not have seen the eyes of a vengeful crustacean, but rather those of the weary chef. For, as Toklas observed in her book, "many first-rate women cooks have tired eyes and a wan smile."[28] To Toklas, however, that look was not a discouraging one. On the contrary, it was a great encouragement, "a happy omen" of the meal to come.

13 Lobster Onstage
Recipes

Even in a perfect world there would not and should not be a definitive recipe for bouillabaisse. We should have freedom of choice, excluding the omission of lobster. The best course of action is to follow an admirable, trustworthy authority, so here is the poet of appetites, as she's been called: M. F. K. Fisher. Her bouillabaisse recipe was published in *The Cooking of Provincial France* in 1968,[1] which was part of the same Time-Life series that carried Claiborne's "stately" *homard à la Parisienne*.

Fisher's bouillabaisse has four parts: (1) stock, or court bouillon; (2) soup that is made by cooking lobster and fish in the strained court bouillon; (3) *croûtes*, rounds of toasted French bread flavored with olive oil and garlic; and (4) rouille, a peppery hot sauce served as a side dish. Both the *croûtes* and the rouille can be prepared while the court bouillon and soup are cooking.

An Adaptation of M. F. K. Fisher's Bouillabaisse[2]

COURT BOUILLON
2 cups thinly sliced onions
1 cup thinly sliced leeks (or another cup of onions)
¾ cup olive oil
8 cups water or 2 cups dry white wine and 6 cups water
2 pounds fish heads, bones and trimmings [or equivalent in whole fish]
3 pounds coarsely chopped ripe tomatoes (about 6 cups)
½ cup fresh fennel or ½ teaspoon dried fennel seeds, crushed
1 teaspoon finely chopped garlic
1 three-inch strip fresh orange peel
1 teaspoon dried thyme
2 parsley sprigs
1 bay leaf

¼ teaspoon crushed saffron threads

salt to taste

freshly ground black pepper to taste

In a heavy 4- to 6-quart saucepan, cook onions (and leeks, if used) in oil over low heat, stirring frequently, for 5 minutes. They should be tender but not brown (additional onions may be substituted for the leeks). Add liquids, fish, tomatoes, herbs, and seasonings, and cook uncovered over moderate heat for 30 minutes.

Strain the liquid through a large, fine sieve into a soup pot or kettle, pressing with the back of a spoon to extract juices before discarding remaining solids.

SOUP

2 lobsters, 1½-pounds each, cut up and cracked[3]

1½ pounds each of three kinds of firm white fish cut into 2-inch
serving pieces (choose from halibut, red snapper, bass, haddock,
Pollack, hake, cod, yellow pike, lake trout, whitefish, rockfish, etc.)

1 eel, cut in 2-inch pieces (optional)

2 pounds live mussels (optional)

2 pounds fresh or frozen sea scallops cut in halves or quarters (optional)

Bring the strained court bouillon to a boil over high heat. Add the lobster. Boil briskly for 5 minutes, add the fish (and eel, if you wish), and cook another 5 minutes. Finally add the mussels and scallops (optional), and boil for 5 minutes longer. Taste for seasoning.

CROÛTES

12 to 16 1-inch thick slices of French bread

2 teaspoons olive oil

1 garlic clove, cut

1 cup grated, imported Swiss cheese or Swiss and freshly grated
Parmesan combined

Preheat the oven to 325 degrees. Spread the slices of bread in one layer on a baking sheet and bake for 15 minutes. With a pastry brush, lightly coat both sides of each slice with olive oil. Then turn the slices over and bake for another 15 minutes, or until the bread is completely dry and lightly browned. Rub each slice with the cut garlic and set aside.[4]

ROUILLE

2 small green peppers, seeded and cut into small squares
1 dry chili pepper, or a few drops Tabasco added to the finished sauce
1 cup water
2 canned pimentos, drained and dried
4 garlic cloves, coarsely chopped
6 tablespoons olive oil
1 to 3 tablespoons fine, dry bread crumbs

In a 6- to 8-cup saucepan, simmer green peppers and chili pepper (optional) in 1 cup of water for 10 minutes, or until they are tender. Drain thoroughly and dry with paper towels. Mash peppers, pimentos, and garlic to a smooth paste, using either a mortar and pestle or a mixing bowl and wooden spoon. Slowly beat in olive oil and enough bread crumbs to make the sauce thick enough to hold its shape in a spoon. Taste and season with Tabasco if you have omitted the chili pepper.

Alternate: Combine peppers, pimento, garlic, and olive oil in a blender. Blend at low speed until smooth, adding more oil if the blender clogs. With a rubber spatula, transfer the sauce to a bowl and stir in enough crumbs to make it thick enough to hold its shape in a spoon. Taste and season with Tabasco if you have omitted the chili pepper.

FINAL ASSEMBLY

When the soup is ready, take the seafood out of the soup with a slotted spoon and put it on a heated platter. Thin the rouille with 2 or 3 teaspoons of soup and put it into a gravy boat. Transfer the soup into a large tureen, then return the seafood to the soup. At the table, place a *croûte* in each individual soup bowl, ladle soup over it, and arrange seafood on top. Pass the rouille separately.

Serves 8 to 10.

This bouillabaisse recipe inspires the imagination of rich aromas. Orange rind, fennel, and saffron especially are so potent that the combination is intoxicating, to say nothing of the pungency of fish and lobster cooking, and the yeasty, garlicky, olive oily smell of the *croûtes*. It makes us realize that recipes should be read carefully, not only to prepare for the complexity or simplicity of a dish but also to examine its plausibility with all the senses. It's not just a question of smell: there is also, for example, the sound of the onions cooking, the color of the tomatoes and green peppers, the tactility of pressing the court bouillon ingredients through a sieve to extract the liquid or mashing pimentos, green peppers, and garlic to make a paste. And, it should go without saying, the taste.

That does not mean you have to follow the recipe through word for word, or ingredient for ingredient. John Thorne has written: "I don't follow recipes; I interact with them."[5] Thorne has an avid following for his newsletter, *Simple Cooking*, and his six published books. Mark Bittman calls Thorne "the antidote to trendy food writing, a literate man who produces pleasurable, instructive, even profound prose, along with satisfying recipes."[6] Thorne writes: "Surely, an important aspect of any recipe is its use as a tool for understanding other recipes. The most familiar example of this, perhaps, is when one recipe is compared to another in a search for the 'perfect' version of a dish."[7]

As for all those bouillabaisse recipes, for the "authentic" Marseille bouillabaisse, *Larousse Gastronomique* lists eleven essential fish, including *rascasse* and spiny lobster. Crabs and other shellfish are listed as a separate category.[8] Craig Claiborne cuts to the chase with his list of seafood ingredients: one small lobster; twelve each of mussels, shrimp, and scallops; and a pound of red snapper or cod.[9] Mark Bittman, who now writes about food for the *New York Times*, pares this down even more to about one pound of almost any seafood (like monkfish, cod, scallops, squid, or shrimp) for "Bouillabaisse with Fennel over Grits."[10] You might say those arguments are challenging one another, as Thorne would have them do. When he cooks, Thorne is likely to appropriate and improvise, "interact" and quarrel with a recipe that captures his fantasy. After a "lifetime of looking through recipes," he writes, "the new recipe that will interest me the most will be the one that I can use to give shape to some nebulous longing that is already alive and stirring within me. This might mean that the true test of a recipe lies somewhere else than in its making."[11]

Like the lobster, the best recipe is in the mind, memory, and emotion of its maker.

Our Darling Clementine

If you have heard of Clementine Paddleford, her name is hard to forget. I had heard of her but couldn't remember why. Who was she? The subtitle of her biography, *Hometown Appetite*, sounds almost accusatory: *The Story of Clementine Paddleford, the Forgotten Food Writer Who Chronicled How America Ate*.[12] Is that our fault or hers? Or is it that times change and we need new heroes every few years?

For many years, Paddleford (1898–1967) was the food editor of the *New York Herald Tribune* — before its demise in 1966, the main rival of the *New York Times* — and of the *Tribune*'s magazine supplement, *This Week*. She was also the author of several books and a multitude of articles in the popular press. In 1953 *Time* referred to her as the best-known food editor in the United States. At that time she had yet to finish her masterwork, *How America Eats*, the culmination of twelve years spent "criss-crossing the United States as roving Food Editor for This Week Magazine — my assignment, tell 'How America Eats.' I have traveled by train, plane, automobile, by mule back, on foot — in all over 800,000 miles."[13]

It was as "June lay gently on the shoulder"[14] that her Maine lobster quest began, in Rockland, which she reminds us — could we ever forget? — is the lobster capital of the United States. From Rockland's harbor she went on a deepwater lobster fishing excursion. At the saltwater farm in Pennellville, Maine, of Robert P. Tristram Coffin, professor of English at Bowdoin College and Pulitzer Prize–winning poet, she inquired about his lobster stew:

"About the recipe, Dr. Coffin," I had my pencil in hand.

"You must know the history of each lobster you cook," said my host, "But if you must pick your lobsters at the local market, the only alternative is to get them lively. Cook in Maine sea water," the Doctor directed.[15]

Here is an adaptation of Coffin's recipe as presented by Paddleford.

Dr. Coffin's Lobster Stew

12 medium lobsters (about 1¼ pounds each)
2 cups Maine sea water or 2 cups fresh water with one tablespoon salt
½ pound butter
3 quarts milk
2 pints heavy cream

Put lobsters in boiling water shell side down so they will cook in their own juices. Cover tightly, steam at high heat 10 to 15 minutes. Remove meat from shell while hot. Remove and discard intestinal vein and lungs. Let picked meat cool overnight.

Next day melt butter in a large pot, add lobster meat and cook only until meat and butter bubble. Then put heat on low and add 1 quart of the milk, "stirring clockwise constantly to keep the mixture from coagulating." When small bubbles begin to form add the second quart of milk a little at a time. Bring to a full froth then immediately stir in the third quart of milk and continue stirring clockwise. Let come to a boil and add 2 pints of cream. Simmer for a few minutes — *do not boil* — then remove from the heat.

Cool 12 to 24 hours allowing flavor to develop. Reheat before serving. Season to taste.

Yield: 10 to 12 portions.[16]

Coffin grew up in Maine and loved and wrote much about that state. He died in 1955. It's only fair to report that in 1944 his own version of the lobster stew recipe was published as a chapter of his book, *Mainstays of Maine*. And it's only right to say that this chapter comes as close to a Paddleford's recipe — or any conventional recipe — as *Paradise Lost* is to *Mary Had a Little Lamb*. It is a warm-hearted and extravagant twelve-page appreciation of "the most moral creature in the universe," the lobster itself, followed by exacting instructions for how to make a stew of it, including: "And this law you must observe above all: Only a half cupful of water to a whole kettle of lobsters."[17] It's way beyond a recipe, but what is it? It's a parable done up in happy, honorific rhetoric.

$4,000?

Before Craig Claiborne and Pierre Franey decided on the restaurant for their "sky's the limit" feast in 1975, they went to Paris to scout out Chez Denis anonymously. They were well pleased. One of the courses they enjoyed was a *chiffonade* of lobster. Claiborne described the dish as "a salad of cold lobster, cubed foie gras, a touch of cognac and, we suspect, cayenne, and a tarragon mayonnaise flavored with tomato, tossed with lettuce."[18]

Chiffonade refers to leafy greens like lettuce and herbs that are sliced thinly into strips. It sounds like an adaptable recipe, and in fact some twelve years later, on June 10, 1987, Franey wrote a column in the *New York Times* describing a quite different lobster *chiffonade*. The lobster preparation is followed by that of the chiffonade. The following is an adaption of Franey's recipe.

Cold Lobster with Basil Vinaigrette

4 quarts water*
1 tablespoon peppercorns
Salt to taste, if desired
½ teaspoon dried thyme
2 bay leaves
¼ teaspoon hot red pepper flakes
4 live lobsters, 1½-pound each
10 or 12 leaves fresh basil, rinsed and patted dry
½ cup olive oil
¼ cup finely chopped shallots
2 tablespoons balsamic vinegar
Three-Salad Chiffonade

*Sea water is best, but omit peppercorns, salt, and herbs if sea water is used.

Use a kettle large enough to hold four lobsters and add the water, peppercorns, salt, thyme, bay leaves, and pepper flakes. Cover and bring to a boil then quickly add lobsters, one at a time, and cover the pot again. When the water returns to a boil cook the lobsters for 10 minutes then drain thoroughly. Once the lobsters are cool enough to handle, break off the tails and crack the large claws. Remove the meat, intact if possible, from each tail and claw. Remove as much meat as you can from remaining claw shells. Put meat in a bowl.

Stack the basil leaves and cut them into fine shreds. There should be about ½ cup. Add to the bowl.

Here is the coup de grace for this salad: to serve, cut each piece of tail meat on the bias into ½-inch-thick medallions. Arrange the slices from one lobster tail on a plate. Arrange two of the large pieces of claw meat at the top of the tail to resemble a lobster's shape. Spoon about a quarter of the dressing over the tail and claw meat. Scatter a quarter of the small pieces of lobster meat and basil around. Garnish each side of the tail meat with a quarter of the recipe for three-salad chiffonade (below). Repeat this composition with the meat from each remaining lobster and garnish each with chiffonade.

Three-Salad Chiffonade

1 head radicchio, core removed, about ¼ pound
2 Kentucky limestone lettuces or bibb lettuces, about ¼ pound
½ pound iceberg lettuce, core removed, about ¼ pound
1 sweet red pepper, about ¼ pound
6 tablespoons olive oil
3½ tablespoons red-wine vinegar
Salt to taste, if desired
Freshly ground pepper to taste

Stack and finely shred the radicchio leaves (should make about 2 cups). Place in a large bowl. Repeat this step with the limestone or bibb lettuces and the iceberg lettuce (about 2 cups of each). Prepare about 1 cup of red pepper, sliced into long thin strips, and add to the salad. Dress the salad with oil, vinegar, salt, and pepper, and toss to blend thoroughly.

For lobster dressing, whisk together olive oil, shallots, vinegar, and salt in a small mixing bowl.

Yield: 4 servings.[19]

What about the lobster that was served at the actual dinner for which American Express footed the bill? On the menu it is listed as *gratin de homard,* or lobster in a cardinal red sauce. Claiborne wrote of the meal that "the food itself was generally exemplary, although there were regrettable lapses . . . The lobster in the gratin was chewy and even the sauce could not compensate."[20]

Surely the lobster would have been cooked too long if it ended up chewy. And what is cardinal sauce? As noted in chapter 12, one recipe is to be found in *The Gourmet Cookbook*. An adaptation of it follows.

Sauce Cardinal

2–3 tablespoons fish *fumet* to 2 cups hot fish *velouté*. (*Fumet* is concentrated stock. *Velouté* is a rich white sauce made, in this case, with fish stock and thickened with cream and egg yolks.) Stir in 1 tablespoon chopped butter that is made with lobster shells plus coral or lobster eggs.[21]

Since the eggs are no longer available, they will have to be omitted. Alas, because the red coloring came from the eggs, the sauce will also have to be renamed. Unless, of course, a dash of red vegetable dye is substituted.

Fear and Transcendence

"I am frightened of many things," the writer Steve Almond tells us. The things he lists are "death, Mormons, Stilton cheese, scorpions, Dick Cheney, the freeways of Los Angeles" — all real threats, to be sure. "But I am perhaps most frightened by lobsters," he adds. "The spiny antennae, the armor-plated cephalothorax, the serrated claws — they are, to my way of thinking, giant aquatic cockroaches that can snap your finger off."[22]

A finger, he ought to know (if he's familiar with the works of Stephen King, Salvador Dalí, and Guillaume Lecasble, among others), should be the least of his worries. Surely he's using the finger as a metaphor.

Almond's essay bears the title "Death by Lobster Pad Thai: A Counter-phobic Paean to Friendship, Crustaceans, and Oral Transcendence." The adventure he describes begins as he is on his way to visit friends in Maine, who traditionally prepare an annual feast of lobster pad Thai. This time, for the first time, he is asked to stop en route and pick up four exceptionally huge lobsters, weighing four and a half pounds each. Those who find Almond's anxiety excessive must understand, he says, that "the true phobia is marked not by the threat of actual harm, but by a fantasy in which the subject imagines harm into being."[23] Yet another signifier of how lobsters and people invade each other's lives.

The meal's preparation is a raucous event washed down with beer, bad jokes, and bizarre ruminations: "It's a strange thing to see the source of your phobia systematically disemboweled. It made me feel guilty again. These lobsters were senior citizens after all. They might have been grandparents. For all I knew they had been involved in the labor movement."[24] Senior citizens, grandparents, union supporters. Dinner!

The source of the lobster pad Thai recipe is a well-known chef, restaurateur, and winner of the James Beard Award, Jasper White. White published *Lobster at Home* in 1998. The book's first chapters are a useful primer on lobster fishing, anatomy, cooking, and disassembly, and the implements needed. The last chapter has recipes from individuals White considers great chefs, and it is there that White discusses Gerald Clare's lobster pad Thai. According to White, it is "off the charts."[25] Here is an adaptation of the recipe.

Lobster Pad Thai

6 live 1½-pound hard shell select lobsters[26]
1 package rice stick noodles, medium width (14 ounces)
4 tablespoons peanut oil
3 tablespoons minced fresh ginger
3 tablespoons minced fresh lemongrass
1 tablespoon chili paste (more if brave, less if timid)
1 tablespoon shrimp paste
4 tablespoons sugar
2 tablespoons fish sauce
juice of 2 limes, plus 1 whole for garnish cut into 6 wedges
juice of 1 lemon
1 bunch scallions, finely chopped
1 large egg, beaten with 2 tablespoons water
3 tablespoons chopped fresh cilantro
3 tablespoons chopped Thai basil, plus 6 sprigs for garnish
1 cup dry roasted unsalted peanuts, ground
1 package bean sprouts (12 ounces)

Fill a pot large enough to cook three lobsters about two-thirds full of water. Add enough salt to make it distinctly salty — as much as ¼ cup salt, or alternately use sea water — and bring to a full boil. Place 3 lobsters in the pot and cook for exactly 4½ minutes. Using tongs, remove them and repeat with remaining three lobsters and allow them to cool.

When lobsters are cool enough to handle, break off the claws with the knuckles attached and remove all their meat. Holding the carapace with one hand, use the other hand to break the tail away, then split the tail in half lengthwise to remove and dispose of the intestine. Cut each half-tail into two pieces. Break the antennae off the lobster carcasses and save for garnish. Discard the green tomalley but reserve the rest of the carcasses for soup.[27] Cover the lobster meat with plastic wrap and refrigerate until ready to use.

To soften rice stick noodles, soak them in warm water for about 20 minutes. Drain well.

Heat the oil over a high flame in a wok or 12-inch sauté pan. Working quickly, add lobster and stir fry for 2 minutes. Then add ginger and lemongrass and cook for 1 minute. Next add chili paste, shrimp paste, and sugar and cook for 1 minute. Lower heat slightly.

Add noodles along with fish sauce, lime juice, and lemon juice. Add scallions and egg and cook 1 or 2 minutes longer, being careful *not to scramble* the egg. Remove from the heat and allow to sit a minute before serving.

Divide pad Thai among 6 plates; distributing the lobster evenly: 2 claws, 2 knuckles, and 4 pieces of tail meat each. Sprinkle each plate with cilantro, chopped basil, ground peanuts, and sprouts. Garnish with a lime wedge and sprigs of Thai basil and crisscross the lobster antennae over the top.

Serves 6 as a main course.[28]

Mysteries

Does "death" in the title of Almond's story refer to his fear or the lobster's fate — or both? Dropping lobsters into boiling water troubles so many people that humane alternatives have become worth their weight in, well, lobsters. Trevor Corson, author of *The Secret Life of Lobsters*, recommends putting the creature in a freezer for fifteen or twenty minutes, long enough to numb it, "then flip it over and split the main body section of the animal in half with the swift stroke of a large kitchen knife."[29] But isn't hypothermia as bad as boiling water? Who can really know what lobsters feel? We don't yet, Corson agrees.

As far as Virginia Rich is concerned, people are the victims of murder and lobsters rapidly boiled are a reward for those who survive to solve the crime. Rich leads the way in the invention of culinary mysteries that include recipes, a literary subgenre that has become popular. When I stopped by the Waldoboro public library to pick up a copy of her *The Baked Bean Supper Murders*, one of the librarians mentioned two or three other authors with the same specialty and another mystery writer whose fans had persuaded her to include recipes in her future works. My informant had tried and enjoyed several crime writers' recipes.

Rich is a journalist and food writer, and her crime solver is a widow named Eugenia Potter. *The Baked Bean Supper Murders* is set in a Maine fishing village called Northcutt's Harbor. The book is dedicated "to Aunt Ada and Aunt Mary and Aunt Emily, to Aunt Tillie, to Aunt Bernice and Aunt Dorothy and Aunt Louise, and to Aunt Stella Hunter." So be prepared not only for good recipes and a clever plotline, but also for many cupfuls of good humor. The story opens at the Grange Hall, where the line of people waiting to be seated for the baked bean supper stretches from the outside doors to the road. Recipe pages in my library book, I should mention, are lightly splashed with small brown drip stains. Many of the recipes are on the inside cover pages of the front and back of the book. Others are part of the story, such as the account of Happenstance Bay Fish Stew, Mrs. Potter's narration of a dinner she cooked that sounds like her personal bouillabaisse . . . with lobster: "Today's catch — a half for each guest and an extra for good measure — fresh from the ocean, hard-shelled, lively, protesting and perfect."[30] Also local clams and haddock, onions, garlic, canned tomatoes, and even some bottled clam juice — it is, as she says, a "forgiving recipe" — and a good pinch of saffron ordered from New York.

Three murders are committed in this small, generally friendly village, and Mrs. Potter is very nearly the next victim. The perpetrator starts to asphyxiate her with a pillow before he is interrupted by one of her friends paying a visit, at which point the murderer manages to escape. It is later, while several friends take turns keeping protective watch over Mrs. Potter, that she tells them, "You know . . . I never heard anything much said about lobster pie, all the years we've lived here." The outcome is an event to rival a Pillsbury bake-off in the quality if not quantity of submissions to "the great lobster pie cook-off." Mrs. Potter gives the blue ribbon to all four versions of the pie: the classic version, a quiche, a lobster seasoned with sherry and paprika in cream sauce, and a puff pastry filled with lobster salad and baked.

For us the winner will be an adaptation of . . .

Classic Lobster Pie

1 9-inch double-crust pastry shell, unbaked
2–3 cups cooked lobster meat
¼ cup butter
⅓ cup flour
½ teaspoon salt
2 cups fish stock or milk
2 teaspoons chopped onion
1 cup cooked vegetables—carrots, peas, celery, or a combination

Melt butter, add flour and salt, and stir until smooth. Still stirring, gradually add liquid and cook until the sauce is thick. Add onions, vegetables, and lobster. Fill an unbaked pie shell with the mixture and top it with second layer of pastry. Pinch the edges, make slits for steam to escape, and bake at 425 degrees until the crust is nicely browned.

On a Roll

Along Coastal Route 1 in Wiscasset, Maine, is a lobster shack about the size of an XXL walk-in closet. It has a bright red-and-white candy-stripe awning in front and a few tables on the ground in back. A big lobster-red sign above the roof says: Red's *Eats*. But if you're trying to get from here to there during the peak months of summer — especially on a Saturday, the conventional first day of vacation and the standard turnover-day for weekly rentals — all you really see, whether traveling north or south, is bumper-to-bumper traffic for miles. For fifty-three years, a bypass around Wiscasset has been under scrutiny. It is what the magazine *Down East* calls a "Neverending Story."[31]

All that for a lobster roll?

Well, probably not quite. But when you do make it to down-town Wiscasset, the bottleneck is pedestrian, with *thick* pedestrian traffic not just in the street itself but also surrounding the crosswalk, where opportunists take advantage of the cars brought to a standstill by mobs of people trying to get their lobster-roll fix. The line already waiting to place an order at Red's Eats looks infinite.

In their book about sandwiches, Jane and Michael Stern praise the lobster roll at Red's Eats as "perhaps the greatest lobster roll on the coast."[32] The recipe they offer for the lobster roll is, how-ever, courtesy of the Maine Diner in Wells, Maine. Red's is repre-sented in the Sterns' book with a recipe for crab salad roll. In the Sterns' well-known coast-to-coast guide, *Roadfood*, they are sim-ilarly noncommittal about Red's, writing: "Many people believe this shack sells the best lobster rolls anywhere."[33]

Such ambivalence — "perhaps" and "many people" — avoids the argumentative context of the bouillabaisse brouhaha. That's ap-propriate because not only are there fewer contenders for the title of "best" lobster roll, but there are also fewer ingredients in said roll, and not many versions of it to choose from: basically, hot or cold. Cold (with mayonnaise) is easier to eat since hot (with but-ter) tends to soak through the bread and fall apart. Red's piles the chunks of lobster on a buttered, grilled hot dog roll served in a foil wrapper. Mayonnaise on the side.

John Thorne has lived, cooked, remembered, and written a lot in Maine. He has left it and returned more than a few times since his childhood, when he summered at his grandparents' home there. He had moved to Maine about 1980 when, with a $100 in-come tax rebate, he began printing and selling pamphlets, starting with "A Treatise on Onion Soup" and "The English Muffin." His newsletter *Simple Cooking* led to a book of the same title, published in 1987; the newsletter has been sporadic since issue number 92 was published in 2004.

Considering Thorne's interest in simple cooking and good Maine food, I hoped to find in his work a straightforward recipe for the lobster roll. Instead I read this:

> When I first moved to Maine, I was puzzled by how easy it was to buy picked crab and how utterly impossible to buy picked lobster. Puzzled because, as good as a crab roll can be, lobster rolls are better. But I won't, can't pick a lobster to make one ... it's just too much labor for too short—however ecstatic—a moment of pleasure. No, the homemade lobster roll is the product of leftover lobster—which means that these days it's just one more traditional Maine lobster dish we rarely see.[34]

Anyone who boils lobster at home to serve straight (dipped in butter, with or without lemon) can easily make lobster rolls the next day *if* there is leftover cooked lobster—which, as Thorne says, is rarely the case. Just chop it, mix it with mayonnaise, toast the hot dog rolls (with a touch of butter, if you like), fill them, and there you go!

What Julia Child said about making bouillabaisse can be said of cooking lobster in general: you can make it as dramatic a production as you like. I find the tastiest lobsters are those that are simply boiled; you just dip the meat in butter and, if you wish, add a touch of lemon. Second best is in a lobster roll. These are also the two simplest lobster meals to serve, in terms of preparation. For lobster drama and even melodrama, I'd suggest going to a restaurant or throwing a party with a lot of friends to pitch in. Like going to the theater, it's more fun if you're not eating lobster alone, and the more the merrier.

Epilogue

Six years have passed since I began to study the lobster, and almost four years have gone by since that freezing day in January 2008 when I watched an eagle fly over the Medomak River, dive, and then disappear as sunset tinted the clouds. I saw but hardly noticed it because I was absorbed by what wasn't there: lobster boats, traps, and buoys, and most of all the lobsters themselves, which had migrated to deeper, calmer, warmer water.

Not that I ever see them in the river, even when they're present in abundance. Still, knowing that they are there, going about their daily lives, is what gives the river its character for much of the year.

Why not the seals? They love to loll on the rocks as the tide recedes, tightly packed side by side, flapping their flippers, and vocalizing. Or the silent sea urchins, mussels, crabs, periwinkles, scallops, and even the armies of little jellyfish, whose excursions take them past our dock from time to time. Not to mention the evasive resident fish: trout, bass, pickerel. Even the crabs, though they are also decapods with claws and taste almost as wonderful as lobsters. Some people prefer crabmeat to lobster. I don't.

No, only the lobster, whether present or absent, haunts our river. Beyond the Medomak, the lobster haunts the arts, fantasy, folklore, cinema, comedy, cuisine, fiction, nonfiction, horror stories, science fiction, history, science, and commerce, of course—every corner of human curiosity and skill. Research has revealed a lot about the behavior of the lobster in and out of its natural environment, but we still think of lobsters as among the strangest creatures in the world—not because they are, but because we make them so.

To Pliny the Elder, the lobster looked like a locust.

To islanders on ancient Seriphos who deified the lobster, it may have symbolized their hero, Perseus.

The biologist Thomas Henry Huxley looked at the lobster and marveled at its bilateral symmetry; it signified to him an aesthetic of science.

John Milton saw that same creature hiding among rocks as an armor-plated hunter, waiting to grab its next meal.

In China and Japan, where the elderly are honored, the curved back of a lobster symbolizes old age and longevity. But the lobster became a token of ferocity in Japanese kabuki theater.

The Holy Scriptures prohibit Jews from eating lobster, but lobsters permeate Jewish humor.

Lobsters are only rarely comedic in the fine arts, but they have symbolized opulence, violence, and misogyny.

They are gangsters, pets, victims, and dancers in literature. Theodore Dreiser used the lobster's predation as a business model in one of his novels.

From ancient Rome to contemporary Rockland, Maine, feasting on lobster ranges from unsurpassable delicacy to gluttonous excess.

Lobsters are portrayed as hybrid monsters and gigantesque creatures larger than whales.

As sexual enticements.

Erotic disasters.

Rock and roll stars and songs.

Creatures of horror and science fiction.

Victims of human plunder and cruelty.

Pilots in space, time travelers.

"We only see what we look for, but we only look for what we can see," as Heinrich Wölfflin wrote.[1] It is also true that we see what we wish to see, or are told to look for. And we see what we do because of everything that contributes to our individuality and our individual frames of reference — everything that makes us part of the place and familial, geographical, social, educational, and cultural time in which we live.

The food writer Alan Davidson singled out one particular type of lobster for its physical attributes:

> If a beauty contest were held in an Asian fish market, the finalists would undoubtedly be some of the numerous spiny lobsters which are found in the Indo-Pacific, especially in the Southeast Asian waters. Their colors . . . do not fade on death — and any-

way they are often sold alive. Unlike the Atlantic lobster, with its sober hue and heavy claws, the spiny lobsters have a fairy-like lightness and rainbow coloration.[2]

His frame of reference: Davidson was a well-traveled British diplomat, who served in the Royal Navy in the Atlantic, the Mediterranean, and the Pacific; and in the diplomatic service in Washington, Cairo, Tunis, and various European cities. He also served as the British ambassador to Laos. His reputation in the culinary world comes from numerous books, including the *Oxford Companion to Food*, *North Atlantic Seafood*, and *Seafood: A Connoisseur's Guide and Cookbook*. The spiny lobster whose good looks he praises is *Panulirus polyphagus*, with "green and brown livery . . . relatively restrained, but pleasingly accentuated by the white cross-bands which mark off the segments of the tail end."[3]

The colored illustrations for *Seafood* are lovely, and *P. polyphagus* is a gem. Even the scientific black-and-white rendering of this species in *Marine Lobsters of the World* is more elegant than most: the antennae rise gracefully above the lobster's head, then arch downward as if designing a heart; while the long, whiplike defensive antennae at rest fall loosely at either side of the carapace, reaching well below the tail fan, and then curl gently in on themselves.[4]

A beauty contest has yet to be held at a fish market as far as I know, and even at its scarlet best, I have not heard of any other lobster, living or dead, described as beautiful. Conceptually Huxley's paragon of symmetry comes close to beauty, but one problem is Huxley's disregard for the asymmetries of *Homarus americanus* and *Homarus gammarus* (or *vulgaris*). I am not referring to the anisotropic molecular structure of chitin, which is invisible to the naked eye, but to the obviously disproportionate sizes of the claws on the lobsters' two front legs — the large, heavy crusher with roughly serrated edges opposing the more streamlined slicer. And there is another problem from a linear perspective: the large claws make these lobsters appear top-heavy and ungainly.

That barely matters in the animal's own environment, where it hunts for prey "nimbly upon the tips of its slender legs," in Francis Herrick's words. When the lobster walks underwater, the size and weight of its claws are inconsequential since they are inactive. The two long antennae or feelers, organs of touch that sprout from the head, wave constantly back and forth, monitoring the surrounding area for any threat that escapes the lobster's vision or its smaller antennules, which are chemical receptors. When it senses danger, the lobster shoots rapidly backward by flexing its abdomen and tail fan, a maneuver called the tail-flip escape behavior. When being pursued, "the lobster rises and flies in another direction, thus zigzagging its way over the bottom until it finds safety in some denser tangle [of seaweed] or rocky crevice," Herrick writes.[5] And if it has to confront the enemy, *then* it raises those big claws in protective defiance.

Once removed from the water, the lobster's eight spindly legs cannot support the weight of its claws and body; it is able to crawl only short distances and with difficulty. This is the source of an Aesop fable about a mother lobster and her daughter who are walking along the beach when the mother chastises the child for walking so crookedly. (In some versions, it is a mother and daughter crab.) The young one asks her mother to demonstrate the proper way to walk, so she might learn by example. The mother takes the lead and, as the daughter observes, moves just as erratically as she had.[6]

This fable illustrates one adage:

Do as I say, not as I do.

And one important lesson:

The lobster never leaves the bottom of its saltwater habitat by choice.

Lobsters are resolutely unlike people. Nevertheless, we look at them and recognize ourselves in what seems like familiar behaviors: fighting for territory, food, and privacy; building shelter; demonstrating bravado; and defending oneself. When it's time to mate, we interpret the event for the lobster as seduction strong enough to change antagonism to compliance. Upon boiling them in water, we imagine their pain as if it had a human equivalent.

To understand lobsters objectively, we structure observations and measurements, and when we cannot observe the animals, we track their movements remotely. We also study characteristics we do not share with them, such as growing new limbs, molting, and the female's long-term storage of sperm until she produces, fertilizes, and finally releases her eggs. Occasionally the information gathered is used to practical advantage, such as prohibiting the capture of "berried" females to protect the future of the species and of the lobster fishery. With or without utilitarian application, lobster knowledge fuels our storytelling.

Ekphrasis

As so often described, lobsters are strange creatures. Strangeness is unsettling, a deviation from normal expectations, like the distortion of looking at oneself in a rippled pool of water or a curved mirror and seeing "This otherness, this / 'Not-being-us'" as in John Ashbery's poem, "Self-Portrait in a Convex Mirror."[7] It is Parmigianino's self-portrait that inspired Ashbery, a portrait painted from Parmigianino's reflection in a convex mirror onto the curved surface of a wooden sphere the same size as the mirror (about nine and a half inches in diameter). Ashbery contemplated Parmigianino's self-portrait for some fifteen years before he wrote his poem about it in the early 1970s. The bowed mirror distorts the reflected image and is mirrored in turn by the curved surface on which it was painted. The effect is mesmerizing: Parmigianino's head and shoulders seem to recede into his studio in the background, while his hand in the foreground appears disproportionately large. It looks like a giant claw:

> The right hand
> Bigger than the head, thrust at the viewer
> And swerving easily away, as though to protect
> What it advertises.[8]

Hand and head seem waterborne, approaching and retreating, the face especially in "a recurring wave of arrival."[9]

I wrote in the introduction that we do not see ourselves only in mirrors. Rather, we see ourselves everywhere and in everything, and — purposefully if not necessarily intentionally — we project ourselves into and onto the world, above ground and under water. Parmigianino used the convex mirror, which allowed several artists — including Jan van Eyck, Anne Vallayer-Coster, and many

Parmigianino (Francesco Mazzola), *Self-Portrait in a Convex Mirror*, circa 1524. Kunsthistorisches Museum, Vienna, Austria. Photo: Foto Marburg / Art Resource, NY.

other still-life painters — to put self-portraits in the background of their compositions. This is a more deft claim of authorship than only a signature because it makes the artist not just a recorder but also a witness to, participant in, and creator of the scene.

Parmigianino took that conceit a great step forward with his self-portrait by becoming the primary subject of the painting. Then, more than four hundred years after the painter took up his brush, the poet took up his pen in a practice known since antiquity as *ekphrasis*, the Greek term for using one artistic medium to describe and discuss another.

In his poem, Ashbery brings Parmigianino's vision to bear on his own life and meditations. The poem is thickly populated — as are the undersea scenarios of Milton, Franco Ferrucci, Bill Holm, and others — with panoramas that bring to life the Jurassic, the aquatic period from which our terrestrial world emerged, and into which both science fiction and forecasts of climate change project its future. It seems right that Ashbery uses swimming and the ocean as descriptive metaphors, though he does not make any allusion to a lobster or any other specific sea creature, with the exception of a whale: Ashbery likens the hand to "a dozing whale on the sea bottom."[10]

Vastly magnified by the curvature of the mirror, the painter's hand has the rounded shape of a whale, but not in relation to the rest of the visible body. Extending Ashbery's concept that the much smaller head and face appear to swim back and forth, and his idea that the hand seems to protect what it advertises, I see a lobster when I look Parmigianino's self-portrait. Ashbery was inspired by Parmigianino to imagine the sea as part of the artist's self-portrait, a filter that leads me to the suggestion of a lobster — not very surprising, considering how many years I've been thinking about lobsters. Many if not most frontal pictures of lobsters show the claws positioned in just the way Parmigianino's hand appears, and the hand and claw are in the same relationship to head and thorax. (There is only one hand/claw in the picture because the artist would have been painting with the other.)

There is a question that has preoccupied and bemused poet, philosopher, anthropologist, and physicist alike: what prevents our world from collapsing from its own weight or falling through space?[11]

An old legend of uncertain origin proclaims that the world rests on the back of an elephant that is, in turn, standing on a great turtle, which stands on another turtle, and so it goes in infinite regress: "Turtles all the way down."

But, as we know, that is not true.

Because it is lobsters.

Besides my own conviction, based on the evidence that is embroidered into the entire tapestry of this book, the only proof I have to offer is a sixteenth-century drawing by Georg (or Joris) Hoefnagel (1542–1601) that was engraved by his son Jacob and published in a collection of their collaborative work two years after

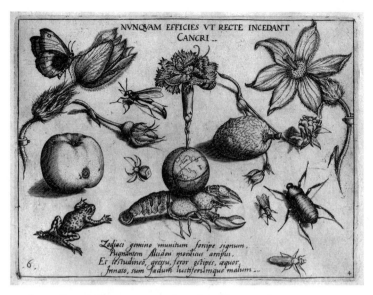

Jacob Hoefnagel after Georg Hoefnagel, *Archetypa studiaque patris*
(Frankfurt, 1592). © The Trustees of the British Museum.

Georg's death: *Archetypa studiaque patris*. Georg Hoefnagel was a
Flemish artist who worked at several European courts, including
that of the Emperor Rudolph II in Prague, known for its enthusiastic embrace of the arts and sciences. Hoefnagel's work combined
the two, being an avid study of nature and eloquent drawings of
plants, insects, and animals with scientific precision: columbine,
tulip, dragonflies, moths, even a cockroach.[12] Not to mention the
lobster in an engraving that is related to the astrological signs.

The title for this particular engraving is taken from Erasmus.
Translated from Latin, it says: "Never can you make it so that
crabs walk straight."[13] Historically lobsters have been substituted
for crabs, and there is no doubt at all that in this illustration it is a
lobster, not a crab — or a turtle — holding up our world.

So it is lobsters, only lobsters, all the way down.

Once we take into account the lobsters' irregular locomotion,
backward and forward, this way and that, it is little wonder that
we must endure prolonged eras of instability in this world of ours.

But consider it philosophically: if they weren't there, it would
only be worse.

ACKNOWLEDGMENTS

Nina and Jim Scott unwittingly started me on the path to this book. They spend their summers in Friendship, Maine, and the rest of the year in Amherst, Massachusetts, where they frequently lead seminars for Five College Learning in Retirement of Western Massachusetts. When my husband, Jack, retired, he and I joined the Scotts' terrific seminar on the subject of lobsters. The text for the course was *The Secret Life of Lobsters*, by Trevor Corson. Everyone in the seminar made a presentation on a lobster-related topic, and mine was a PowerPoint exhibit and discussion of lobsters in art. Who knew it would end this way!

The architectural historian Helen Searing, a cherished friend for over fifty years, not only gave me a unique rope necklace with dangling red lobsters, but she also put me on the trail of Salvador Dalí's *Lobster Telephone*. What a trip that turned out to be.

And how lucky I am to have a Milton scholar for a friend. A few years ago, when the geese were honking madly, Kathleen Swaim smiled and said, "They are 'intelligent of seasons.'" I was puzzled. Then she said, "Milton." The phrase tucked itself somewhere in my brain, buzzing now and then as the weather changed and geese were on the wing again, until the day I learned about the extraordinary marching formation of the migrating spiny lobsters, *Panulirus argus*. Then, thanks to Kathy, I found a Miltonic connection between lobsters and geese.

When Kathy and Margo Culley—the professor who shepherded me through my doctoral studies and a generous, constant friend—visited Maine over the years they brought me lobsters: on a cap or a T-shirt, in books, and masquerading as soft and fuzzy toys. Margo also brought back word of the unforgettable bumper sticker illustrated with a lobster and inscribed with the ironic double-entendre "Say No to Pot!"

Thanks to other friends for their gifts of everything from good ideas and help to tchotchkes: Ann Connolly; Sonia Sofield; Ann Grose; Jill Franks and her father, Lewis; Kathleen Scott; and Shirley Keech. Thanks to all the friends who tolerated my Decapoda obsession. I am grateful to family members, especially Jack, who have managed—so far, at least—to survive the ups and downs of my life as a lobster. Special mention for my seven-year-old grandson, Davidcito, who is always on the lookout for lobster treasures, the most recent of which is a jaunty, magnetized specimen with antennae that jiggle whenever the refrigerator door is opened or closed.

The art historian John Varriano's book, *Tastes and Temptations*, introduced me to Zanino di Pietro's *Last Supper* with lobsters. A year later, I met
John for the first time. We had lunch at a local seafood restaurant and sat in
a booth talking about art and books over lobster rolls. It was John who told
me about the sixteenth-century recipe book by Bartolomeo Scappi, chef to
Pope Pius V.

My neighbors in Maine, Nadia and Ron Colvin, introduced me to their
friend Mark Wallace, a skilled and highly successful lobsterman who had
been a member of Maine's Lobster Advisory Council. Mark was generous
with his time and answered my questions with patience and good humor.
The marine biologists William Herrnkind, of Florida State University, and
Carl Wilson, of the Maine Department of Marine Resources, also took time
to give me valuable information.

Just as Kathy's words from Milton enriched other discoveries, so did the
observations of Craig Harbison, an art historian with whom I studied. In
one of his classes, Craig mentioned the ancient question of infinite regress
residing in the idea that the world rests on the back of a turtle that stands on
another turtle . . . ad infinitum. The turtles metamorphosed when I discovered Georg Hoefnagel's fifteenth-century engraving of the world supported
on the back of a lobster, which revealed the truth of the matter: it's not turtles, it's lobsters all the way down.

It was an honor to have my first lobster article, "Salvador Dalí's Lobsters:
Feast, Phobia, and Freudian Slip," published in *Gastronomica*, edited by
Darra Goldstein.

I appreciate Steve Hull, my editor at the University Press of New England. His challenges greatly improved this book.

These are some of the high points of writing *I, Lobster*. The low point is
that my agent, Ed Knappman, died unexpectedly and much too young, while
I was writing this book.

Nancy Frazier

NOTES

Introduction

1. Frans Snyders, *Still Life*, Mead Art Museum, Amherst College, http://museums.fivecolleges.edu.

2. Corson, *The Secret Life of Lobsters*.

3. Randall Bytwerk, "The German Propaganda Archive," www.calvin .edu/academic/cas/gpa/. Bytwerk, a professor of communication arts and sciences at Calvin College, has published books and articles on German propaganda. He found "Hitler Advances" in a book of cartoons of Ernst Hanfstaengl, *Hitler in der Karikatur der Welt: Tat gegen Tinte* (Berlin: Verlag Braune Bücher Carl Rentsch, 1933).

4. Braddy, Poschmann, and Tetlie, "Giant Claw Reveals the Largest Ever Arthropod."

5. MacKenzie and Moring, *Species Profiles*, 1.

6. Ibid., 2.

7. Herrnkind, "Queuing Behavior of Spiny Lobsters."

8. Campbell and Stasko, "Movements of Lobsters (*Homarus americanus*) Tagged in the Bay of Fundy, Canada." The researchers released 18,358 tagged American lobsters in the Bay of Fundy between 1977 and 1980. The movements of tagged *Homarus americanus* are tracked by sensors. Migrations of *Panulirus argus* have been captured on film.

9. Greenlaw, *The Lobster Chronicles*, 147.

10. Pliny the Elder, *The Naturall Historie of C. Plinius Secundus*, 9:30.

11. Deut. 14:9, *Tanakh*, 297.

12. Varriano, *Tastes and Temptations*, 101.

13. Ibid., 102.

14. For reproductions and discussions of interpretations of the Last Supper by Zanino, Leonardo, and others, see ibid., 94–107.

15. Wölfflin, *Principles of Art History*, 230.

16. Ibid., ix.

17. L. Carroll, *The Annotated Alice*, 100.

Consider the Cult of the Lobster

1. Pausanias, *Pausanias's Description of Greece*, 4:153.

2. Bent, *The Cyclades*, 4–5.

3. Ibid., 6–7.

4. Elworthy, "A Solution of the Gorgon Myth," 215.

5. Ibid.

6. Pliny the Elder, *The Naturall Historie of C. Plinius Secundus*, 9:62.

7. The eel — *Muraena helena*, known as the Mediterranean or eastern Atlantic eel and in the moray family — has a dark brown body mottled with yellow.

8. Oppian, "Halieuticks," 309–11.

9. Ibid., 315–17.

10. Hesiod, *Theogony*, 74.

11. Lee, *The Octopus*, 7.

12. Cunningham, "Octopus," 19:993.

13. Pausanias, *Pausanias's Description of Greece*, 3:187.

14. Milton, *Paradise Lost*, 15.

15. Ibid.

16. Ibid.

17. Ferrucci, *The Life of God*, 5.

18. Ibid, 7.

19. Ibid., 8.

20. Ibid., 17.

21. Ibid., 19.

22. Ibid., 19–20.

23. Holm, "New Religion," in *The Chain Letter of the Soul*, 66.

24. Nakamura, *Kabuki Backstage, Onstage*, 21–23.

25. Kominz, *Avatars of Vengeance*, 206.

26. Leiter, *Historical Dictionary of Japanese Traditional Theatre*, 23.

27. Kominz, *Avatars of Vengeance*, 206.

28. Langsdorff, *Voyages and Travels in Various Parts of the World*, 246.

29. Ando Hiroshige, *Lobster and Shrimps*, Hermitage Musem, www.arthermitage.org.

30. Check out the Maine Lobster Festival's website at www.mainelobsterfestival.com/about.

31. The yield of meat changes according to the lobster's size and whether it has a hard or soft shell. According to an online fact sheet (http://www.ciaprochef.com) from the Culinary Institute of America, a leading culinary college, a one-pound, hard-shell live lobster yields 3.84 ounces of meat.

32. Claesson, Ronertson, and Hall-Arber, "Fishing Heritage Festivals."

33. Wallace, "Consider the Lobster," 255.

34. James Ensor, *Christ's Entry into Brussels in 1889*, is at the J. Paul Getty Museum (http://www.getty.edu/museum).

35. Wallace, "Consider the Lobster," 263.

36. Ibid., 259.

37. Ibid., 264.

38. Ibid., 267.

39. Ibid., 269.

40. Though this is vivid in my memory, I cannot find any reference to this advertisement.

41. Wallace, "Consider the Lobster," 255.

42. Ibid., 262.

43. Ibid., 256.

44. Wallace was a teacher and wrote fiction and nonfiction that won him a multitude of admirers. But his unbearable bouts of depression and problems with medication caused him to take his own life in the fall of 2008, at the age of forty-six.

Celebrations, Seductions, and Crimes

1. Katherine Dunbabin writes: "The type of mosaic known as *asarotos oikos* or 'unswept room' goes back to a Hellenistic concept devised, as Pliny tells us, by the mosaicist Soso at Pergamon. This original is lost, but a handful of later mosaics imitate or adapt the concept, the earliest of the first century BC" (*The Roman Banquet*, 64).

2. Grafton, "Petronius and Neo-Latin Satire," 241.

3. Recipes adapted from Apicius, *Cookery and Dining in Imperial Rome*, 210.

4. Ibid., 209.

5. Ibid., 210.

6. Scappi, *The Opera of Bartolomeo Scappi*, 340.

7. Ibid., 282.

8. Rosenberg, Slive, and ter Kuile, *Dutch Art and Architecture, 1600 to 1800*, 330.

9. Jan Davidsz. de Heem, *Still Life with Fruit and Lobster*, http://www.imagiva.com/heem-jan-davidsz-de/.

10. Ember, *Delights of the Senses*, 26. See also Malaguzzi, *Food and Feasting in Art*, 177.

11. Quoted in Barnes and Rose, *Matters of Taste*, 140.

12. Smith, *The Oxford Companion to American Food and Drink*, 186.

13. Batterberry and Batterberry, *On the Town in New York*, 141.

14. Ibid., 170.

15. Quoted in Bloom, *Broadway*, 428.

16. Quoted in Jeffers, *Diamond Jim Brady*, 2.

17. Ibid., 208.

18. Quoted in Woolf, "Mencken as Etymologist," 233.

19. Darren McGrady, *Eating Royally*, 94.

20. The restaurant, in Waycross, Georgia, has expanded and is now managed by Bill Darden Jr. and Jet Darden, sons of Bill Darden Sr.

21. The statistics are from http://investing.businessweek.com.

22. To see pictures of the redesigned restaurants, go to www.redlobster .com/bar_harbor.

23. Queenan, *Red Lobster, White Trash and the Blue Lagoon*, 2.

24. Ibid., 3

25. Ibid., 10-11.

26. Wallace, "Consider the Lobster," 255.

27. Quoted in Sandra Pedicini, "Red Lobster Fishes for Upscale Diners," *Orlando Sentinel*, February 16, 2009 (www.orlandosentinel.com).

"Natural" History

1. Pliny the Elder, *The Naturall Historie of C. Plinius Secundus*, 9:2.

2. Ibid.

3. Ibid.

4. Kornfield, Williams, and Steneck, "Assignment of *Homarus capensis* (Herbst, 1792)." 97.

5. Saussure, *Course in General Linguistics*, 172–73. The suffix *-ard* sometimes has a pejorative effect in French, as in *bâtard* (bastard), the slang usage of *canard* (false news; a duck is also called a *canard*), *couard* (coward), and *mouchard* (denouncer) — and perhaps, by unfortunate association, *homard*.

6. Gould, "The Man Who Invented Natural History," 84.

7. Ibid., 83.

8. Ibid., 86.

9. Quoted in Sloan, "The Buffon-Linnaeus Controversy," 359.

10. Quoted in ibid.

11. Quoted in ibid., 360.

12. Buffon, *A Natural History of the Globe*, 4:5–6.

13. Huxley, *Autobiography and Essays*, 72.

14. Ibid.

15. Ibid.

16. Ibid.

17. Ibid., 75.

18. This is the first of four episodes of *Pulse of the Planet*, produced by Jim Matzner and first aired on National Public Radio on January 13, 2006. The transcript is available at http://www.pulseplanet.com/dailyprogram/ dailies.php?POP=3620 (accessed January 26, 2012).

19. *Pulse of the Planet*, January 20, 2006. The transcript is available

at http://www.pulseplanet.com/dailyprogram/dailies.php?POP=3625 (accessed January 26, 2012.

20. Information about the Lobster Conservancy is available at its website (http://www.lobsters.org/).

21. This information is from the Lobster Conservancy's Spring 2010 newsletter, signed by Diane Cowan, available on the conservancy's website.

22. Ibid.

23. Ibid.

Life, Death, and Medical Conditions

1. Aesop, *The Book of Fables*, 164.

2. Fabritius et al., "Chitin in the Exoskeletons of Arthropoda."

3. Ibid.

4. Austin, Brine, Castle, and Zikakis, "Chitin," 749.

5. These and other applications are explored by Riccardo Muzzarelli in his recently published book, *Chitosan for Biomaterials II*, and online (www.chitin.it/).

6. See www.patents.com/us-4392916.html.

7. Linda Wilson Fuoco, "Bacterial Infection Sank Bubba, the Huge Lobster," *Pittsburgh Post-Gazette*, April 6, 2005.

8. Irwin Fisher, "Seafood Lover Jailed," *Weekly World News*, December 5, 1989.

9. Ibid.

10. A drop in lobster catches in 2008 has been attributed to such pollutants (Doug Fraser, "Man-Made Chemicals Tied to Sick Lobsters," *Cape Cod Times*, August 22, 2008).

11. Galen, *Galen on Food and Diet*, 185.

12. Lobster Conservancy, "Lobster Biology," http://www.lobsters.org/.

13. Burton, *The Anatomy of Melancholy*, 251.

14. Foucault, *Madness and Civilization*, 156–57.

15. Quoted in Gould, *The Flamingo's Smile*, 339.

16. Dobell, *On Diet and Regimen in Sickness and Health*, 183.

17. Bibley, "Perforating Ulcer of the Stomach," 467.

18. The paper was published as Schram, "A Case of Poisoning from Eating Lobster."

19. Atwell, "Some Little Bug Is Going to Find You."

20. Gulf of Maine Research Institute, "How to Eat Lobster and Other Items to Discuss Over Lobster," www.gma.org/lobsters/eatingetc.html. The institute's website also answers questions such as "What is the best lobster to eat?" and includes step-by-step drawings of the correct way to take a lobster apart in order to eat it.

21. On July 28, 2008, the Food and Drug Administration issued a press release with the headline, "FDA Advises against Consumption of Tomalley from American Lobster (also known as 'Maine Lobster')" (www.fda .gov). On August 1, 2008, the release was revised to include the reassuring statement: "This advisory applies only to tomalley and not to lobster meat."

22. Thomas Becnel, "Everybody Fits In In 'Gib-town,'" *Sarasota Herald-Tribune*, February 23, 2008.

23. Stuart McIver tells the sordid story of the Lobster Boy in *Murder in the Tropics* (41–52).

24. Chemers, *Staging Stigma*, 116.

25. Quoted in Gerber, "Pornography or Entertainment?," 16.

Man-Eating Monsters

1. King, *The Drawing of the Three*, 15.

2. Ibid. See also the chapter titled "Shuffle," 183–211.

3. Bailey, *The Universal Etymological English Dictionary*, n.p.

4. "Mythology And Teratology," 671–72.

5. Ibid.

6. King, *On Writing*, 68.

7. King, *The Drawing of the Three*, 189.

8. Furth, *Stephen King's The Dark Tower*, 236–37.

9. Asma, *On Monsters*, 20–21.

10. Terrence Rafferty, "Zombie Resurrection," *New York Times Book Review*, August 7, 2011.

11. See, for example, Gerdes, Uhl, and Alpers, "Spiders Are Special."

12. Johannesson, *The Renaissance of the Goths in Sixteenth-Century Sweden*, 175 and 245, note 135.

13. Granlund and Crone, "The 'Carta Marina' of Olaus Magnus," 36.

14. The James Ford Bell Library at the University of Minnesota has online reproductions of Olaus Magnus's map (http://www.lib.umn.edu).

15. Ullman and Wade, *Shock and Awe*, xxiv.

16. Johannesson, *The Renaissance of the Goths in Sixteenth-Century Sweden*, xvii.

17. After Johannes died in 1544, Olaus was given the nominal title of archbishop of Uppsala.

18. Johannesson, *The Renaissance of the Goths in Sixteenth-Century Sweden*, 69.

19. Foote, introduction, xxv. Granlund and Crone also make Olaus's intentions explicit: "In his autobiographical notes Olaus Magnus mentioned that one of the aims of his work was to place his map at the service of the militant Catholic Church" ("The 'Carta Marina' of Olaus Magnus," 42).

20. Granlund and Crone, "The 'Carta Marina' of Olaus Magnus," 37.

21. Magnus, *Description of the Northern Peoples*, 3:1119.

22. Sartre, preface, lviii.

23. Boeck, "The Norwegian Lobster-Fishery and its History," 223–24.

24. Ibid., 223.

25. Ibid.

SF: Are We All Lobsters Yet?

1. N. Carroll, "The Nature of Horror," 51.

2. Ibid., 52.

3. Lucian, *Lucian*, 1:253.

4. Ibid., 1:285.

5. Ibid., 1:293.

6. Georgiadou and Larmour, *Lucian's Science Fiction Novel, True Histories*, 168.

7. Aristotle, *Aristotle's History of Animals*, 7:198.

8. Lucian, *Lucian*, 1:253.

9. *Weird Tales*, http://weirdtales.net/wordpress/about/.

10. Hamilton, *Outside the Universe*, chapter 1.

11. Ibid.

12. Lorimer, "Homer's Use of the Past," 155–56.

13. Ibid., 157.

14. Quoted in "Moore on His Methods," *Christian Science Monitor*, March 24, 1967. A photograph of Moore's *The Helmet* is shown on the website of The Scottish National Gallery of Modern Art (www .nationalgalleries.org/modernartgalleries).

15. Evans, "The Origins of Science Fiction Criticism," 179.

16. Quoted in Stover, "Applied Natural History," 125.

17. The *Oxford English Dictionary* defines *selenite* as both a stone known to the ancients and, dating back to 1650, a supposed inhabitant of the moon.

18. Wells, *The First Men in the Moon*, 219–21.

19. Quoted in Chambers and Chambers, *Chambers's Journal of Popular Literature, Science and Arts*, 124.

20. Wagar, *H. G. Wells*, 58–59.

21. Ibid., 60.

22. Wilson, *A Little Earnest Book upon a Great Old Subject*, 138.

23. Ibid., 168.

24. Poole, "A Hand From the Deep."

25. Quoted in Herrick, *The American Lobster*, 103.

26. Van Dommelen, "Biology in Science Fiction," 729.

27. Ibid. The story about "wireheads" is Thomas Easton's "When Life Hands You a Lemming."

28. Silverberg, "Homefaring: An Introduction," 86.

29. Silverberg, "Homefaring," 90.

30. Ibid., 99.

31. Ibid., 126.

32. Stross, "Lobsters," 9.

33. Ibid. 23.

34. Ibid., 23–24.

The Palinurus/Palinurus Problem

1. Connolly, *The Unquiet Grave*, 9.

2. Another magazine called *Horizon* was published in the United States from 1958 to 1989.

3. Quoted in Connolly, *The Unquiet Grave*, 127.

4. Ibid., 130.

5. Ibid.

6. Ibid., 132–33.

7. Ibid., 11.

8. Virgil, *Aeneid*, 362, note 842.

9. Jones, *An Aeneid Commentary*, 35, note 67.

10. Ambrose, "The Etymology and Genealogy of Palinurus."

11. Scott, *Marmion*, 6.

12. Knoppers, *Constructing Cromwell*, 90–91.

13. Longfellow, *The Letters of Henry Wadsworth Longfellow 1814–1843*, 1:154.

14. Longfellow, 1:232.

15. Longfellow, 1:456.

16. Scott, *Marmion*, 192.

17. Hanne, " Ungaretti's la Terra Promessa and the Aeneid," 8.

18. Ibid., 10–11.

19. Paso, *Palinuro of Mexico*. For a good critical interpretation of this book, see Sánchez-Prado, "Dying Mirrors, Medieval Moralists, and Tristram Shandies."

20. Hemming, *Opinions and Declarations Rendered by the International Commission on Zoological Nomenclature*, vol. 19, part 6, 149.

21. Kanciruk and Herrnkind, "Mass Migration of Spiny Lobster."

22. Milton, *Paradise Lost*, 16.

23. Cousteau and Schiefelbein, *The Human, the Orchid, and the Octopus*, 280–81.

24. Ibid., 281.

25. "Lobster Telescope Has an Eye for X-Rays," April 2006, http://www2.le.ac.uk/news.

26. Quoted in ibid.

"Secrets of the Sea"

1. Dedalus Books, http://www.dedalusbooks.com/about.html.

2. Ibid.

3. Nicholas Lezard, "Cooked to Perfection," *Guardian*, July 9, 2005.

4. "The Manchester Guardian, Born 5 May 1821: 190 years — work in progress," *Guardian*, May 4, 2011.

5. Lecasble, *Lobster*, 9.

6. McIver, *Murder in the Tropics*, 47.

7. A version of *Lobster Telephone* is at the Tate Collection in London (www.tate.org.uk/collection).

8. Quoted in Gibson, *The Shameful Life of Salvador Dalí*, 371.

9. Quoted in Soby, *Salvador Dalí*, 11.

10. Anamorphosis, from the Greek word word for "transform," describes a pictorial distortion of something seen from a radical perspective or point of view.

11. Ades and Taylor, *Dalí*, 198. By way of explanation, the catalog entry also notes that Millet's *Angelus*, which Dalí reproduced over the door in his painting, "was to Dalí a monstrous example of disguised sexual repression and violence" (ibid.). Dalí's painting is owned by the National Gallery of Canada, in Ottawa.

12. Ibid.

13. The Harpo Marx drawing is owned by the Philadelphia Museum of Art.

14. Dalí, *The Secret Life Salvador of Dalí*, 377.

15. Rubin, *Dada, Surrealism, and Their Heritage*, 148.

16. Pennington, "Joseph Cornell: Dime Store Connoisseur."

17. Hartigan, *Joseph Cornell*.

18. Eggener, "'An Amusing Lack of Logic,'" 31.

19. There is a small reproduction of this box online, at www.twoartiststalkingarchives.blogspot.com/ (accessed January 12, 2012).

20. The phrase ("To arms, citizens!") begins the chorus of "La Marseillaise," the French national anthem.

21. Chambers and Chambers, "The Mid-Day Signal of the Palais-Royal," 90.

22. The followers of symbolism, a movement that preceded and influenced surrealism, used indirect and symbolic suggestion to express their thoughts and states of mind.

23. Nerval, "Aurélia," 115.

24. Breton, *Manifestoes of Surrealism*, 25.

25. Quoted in Knowles, *The Oxford Dictionary of Quotations*, 541.

26. A. Davis, "The Lobster Sestinas," 168–69.

27. Dennett, *Consciousness Explained*, 427

28. Quoted in Straley, "Of Beasts and Boys," 583.

29. Kingsley, *The Water Babies*, 109–10.

30. Ibid., 115.

31. Ibid., 135.

32. Beckett, "Dante and the Lobster," 77.

33. Ibid., 87–88.

34. Shapiro, "Literary Production as a Politicizing Practice," 407.

35. Nemerov, *The Collected Poems of Howard Nemerov*, 361–62.

36. L. Carroll, *The Annotated Alice*.

37. Ibid., 101.

38. Ibid., 105.

39. Ibid., 106.

40. For a mention of a portrait of Scott with powdered hair, see Humphreys, "The Bartholdi Loan Association Exhibition," 123. There is a parody of Scotts' "Bonny Dundee" in *Through the Looking-Glass* (Carroll, *The Annotated Alice*, 260).

41. The Tenniel illustrations for *Alice in Wonderland* are available online from Project Gutenberg (http://www.gutenberg.org/ebooks/114).

A Metaphor for People

1. Koons's *Lobster* is shown online at http://www.afterartnews.com.

2. Elaine Scoliano, "At Versailles, an Invasion of American Art," *New York Times*, September 11, 2008.

3. Quoted in Hyde and Milam, *Women, Art and the Politics of Identity in Eighteenth-Century Europe*, 1.

4. Chadwick, *Women, Art, and Society*, 158–59.

5. Harbison, *Jan Van Eyck*, 181.

6. Calman, "Barnacle."

7. See Garrard, "Here's Looking at Me."

8. McTighe, "Foods and the Body in Italian Genre Paintings, about 1580," 319.

9. Ibid.

10. Quoted in Gill, "Method and Metaphysics in Plato's Sophist and Statesman."

11. Delacroix, *Selected Letters*, 9.

12. Quoted in Golding, *Visions of the Modern*, 86.

13. Pablo Picasso, *Lobster and Cat*, www.guggenheim.org.

14. Fred Licht, comments on Picasso, *Lobster and Cat*, www.guggenheim.org.

15. Ibid.

16. Willem de Kooning, *Woman 1*, www.moma.org.

17. Willem de Kooning, *Lobster Woman*, http://hirshhorn.si.edu.

18. Quoted in C. Martin and West, *Distant Shores*, 20.

19. Rockwell Kent, "Toilers of the Sea," www.tfaoi.com/newsmu/nmus36a.htm (accessed February 2, 2012).

20. Quoted in Perlman, *Robert Henri*, 59.

21. Quoted in MacAdam, *Marks of Distinction*, 138.

22. George Bellows, Fish Wharf, *Matinicus Island*, www.the-athenaeum.org.

23. N. C. Wyeth, *Deep Cove Lobster Man*, http://www.pafa.org/Museum/The-Collection/View-All-Works/Collection-Detail/89/PageIndex__93/colId__6747/ (accessed February 2, 2012).

24. Due to copyright protection, these paintings cannot be seen online.

25. Tatham, *Winslow Homer and the Pictorial Press*. 195–96.

26. Hughes, *American Visions*, 311.

27. Wölfflin, *Principles of Art History*, ix.

The Bartender and the Lobster

1. Corson, *The Secret Life of Lobsters*, 217.

2. Ellen Ruppel Shell, "Lives: Capsized," *New York Times Magazine*, January 24, 2010.

3. Ibid.

4. Dorson, "Collecting Folklore in Jonesport, Maine," 271.

5. Quoted in ibid., 275.

6. Quoted in Dorson, *Buying the Wind*, 27–28.

7. Quoted in ibid., 28.

8. Ibid., 28.

9. Quoted in ibid., 29.

10. Quoted in ibid., 33.

11. Quoted in ibid., 73.

12. Quoted in ibid., 74.

13. Dorson, *Folklore and Fakelore*, 12.

14. Ibid., 340, note 8.

15. Paredes, "Tag, You're It."

16. Brooks, "My Movies," 61.

17. Ibid.

18. Ibid.

19. Allen, "Tails of Manhattan."

20. Ibid.

21. Twain, *The Jumping Frog and 18 Other Stories*, 102.

22. Powell, "Lobster Killer."

23. Ibid., 147.

24. Ibid., 148.

25. Ibid., 149.

26. Child, *Mastering the Art of French Cooking*, 221.

27. Powell, *Lobster Killer*, 150.

28. Ibid., 151.

29. Ibid., 152.

30. This story is told by Sally Quinn in her appropriately named *The Party: A Guide to Adventurous Entertaining* (102). In Ephron's version of the event, the wine dousing is changed to a pie in the face (*Heartburn*, 175).

31. J. Martin, *Miss Manners' Guide to Excruciatingly Correct Behavior*, 193.

32. Ed Pilkington, "My Murdered Uncle Would Not Have Wanted Ronnie Lee Gardner Murdered," *Guardian*, June 18, 2010; Ray Sanchez, "Ronnie Lee Gardner Faces Firing Squad in Utah," June 17, 2010, abcnews.com.

33. Bob Greene, "Who Weeps for the Blood of the Weiler Family?," *Chicago Tribune*, June 14, 1999.

34. Untiedt, *Texas Folklore Society*, 122–23.

35. Liebling, "Elijah and Sinbad," 138.

36. Quoted in Karvoski, *The Movie Queen Quiz Book*, 156.

37. Borowitz, "Painted Smiles," 26–27.

38. "Lobsters Are Like People."

Welcome to the Lobster Hotel

1. Rosier, *Rosier's Narrative of Waymouth's Voyage to the Coast of Maine, in 1605*, 30.

2. *Sailors Narratives of Voyages along the New England Coast*, 36.

3. George, "Cod."

4. Rosier, *Rosier's Narrative of Waymouth's Voyage to the Coast of Maine, in 1605*, 21.

5. Josselyn, *An Account of Two Voyages to New England Made during the Years 1638, 1663*, 109.

6. Rosier, *Rosier's Narrative of Waymouth's Voyage to the Coast of Maine, in 1605*, 40.

7. Ibid., 38.

8. Quoted in Woodard, *The Lobster Coast*, 80.

9. Herrick, *The American Lobster*, 12.

10. Lord, *Crab, Shrimp, and Lobster Lore*, 96–97.

11. Woodard, *The Lobster Coast*, 179.

12. Cobb, *The Lobster Fishery of Maine*, 253.

13. Dreiser, *The Financier*, 4–5.

14. Ibid., 4.

15. Ibid., 4–6.

16. Kurlansky, *Cod*.

17. Cristina Fox Fernandez, e-mail to author, September 8, 2010.

18. Thoreau, *Cape Cod*, 219.

19. The National Marine Fisheries Service is a federal agency affiliated with the National Oceanic and Atmospheric Administration and a division of the Department of Commerce. It is responsible for managing, conserving, and protecting the United States's living marine resources in waters three to two hundred miles offshore.

20. Conkling, "From Many Fish at Low Prices to Fewer Fish for More Money."

21. Coffin, "Down East Breakfast," 124.

22. Acheson, *The Lobster Gangs of Maine*, 3.

23. Ibid., 2.

24. Monhegan has a "closed season": by law, there is no fishing in Monhegan waters from the end of June until the first of January. One benefit of this regulation is that during the height of summer, when lobsters molt and are especially vulnerable, they are not trapped. Another is that fishermen and women can find other gainful employment during the busy tourist season.

25. Acheson, *Capturing the Commons*, 2.

26. Ibid., 235.

27. Adapted from Dinsmore, "Deciphering Mysterious World of Lobster Pricing."

28. Mark Wallace, conversation with author, September 16, 2010.

29. Carl Wilson, conversation with author, September 21, 2010.

30. McPhee, "Out in the Sort," 161.

31. Ibid. 163.

32. "Processing Facilities," www.clearwater.ca.

33. Conkling, "Cheer Up, Things Could be Worse."

Bouillabaisse

1. Child, *My Life in France*, 173.

2. Ibid., 151.

3. Ibid., 174.

4. Toklas, *The Alice B. Toklas Cook Book*, 88.

5. Ibid.

6. McGee, *On Food and Cooking*, 628.

7. David, *French Provincial Cooking*, 298.

8. David, *A Book of Mediterranean Food*, 60.

9. Quoted in ibid., 61–62.

10. Liebling, "The Soul of Bouillabaisse," 189.

11. Quoted in ibid., 201.

12. Root, *The Food of France*, 352.

13. Ibid. 315.

14. Ibid. 348.

15. Ibid., 349.

16. Ibid., 350.

17. Thackeray, *The Works of William Makepeace Thackeray*, 11:424.

18. Ibid.

19. Quoted in Pollman, *Bottled Wisdom*, 9.

20. Quoted in Fisher and Lazar, *Conversations with M. F. K. Fisher*, 70.

21. Fisher, "A Considerable Town," 124.

22. Fisher, *The Gastronomical Me*, 119.

23. There is a recipe for the sauce, called sauce cardinal, in *The Gourmet Cookbook* (506), and a recipe for a similar sauce, lobster butter (514). See chapter 13 for the first recipe.

24. My information about Claiborne's meal draws on Mitchell Davis's "Power Meal," a long, thoughtful investigation.

25. Toklas, *The Alice B. Toklas Cook Book*, 11.

26. Southgate, *Things a Lady Would Like to Know Concerning Domestic Management and Expenditure*, 143.

27. Claiborne and Franey, *Classic French Cooking*, 12–13.

28. Toklas, *The Alice B. Toklas Cook Book*, 82.

Lobster Onstage: Recipes

1. Fisher and the editors of Time-Life Books, *The Cooking of Provincial France*, 94–95.

2. In Fisher's recipe the ingredients are separated from the instructions. I've combined ingredients and recipes and edited accordingly. I've included the recipe for *croûtes* that appears earlier in her book.

3. Yes, unless you have the fish dealer do it (and run home with the newly slaughtered package), that means you cut up and crack the live lobster. "Just remember that there is a first time for everything," is Fisher's instructional consolation. Alternately, put the whole live lobsters in the boiling court bouillon and cut and crack them later. There is a pictorial demonstration (called "A Winning Technique") of dissecting a live lobster

in Fisher and the editors of Time-Life Books, *The Cooking of Provincial France*, 114–15.

4. Ibid., 88.

5. Thorne, *Mouth Wide Open*, xi.

6. Quoted on the dust jacket of ibid.

7. Ibid., 34.

8. Montagné, *Larousse Gastronomique*, 161–63.

9. Claiborne, *The New York Times Cook Book*, 265.

10. Bittman, *The Food Matters Cook Book*, 317–18.

11. Thorne, *Mouth Wide Open*, 35.

12. Alexander and Harris, *Hometown Appetites*.

13. Paddleford, *How America Eats*, v.

14. Ibid., 3.

15. Ibid., 6.

16. Ibid.

17. Coffin, *Mainstays of Maine*, 1–12.

18. Claiborne, "Just a Quiet Dinner for Two," 358–59.

19. Pierre Franey, "Cold Lobster with Basil Vinaigrette," *The New York Times*, June 10, 1987.

20. Claiborne, "Just a Quiet Dinner for Two," 362.

21. Adapted from *The Gourmet Cookbook*, 506.

22. Almond, "Death by Lobster Pad Thai," 189.

23. Ibid., 190.

24. Ibid., 196.

25. White, *Lobster at Home*, 204.

26. Select lobsters are 1½ to 2 pounds. Shorts are lobsters under legal size in the United States. Chicken lobsters are the smallest allowable lobsters in the United States: at least 1 pound and 3½ inches from behind the eyes to the end of carapace. Jumbos are 2½ pounds and up.

27. As noted in chapter 4, it is no longer advisable to eat tomalley. In July 2008 the Food and Drug Administration advised that dangerous levels of toxins responsible for Paralytic Shellfish Poisoning had been found in tomalley. The poison does not affect the lobster's white meat.

28. White, *Lobster at Home*, 204–5.

29. Corson, "How to Kill a Lobster Humanely."

30. Rich, *The Baked Bean Supper Murders*, 55.

31. "Neverending Story," 14–15. If the bypass were to be built, it would cost $100,000,000 and take at least ten years to build. The "amount of money we're willing to bet that we'll see a Wiscasset bypass in our lifetime," the item concludes, is "0."

32. Stern and Stern, *Roadfood Sandwiches*, 50.

33. Stern and Stern, *Roadfood*, 44.

34. Thorne, *Serious Pig*, 59.

Epilogue

1. Wölfflin, *Principles of Art History*, 230.

2. Davidson, *Seafood*, 128.

3. Ibid.

4. Holthuis, *Marine Lobsters of the World*. The work is a comprehensive account of all marine lobsters of interest to fisheries.

5. Herrick, *The American Lobster*, 18–19.

6. Aesop, *The Book of Fables*, 35. As often happens, crabs and lobsters are substituted for each other. In this version, mother and daughter are called crabs.

7. Ashbery, *Self-Portrait in a Convex Mirror*, 81.

8. Ibid., 68.

9. Ibid.

10. Ibid., 70.

11. See, for example, Locke, *An Essay Concerning Human Understanding*, 2:104; Geertz, *The Interpretation of Cultures*, 29; Hawking, *A Brief History of Time*, 1.

12. Hoefnagel, *Archetypa studiaque patris*, 2:1.

13. I am grateful to Stephen Harris of the Department of Languages, Literatures, and Cultures, College of Arts and Humanities, at the University of Massachusetts Amherst for this translation — which, Harris mentioned, is from Erasmus. Thanks also to John Higgins, a Latin teacher, for his translation of the accompanying couplets: "The sign of the Zodiac defended by a pair of pincers, I defeated the fighting Hercules by pinching him. / And I am borne, eight-footed, in my carapaced step, swimming in the sea. I am a foul, grief-bearing evil thing."

REFERENCES

Acheson, James M. *Capturing the Commons: Devising Institutions to Manage the Maine Lobster Industry*. Hanover, NH: University Press of New England, 2003.

———. *The Lobster Gangs of Maine*. Hanover, NH: University Press of New England, 1988.

Ades, Dawn, and Michael R. Taylor, with the assistance of Montset Aguer. *Dalí*. New York: Rizzoli; 2004.

Aesop. *The Book of Fables: Containing Aesop's Fables*. New York: American Book Exchange, 1880.

Agulló, Enrique, et al. "Present and Future Role of Chitin." *Macromolecular Bioscience* 3, no. 10 (October 2003): 521–30.

Alexander, Kelly, and Cynthia Harris. *Hometown Appetites: The Story of Clementine Paddleford, the Forgotten Food Writer Who Chronicled How America Ate*. New York: Gotham, 2008.

Allen, Woody. "Tails of Manhattan." *New Yorker*, March 30, 2009, 29.

Almond, Steve. "Death by Lobster Pad Thai: A Counter-Phobic Paean to Friendship, Crustaceans, and Oral Transcendence." In Steve Almond, *Not That You Asked: Rants, Exploits, and Obsessions*, 189–98. New York: Random House, 2008.

Ambrose, Z. Philip. "The Etymology and Genealogy of Palinurus." *American Journal of Philology* 101, no. 4 (1980): 449–57.

Apicius. *Cookery and Dining in Imperial Rome: A Bibliography, Critical Review, and Translation of the Ancient Book known as Apicius de re Coquinaria: Now for the First Time Rendered into English by Joseph Dommers Vehling*. New York: Dover, 1977.

Aristotle. *Aristotle's History of Animals*. Translated by Richard Cresswell from the text of Johann Gottlob Schneider. 10 vols. London: Bell, 1878.

Ashbery, John. *Self-Portrait in a Convex Mirror: Poems*. New York: Penguin, 1975.

Asma, Stephen T. *On Monsters: An Unnatural History of Our Worst Fears*. New York: Oxford University Press, 2009.

Atwell, Roy. "Some Little Bug Is Going to Find You." In *Such Nonsense! An Anthology*, edited by Carolyn Wells, 112. New York: George H. Doran, 1918.

Austin, P. R., C. J. Brine, J. E. Castle, and J. P. Zikakis. 1981. "Chitin: New Facets of Research." *Science* 212, no. 4496 (1981): 749–53.

Bailey, Nathan. *The Universal Etymological English Dictionary*. London: Thomas Cox, 1731.

Barnes, Donna R., and Peter G. Rose. *Matters of Taste: Food and Drink in Seventeenth-Century Dutch Art and Life, with Essays by Charles T. Gehring and Nancy T. Minty and Supplementary Cookbook by Peter G. Rose.* Albany, NY: Albany Institute of History and Art, 2002.

Batterberry, Michael, and Ariane Ruskin Batterberry. *On the Town in New York: The Landmark History of Eating, Drinking, and Entertainments from the American Revolution to the Food Revolution.* New York: Routledge, 1999.

Beckett, Samuel. "Dante and the Lobster." In *Samuel Beckett: Poems, Short Fiction, and Criticism*, edited by Paul Auster, 77–88. Grove Centenary Edition. New York: Grove, 2006.

Bent, J. Theodore. *The Cyclades, or Life among the Insular Greeks.* London: Longmans, Green, 1885.

Bibley, Samuel H. "Perforating Ulcer of the Stomach." *London Medical Gazette*, June 9, 1838, 467–68.

Bittman, Mark. *The Food Matters Cook Book: 500 Revolutionary Recipes for Better Living.* New York: Simon and Schuster, 2010.

Bloom, Ken. *Broadway: Its History, People, and Places; An Encyclopedia.* New York: Routledge, 2004.

Boeck, Axel. "The Norwegian Lobster-Fishery and Its History." In *United States Commission of Fish and Fisheries, Part III; Report of the Commissioner for 1873–4 and 1874–5*, 223–58. Washington: Government Printing Office, 1876.

Borowitz, Helen O. "Painted Smiles: Sad Clowns in French Art and Literature." *Bulletin of the Cleveland Museum of Art* 71, no. 1 (1984): 23–35.

Braddy, Simon J., Markus Poschmann, and O. Erik Tetlie. "Giant Claw Reveals the Largest Ever Arthropod." *Biology Letters* 4, no. 1 (2008): 106–9.

Breton, Andreì. *Manifestoes of Surrealism.* Translated by Richard Seaver and Helen R. Lane. Ann Arbor: University of Michigan Press, 1969.

Brooks, Mel. "My Movies: The Collision of Art and Money." In *The Movie Business Book*, edited by Jason E. Squire, 57–66. 2nd ed. New York: Fireside, 1983.

Buffon, Georges Louis Leclerc, comte de. *A Natural History of the Globe, and of Man, Beasts, Birds, Fishes, Reptiles, and Insects.* 4 vols. Edited by John Wright. London: Thomas Tegg, 1831.

Burton, Robert. *The Anatomy of Melancholy.* Edited by Arthur R. Shilleto. London: George Bell, 1903.

Calman, William Thomas. "Barnacle." In *The Encyclopaedia Britannica*, 3:409. 11th ed. New York: Encyclopaedia Britannica, 1911.

Campbell, Alan, and Alvars B. Stasko. "Movements of Lobsters (*Homarus americanus*) Tagged in the Bay of Fundy, Canada." *Marine Biology* 92, no. 3 (1986): 393–404.

Carroll, Lewis. *The Annotated Alice: Alice's Adventures in Wonderland & Through the Looking-Glass*. Illustrations by John Tenniel. Introduction and notes by Martin Gardner. Definitive ed. New York: Norton, 2000.

Carroll, Noel. "The Nature of Horror." *Journal of Aesthetics and Art Criticism* 46, no. 1 (1987): 51–59.

Chadwick, Whitney. *Women, Art, and Society*. New York: Thames and Hudson, 1990.

Chambers, William, and Robert Chambers. *Chambers's Journal of Popular Literature, Science and Arts*, June 1857, 124.

———. "The Mid-Day Signal of the Palais-Royal." *Chambers's Pocket Miscellany*, 1854, 86–91.

Chemers, Michael M. *Staging Stigma: A Critical Examination of the American Freak Show*. New York: Palgrave and Macmillan, 2008.

Child, Julia, with Simone Beck and Louisette Bertholle. *Mastering the Art of French Cooking*. New York: Knopf, 1965.

———, with Alex Prud'homme. *My Life in France*. New York: Knopf, 2006.

Claesson, Stefan, Robert A. Ronertson, and Madeleine Hall-Arbe. "Fishing Heritage Festivals, Tourism, and Community Development in the Gulf of Maine." In *Proceedings of the 2005 Northeatern Recreation Research Symposium*, edited by John G. Peden and Rudy M. Schuster, 420–28. Newtown Square, PA: US Department of Agriculture, Forest Service, Northeastern Research Station, 2006.

Claiborne, Craig. "Just a Quiet Dinner for Two." In *A Food Lover's Companion*, edited by Evan Jones, 357–63. New York: Harper and Row, 1979.

———. *The New York Times Cook Book*. New York: Harper and Row, 1961.

———, Pierre Franey, and the editors of Time-Life Books. *Classic French Cooking*. New York: Time-Life Books, 1970.

Cobb, John N. *The Lobster Fishery of Maine*. Washington: Government Printing Office, 1900.

Coffin, Robert P. T. "Down East Breakfast." In *Endless Feasts: Sixty Years of Writing from Gourmet*, edited by Ruth Reichl, 123–29. New York: Modern Library, 2003.

———. *Mainstays of Maine*. New York: Macmillan, 1944.

Conkling, Philip. "Cheer Up, Things Could Be Worse." *Working Waterfront*, September 2008, workingwaterfront.com.

————. "From Many Fish at Low Prices to Fewer Fish for More Money." *Working Waterfront*, August 2008, workingwaterfront.com.

Connolly, Cyril. *The Unquiet Grave: A Word Cycle by Palinurus*. Rev. ed. New York: Persea, 1981.

Corson, Trevor. "How to Kill a Lobster Humanely." *Atlantic*, July 2009. www.theatlantic.com.

————. *The Secret Life of Lobsters: How Fishermen and Scientists Are Unraveling the Mysteries of Our Favorite Crustacean*. New York: HarperCollins, 2004.

Cousteau, Jacques, and Susan Schiefelbein. *The Human, the Orchid, and the Octopus: Exploring and Conserving Our Natural World*. New York: Bloomsbury, 2007.

Cunningham, Joseph Thomas. "Octopus." In *Encyclopaedia Britannica*, 19:993. 11th ed. New York: Encyclopaedia Britannica, 1911.

Dalí, Salvador. *The Secret Life of Salvador Dalí*. New York: Dial, 1942.

David, Elizabeth. *A Book of Mediterranean Food*. New York: Knopf, 1980.

————. *French Provincial Cooking*. New York: Penguin, 1999.

Davidson, Alan. *Seafood: A Connoisseur's Guide and Cookbook*. New York: Simon and Schuster, 1989.

Davis, Angela J. "The Lobster Sestinas." *Antioch Review* 54, no. 2 (1996): 168–71.

Davis, Mitchell. "Power Meal: Craig Claiborne's Last Supper for the New York Times." *Gastronomica* 4, no. 3 (2004): 60–72.

Delacroix, Eugene. *Selected Letters, 1813-1861*. Edited by Jean Stewart. Boston: MFA, 2001.

Dennett, Daniel C. *Consciousness Explained*. Boston: Little, Brown, 1991.

Dinsmore, Sandra. "Deciphering Mysterious World of Lobster Pricing." *Working Waterfront*, September 2008, workingwaterfront.com.

Dobell, Horace Benge. *On Diet and Regimen in Sickness and Health, and on the Interdependence and Prevention of Diseases and the Diminution of their Fatality*. 7th ed. London: H. K. Lewis, 1882.

Dorson, Richard M. *Buying the Wind: Regional Folklore in the United States*. Chicago: University of Chicago Press, 1964.

————. "Collecting Folklore in Jonesport, Maine." *Proceedings of the American Philosophical Society* 101, no. 3 (1957): 270–89.

————. *Folklore and Fakelore: Essays Toward a Discipline of Folk Studies*. Cambridge: Harvard University Press, 1976.

Dreiser, Theodore. *The Financier*. Cleveland, OH: World, 1912.

Dunbabin, Katherine M. D. *The Roman Banquet: Images of Conviviality*. Cambridge: Cambridge University Press, 2003.

Easton, Thomas A. "When Life Hands You a Lemming." *Analog*, May 1989, 92–101.

Eggener, Keith L. "'An Amusing Lack of Logic': Surrealism and Popular Entertainment." *American Art* 7, no. 4 (1993): 30–45.

Elworthy, F. T. "A Solution of the Gorgon Myth." *Folklore* 14, no. 3 (1903): 212–42.

Ember, Ildikoì. *Delights for the Senses: Dutch and Flemish Still-Life Paintings from Budapest.* Wausau (WI): Leigh Yawkey Woodson Art Museum, 1989.

Ephron, Nora. *Heartburn.* New York: Knopf, 1983.

Evans, Arthur B. "The Origins of Science Fiction Criticism: From Kepler to Wells." *Science Fiction Studies* 26, no. 2 (1990): 163–86.

Fabritius, Helge, et al. "Chitin in the Exoskeletons of Arthropoda: From Ancient Design to Novel Materials Science." http://www.mpie.de/index .php?id=2957.

Ferrucci, Franco. *The Life of God (as Told by Himself).* Translated by Raymond Rosenthal and Franco Ferrucci. Chicago: University of Chicago Press, 1996.

Fisher, M. F. K. "A Considerable Town." In M. F. K. Fisher, *Two Towns in Provence*, 3–208. New York: Vintage, 1983.

———. *The Gastronomical Me.* New York: Farrar, Straus and Giroux, 1943.

———and the editors of Time-Life Books. *The Cooking of Provincial France.* New York: Time-Life Books, 1968.

Fisher, M. F. K., and David Lazar. *Conversations with M. F. K. Fisher.* Jackson: University Press of Mississippi, 1992.

Foote, Peter. Introduction to Olaus Magnus, *Description of the Northern Peoples*, translated by Peter Fisher and Humphrey Higgens and edited by Peter Foote. 3 vols. London: Hakluyt Society, 1996–98.

Foucault, Michel. *Madness and Civilization: A History of Insanity in the Age of Reason.* Translated by Richard Howard. 2nd ed. London: Routledge, 2001.

Furth, Robin. *Stephen King's The Dark Tower: A Concordance.* Vol. 1. New York: Scribner, 2003.

Galen. *Galen: On Food and Diet.* Translated by Mark Grant. London: Routledge, 2000.

Garrard, Mary D. "Here's Looking at Me: Sofonisba Anguissola and the Problem of the Woman Artist." *Renaissance Quarterly* 47, no. 3 (1994): 556–622.

Geertz, Clifford. *The Interpretation of Cultures: Selected essays.* New York: Basic, 1973.

George, A. Boulenger. "Cod." In *The Encyclopaedia Britannica,* 6:632. 11th ed. New York: Encyclopaedia Britannica, 1911.

Georgiadou, Aristoula, and David H. J. Larmour. *Lucian's Science Fiction Novel, True Histories: Interpretation and Commentary.* Leiden: Brill, 1998.

Gerber, David. "Pornography or Entertainment? The Rise and Fall of the Freak Show." *Reviews in American History* 18, no. 1 (1990): 15–21.

Gerdes, Antje B. M., Gabriele Uhl, and Georg W. Alpers. "Spiders Are Special: Fear and Disgust Evoked by Pictures of Arthropods." *Evolution and Human Behavior* 30, no. 1 (2009): 66–73.

Gibson, Ian. *The Shameful Life of Salvador Dalí.* New York: Norton, 1998.

Gill, Mary Louise. "Method and Metaphysics in Plato's Sophist and Statesman." In Stanford Encyclopedia of Philosophy, Winter 2009, http://plato.stanford.edu/archives/win2009/entries/plato-sophstate (accessed February 9, 2012).

Golding, John. *Visions of the Modern.* Berkeley: University of California Press, 1994.

Gould, Stephen Jay. *The Flamingo's Smile: Reflections in Natural History.* New York: Norton, 1987.

———. "The Man Who Invented Natural History." *New York Review of Books,* October 22, 1998, 83–86.

The Gourmet Cookbook. Vol. 1. New York: Gourmet, 1950.

Grafton, Anthony. "Petronius and Neo-Latin Satire: The Reception of the Cena Trimalchios." *Journal of the Warburg and Courtauld Institutes* 53 (1990): 237–49.

Granlund, John, and G. R. Crone. "The 'Carta Marina' of Olaus Magnus." *Imago Mundi* 8 (1951): 35-43.

Greenlaw, Linda. *The Lobster Chronicles: Life on a Very Small Island.* New York: Hyperion, 2002.

Hamilton, Edmond. *Outside the Universe.* http://freesf.blogspot.com/2009/10/outside-universe-edmond-hamilton.html (accessed February 2, 2012).

Hanne, Michael. "Ungaretti's la Terra Promessa and the Aeneid." *Italica* 50, no. 1 (1973): 3–25.

Harbison, Craig. 1991. *Jan Van Eyck: The Play of Realism.* London: Reaktion, 1991.

Hartigan, Lynda Roscoe. *Joseph Cornell: Navigating the Imagination.* New Haven, CT: Yale University Press, 2007.

Hawking, Stephen M. *A Brief History of Time: From the Big Bang to Black Holes.* New York: Bantam, 1988.

Hemming, Francis, ed. *Opinions and Declarations Rendered by the International Commission on Zoological Nomenclature.* Vol. 19, part 6.

London: International Commission on Zoological Nomenclature, 1958.

Herrick, Francis Hobart. *The American Lobster: A Study of Its Habits and Development*. Washington: Government Printing Office, 1895.

Herrnkind, William. "Queuing Behavior of Spiny Lobsters. *Science* 164, no. 3886 (1969): 1425–27.

Hesiod. *Theogony; Works and Days; Shield*. Introduction, translation, and notes by Apostolos N. Athanassakis. Baltimore, MD: Johns Hopkins University Press, 1983.

Hoefnagel, Jacob, after Georg Hoefnagel. *Archetypa studiaque patris*. Frankfurt, 1592.

Holm, Bill. *The Chain Letter of the Soul: New and Selected Poems*. Minneapolis: Milkweed, 2009.

Holthuis, L. B. *Marine Lobsters of the World: An Annotated and Illustrated Catalogue of Species of Interest to Fisheries Known to Date*. Rome: Food and Agriculture Organization of the United Nations, 1991. http://species-identification.org.

Hughes, Robert. *American Visions: The Epic History of Art in America*. New York: Knopf, 1997.

Humphreys, Mary Gay. "The Bartholdi Loan Association Exhibition." *Decorator and Furnisher* 3, no. 4 (1884): 123–25.

Hurley, David. *Lobster Tales*. Camden, ME: Down East Books, 1997.

Huxley, Thomas Henry. *Autobiography and Essays*. Edited by Brander Matthews. New York: Gregg, 1969.

Hyde, Melissa Lee, and Jennifer Dawn Milam, eds. *Women, Art and the Politics of Identity in Eighteenth-Century Europe*. Burlington, VT: Ashgate, 2003.

Jeffers, H. Paul. *Diamond Jim Brady: Prince of the Gilded Age*. New York: Wiley, 2001.

Johannesson, Kurt. *The Renaissance of the Goths in Sixteenth-Century Sweden: Johannes and Olaus Magnus as Politicians and Historians*. Translated and edited by James Larson. Berkeley: University of California Press, 1991.

Jones, Julian Ward. *An Aeneid Commentary of Mixed Type: The Glosses in MSS Harley 4946 and Ambrosianus G111 Inf*. Toronto: Pontifical Institute of Mediaeval Studies, 1996.

Josselyn, John. *An Account of Two Voyages to New England Made during the Years 1638, 1663*. Boston: William Veazie, 1865.

Kanciruk, Paul, and William Herrnkind. "Mass Migration of Spiny Lobster, *Panulirus argus* (Crustacea: Palinuridae): Behavior and Environmental Correlates." *Bulletin of Marine Science* 28, no. 4 (1978): 601–23.

Karvoski, Ed, Jr. *The Movie Queen Quiz Book: A Trivia Test Dedicated to Fabulous Female Film Stars*. Lincoln, NE: Writers Club, 2002.

King, Stephen. *The Drawing of the Three*. New York: Signet, 2003.

———. *The Mist*. New York: Signet, 2007.

———. *On Writing: A Memoir of the Craft*. New York: Scribner, 2000.

Kingsley, Charles. *The Water Babies: A Fairy-Tale for a Land-Baby*. London: J. M. Dent, 1957.

Knoppers, Laura Lunger. *Constructing Cromwell: Ceremony, Portrait, and Print, 1645-1661*. Cambridge: Cambridge University Press, 2000.

Knowles, Elizabeth M., ed. *The Oxford Dictionary of Quotations*. 5th ed. Oxford: Oxford University Press, 1999.

Kominz, Laurence R. *Avatars of Vengeance: Japanese Drama and the Soga Literary Tradition*. Ann Arbor: Center for Japanese Studies, University of Michigan, 1995.

Kornfield, Irv, Austin B. Williams, and Robert S. Steneck. "Assignment of *Homarus capensis* (Herbst, 1792), the Cape Lobster of South Africa, to the New Genus *Homarinus* (Decapoda: Nephropidae)." *Fishery Bulletin* 93, no. 1 (1995): 97–102.

Kurlansky, Mark. *Cod: A Biography of the Fish That Changed the World*. New York: Penguin, 1997.

Langsdorff, Georg Heinrich von. *Voyages and Travels in Various Parts of the World, during the Years 1803, 1804, 1805, 1806, and 1807*. Carlisle, PA: George Phillips, 1817.

Lecasble, Guillaume. *Lobster*. Translated by Polly McLean. Sawtry, England: Dedalus, 2005.

Lee, Henry. *The Octopus, or, the "Devil-Fish" of Fiction and of Fact*. London: Chapman and Hall, 1875.

Leiter, Samuel L. *Historical Dictionary of Japanese Traditional Theatre*. Lanham, MD: Scarecrow, 2006.

Liebling, A. J. "Elijah and Sinbad: 1961." In *The Most of A. J. Liebling*, selected by William Cole, 135–39. New York: Simon and Schuster, 1963.

———. "The Soul of Bouillabaisse." *New Yorker*, October 27, 1962, 189–201.

"Lobsters Are Like People." *Popular Mechanics*, June 1952. modernmechanix.com/2006/03/30/lobsters.

Locke, John. *An Essay Concerning Human Understanding*. London: William Tegg, 1849.

Longfellow, Henry Wadsworth. *The Letters of Henry Wadsworth Longfellow 1814–1843*, vol. 1, edited by Andrew R. Hilen. Cambridge: Belknap Press of Harvard University Press, 1967.

Lord, William Barry. *Crab, Shrimp, and Lobster Lore*. London: George Routledge, 1867.

Lorimer, H. L. "Homer's Use of the Past." *Journal of Hellenic Studies* 49, part 2 (1929): 145–59.

Lucian, of Samosata. *Lucian*. Translated by A. M. Harmon. 8 vols. London: W. Heinemann, 1913.

MacAdam, Barbara J. *Marks of Distinction: Two Hundred Years of American Drawings and Watercolors from the Hood Museum of Art, 1769–1969*. New York: Hudson Hills, 2005.

MacKenzie, Chet, and John R. Moring. *Species Profiles: Life Histories and Environmental Requirements of Coastal Fishes and Invertebrates (North Atlantic): American Lobster*. Biological Report 82 (11.33). Washington: US Fish and Wildlife Services, April 1985.

Magnus, Olaus. *Description of the Northern Peoples*. Translated by Peter Fisher and Humphrey Higgens. Edited by Peter Foote. 3 vols. London: Hakluyt Society, 1996–98.

Malaguzzi, Silvia. *Food and Feasting in Art*. Los Angeles: Getty, 2008.

Martin, Constance, and Richard V. West. *Distant Shores: The Odyssey of Rockwell Kent*. Berkeley: University of California Press, 2000.

Martin, Judith. *Miss Manners' Guide to Excruciatingly Correct Behavior*. New York: Norton, 2005.

McGee, Harold. *On Food and Cooking: The Science and Lore of the Kitchen*. New York: Scribner, 1984.

McGrady, Darren. *Eating Royally*. Nashville, TN: Thomas Nelson, 2007.

McIver, Stuart B. *Murder in the Tropics*. Sarasota, FL: Pineapple, 1995.

McPhee, John. "Out in the Sort: Lobsters, Bats, and Bentleys in the UPS Hub." *New Yorker*, April 18, 2005, 161–75.

McTighe, Sheila. "Foods and the Body in Italian Genre Paintings, about 1580: Campi, Passarotti, Carrachi." *Art Bulletin* 86, no. 2 (2004): 301–23.

Milton, John. *Paradise Lost*. Cambridge: Cambridge University Press, 1902.

Montagne, Prosper. *Larousse Gastronomique: The Encyclopedia of Food, Wine and Cookery*. Edited by Charlotte Turgeon and Nina Froud. Translated by Nina Froud and others. New York: Crown, 1961.

Muzzarelli, Riccardo. *Chitosan for Biomaterials II*. Berlin: Springer, 2011.

"Mythology and Teratology." *British Medical Journal* 1, no. 2150 (1902): 671–72.

Nakamura, Matazō. *Kabuki Backstage, Onstage: An Actor's Life*. Translated by Mark Oshima. Tokyo: Kodansha International, 1990.

Nemerov, Howard. *The Collected Poems of Howard Nemerov*. Chicago: University of Chicago Press, 1977.

Nerval, Gérard de. "Aurélia." In *Selected Writing of Gérard de Nerval*, translated by Geoffrey Wagner. New York: Grove Press, 1957, 111–78.

"Neverending Story: The Effort to Build a Bypass around Wiscasset Has Stalled; What Were the Odds?" *Down East*, February 2011, 14–15.

Oppian. "Halieuticks, of the Nature of Fish and Fishing." In *Oppian,
Colluthus, Tryphiodorus*, translated by A. W. Mair, 201–401. London:
William Heinemann, 1928.

Paddleford, Clementine. *How America Eats*. New York: Scribner's, 1960.

Paredes, Americo. "Tag, You're It." *Journal of American Folklore* 73, no. 288
(1960): 157–58.

Paso, Fernando del. *Palinuro of Mexico*. Translated by Elizabeth Plaister.
Normal, IL: Dalkey Archive Press, 1996.

Pausanias. *Pausanias's Description of Greece*. Translated by James George
Frazer. 2nd ed. London: Macmillan, 1913.

Pennington, Estill Curtis (Buck). "Joseph Cornell: Dime Store
Connoisseur." *Archives of American Art Journal* 23, no. 3 (1983): 13–20.

Perlman, Bennard B. *Robert Henri: His Life and Art*, Mineola, NY: Dover,
1991.

Pliny the Elder. *The Naturall Historie of C. Plinius Secundus*. 37 vols.
Translated by Philemon Holand, 1601. Edited by the Wernerian Club.
London: George Barclay, 1847–48. http://penelope.uchicago.edu/
holland/index.htm.

Pollman, Mark. *Bottled Wisdom: Over 1,000 Spirited Quotations and
Anecdotes*. St. Louis, MO: Wildstone, 1998.

Poole, Romeo. "A Hand from the Deep." In *Not at Night*, edited by Herbert
Asbury, 53–66. New York: Vanguard, 1928.

Powell, Julie. "Lobster Killer." In *Best Food Writing 2006*, edited by Holly
Hughes, 147–54. New York: Avalon, 2006.

Queenan, Joe. 1998. *Red Lobster, White Trash, and the Blue Lagoon: Joe
Queenan's America*. New York: Hyperion, 1998.

Quinn, Sally. *The Party: A Guide to Adventurous Entertaining*. New York:
Fireside, 1998.

Rich, Virginia. *The Baked Bean Supper Murders*. New York: Dutton, 1983.

Root, Waverley. *The Food of France*. New York: Knopf, 1958.

Rosenberg, Jakob, Seymour Slive, and E. H. ter Kuile. *Dutch Art and
Architecture, 1600 to 1800*. Baltimore, MD: Penguin, 1966.

Rosier, James. *Rosier's Narrative of Waymouth's Voyage to the Coast of Maine,
in 1605*. Edited by George Prince. Bath, ME: Eastern Times, 1860.

Rubin, William S. *Dada, Surrealism, and Their Heritage*. New York:
Museum Of Modern Art, 1968.

Sailors Narratives of Voyages along the New England Coast, 1524–1624. With
notes by George Parker Winship. Boston: Houghton Mifflin, 1905.

Sánchez-Prado, Ignacio M. "Dying Mirrors, Medieval Moralists, and
Tristram Shandies: The Literary Traditions of Fernando del Paso's
Palinuro of Mexico." *Comparative Literature* 60, no. 2 (2008.): 142–63.

Sartre, Jean-Paul. Preface to Frantz Fanon, *The Wretched of the Earth*, xliii–lxii. Translated by Constance Farrington. New York: Grove, 1965.

Saussure, Ferdinand de. *Course in General Linguistics*. Edited by Charles Bally. Translated by Roy Harris. Peru, IL: Open Court, 1983.

Scappi, Bartolomeo. *The Opera of Bartolomeo Scappi (1570): L'Arte et Prudenza d'un Maestro Cuoco*. Translated with commentary by Terence Scully. Toronto: University of Toronto Press, 2008.

Schram, Charles. "A Case of Poisoning from Eating Lobster." *Medical News* 71 (June–December 1897): 659–60.

Scott, Sir Walter. *Marmion: A Tale of Flodden Field*. Edited by George B. Aiton. New York: Macmillan, 1922.

Shapiro, Michael J. "Literary Production as a Politicizing Practice." *Political Theory* 12, no. 3 (1984): 387–422.

Sherwood, Shirley, Stephen Harris, and Barrie E. Juniper. *A New Flowering: 1,000 Years of Botanical Art*. Oxford: Ashmolean Museum, 2005.

Silverberg, Robert. "Homefaring." In Robert Silverberg, *Sailing to Byzantium*, 90–166. New York: Ibooks, 2000.

———. "Homefaring: An Introduction." In Robert Silverberg, *Sailing to Byzantium*, 86–88. New York: Ibooks, 2000.

Sloan, Phillip R. "The Buffon-Linnaeus Controversy." *Isis* 67, no. 3 (1976): 356–75.

Smith, Andrew F. *The Oxford Companion to American Food and Drink*. New York: Oxford University Press, 2007.

Soby, James Thrall. *Salvador Dalí*. New York: Museum of Modern Art, 1946.

Southgate, Henry. *Things a Lady Would Like to Know Concerning Domestic Management and Expenditure: Arranged for Daily Reference with Hints Regarding the Intellectual as Well as the Physical Life*. London: William P. Nimmo, 1875.

Stern, Jane, and Michael Stern. *Roadfood: The Coast-to-Coast Guide to 700 of the Best Barbecue Joints, Lobster Shacks, Ice Cream Parlors, Highway Diners, and Much, Much More*. New York: Broadway, 2008.

———. *Roadfood Sandwiches: Recipes and Lore from Our Favorite Shops Coast to Coast*. Boston: Houghton Mifflin, 2007.

Stover, Leon. "Applied Natural History: Wells vs. Huxley." In *H. G. Wells under Revision: Proceedings of the International H. G. Wells Symposium London, July 1986*, edited by Patrick Parrinder and Christopher Rolfe, 125–33. Cranbury, NJ: Associated University Presses, 1990.

Straley, Jessica. "Of Beasts and Boys: Kingsley, Spencer, and the Theory of Recapitulation." *Victorian Studies* 49, no. 4 (2008): 583–609.

Stross, Charles. "Lobsters." In Charles Stross, *Accelerando*, 3–32. New York: Ace, 2005.

Tanakh: The Holy Scriptures. Philadelphia: Jewish Publication Society, 1985.

Tatham, David. *Winslow Homer and the Pictorial Press.* Syracuse, NY: Syracuse University Press, 2003.

Thackeray, William Makepeace. *The Works of William Makepeace Thackeray.* Vol. 11. Boston: James R. Osgood, 1872.

Thoreau, Henry David. *Cape Cod.* New York: Crowell, 1908.

Thorne, John, with Matt Lewis Thorne. *Mouth Wide Open: A Cook and His Appetite.* New York: North Point, 2007.

———. *Serious Pig: An American Cook in Search of His Roots.* New York: North Point, 1996.

Toklas, Alice B. *The Alice B. Toklas Cook Book.* New York: Harper and Row, 1984.

Twain, Mark. *The Jumping Frog and 18 Other Stories.* Escondido, CA: Book Tree, 2000.

Ullman, Harlan, and James P. Wade. *Shock and Awe: Achieving Rapid Dominance.* Washington: Center for Advanced Concepts and Technology, 1996.

Untiedt, Kenneth L. *Texas Folklore Society.* Denton: University of North Texas Press, 2008.

Van Dommelen, Erica. "Biology in Science Fiction." *BioScience* 39, no. 10 (1989): 729–31.

Varriano, John L. *Tastes and Temptations: Food and Art in Renaissance Italy.* Berkeley: University of California Press, 2009.

Virgil. *Aeneid.* Translated by Frederick Ahl. Oxford: Oxford University Press, 2007.

Wagar, W. Warren. *H. G. Wells: Traversing Time.* Middletown, CT: Wesleyan University Press, 2004.

Wallace, David Foster. "Consider the Lobster." In *The Best American Essays,* edited by Susan Orlean, 255–69. Boston: Houghton Mifflin, 2005.

Wells, H. G. *The First Men in the Moon.* London: Collins, 1901.

White, Jasper. *Lobster at Home.* New York: Scribner, 1998.

Wilson, William. *A Little Earnest Book upon a Great Old Subject.* London: Darton, 1851.

Wölfflin, Heinrich. *Principles of Art History: The Problem of the Development of Style in Later Art.* Translated by M. D. Hottinger. New York: Dover, 1932.

Woodard, Colin. *The Lobster Coast: Rebels, Rusticators, and the Struggle for a Forgotten Frontier.* New York: Penguin, 2004.

Woolf, H. B. "Mencken as Etymologist: Charley Horse and Lobster Trick." *American Speech* 48, nos. 3–4 (1973): 229–38.

INDEX